京西路

乔争月 著
Michelle Qiao

上海三联书店

The Bubbling
Well Road

静安寺路

素描

白华《沪西风景线·静安寺路素描》1937

华山路
Huashan Road

常德路
Changde Road

铜仁路
Tongren Road

沪西的风景，其幽静与繁嚣，和热闹的都市划开了一条鸿沟。静安寺路上，充分地给人以清静的美感，真是"静"而且"安"。这儿住的，大都是些高贵的现代贵人：欧美风度的哈同花园，文化枢纽的中华书局，惨淡氛围的万国墓园，中世纪风静安古寺等主题建筑，也都陈列在一带榆树飘拂的绿荫地下。有闲的红男绿女，也很高兴在那条路面上踩着，像踩公园一样地有清闲的趣味。若干时候以前，我也常有机会踟蹰在这广宽的道上，悠闲地，望着榆树梢头浮动着的夕阳，白云，可以陶醉一个傍晚或早晨。

上海犹太学校

陕西北路
North Shaanxi Road

泰兴路
Taixing Road

石门二路
Shiemener Road

成都路
Chengdu Road

锺义大楼

泰兴大楼

张园

同孚大楼

华山路
Huashan Road

常德路
Changde Road

铜仁路
Tongren Road

AVENUE APARTMENTS

绿房子·四层平台的流畅曲线

绿房子·餐厅内景

绿房子·从花园西南角望住宅全景

泰兴路
Taixing Road

石门二路
Shiemener Road

陕西北路
North Shaanxi Road

成都路
Chengdu Road

雷士德医学研究院 · 大楼

雷士德医学研究院 · 图书馆

雷士德医学研究院 · 大礼堂

爱俪园现在上海展览中心

华山路
Huashan Road

常德路
Changde Road

铜仁路
Tongren Road

静安寺

嘉道理故居

静安公园

泰兴路
Taixing Road

石门二路
Shiemener Road

陕西北路
North Shaanxi Road

成都路
Chengdu Road

常德公寓

共济会堂

共济会堂

百乐门

静安公园

科学教会堂

Annual Basket Fair Back Again

Excerpt from the *North-China Herald*, on May 8, 1935

To the uninitiated, the sullying with yellow paint of the pavements on all the roads around Bubbling Well and St. George's for the last week or so now has a meaning, but to initiate it has meant all along that the Basket Fair of Bubbling Well Temple was due again. On Sunday, seemingly springing out of thin air, the fair was there, thronged with people, of all nationalities and all classes.

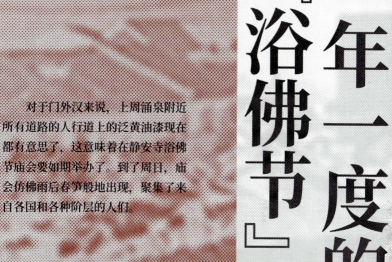

一年一度的『浴佛节』归来

对于门外汉来说，上周涌泉附近所有道路的人行道上的泛黄油漆现在都有意思了，这意味着在静安寺浴佛节庙会要如期举办了。到了周日，庙会仿佛雨后春笋般地出现，聚集了来自各国和各种阶层的人们。

摘自 1935 年 5 月 8 日《北华捷报》

It is an annual show, this fair. For one week
it blossoms from nowhere, to disappear as
mysteriously as it came. For one week houses
and shops are blotted out by mat sheds
erected against them. Piles of merchandise
clutter the pavements, forcing pedestrians
into the roadway. Merchants clutter the roads,
living in the midst of their goods for the seven
days. And overall there is an atmosphere of
calm excitement, or order despite the seeming
chaos.

这是一年一度的盛会。一个星期来，它无中生有般地绽放，又同样神秘地消失。在一周内，房屋和商店都被前面的棚子遮住了。成堆的商品乱堆在人行道上，迫使行人走到车道上。商贩们也凌乱地塞满道路，他们在自己的货品堆里生活 7 天。总体而言，尽管看上去很混乱，但还是有一种平静的兴奋的气氛或秩序存在。

The origin of the fair goes back for generations. It started with the an nual pilgrimage to the ancient Bubbling Well Temple, now almost lost in the midst of the modern buildings which surround it, this pilgrimage being in celebration of the legendary birthday of Buddha which, according to Chinese calculations, falls on the 8th day of the 4th moon, or May 10 this year. With this pilgrimage, peasants and artisans for many miles around used to bring with them bamboo work, baskets, and other specimens of their work in order to sell them to pay for the cost of their pilgrimage. From this the fair has grown till now it is almost entirely a commercial undertaking.

庙会的历史可以追溯到几代人之前。它始于每年一次的静安寺礼佛之旅，如今被现代建筑围绕的静安寺几乎都要隐没了。礼佛之旅是为了庆祝佛陀的传奇生日，根据中国人的计算方式为 4 月 8 日，或今年 5 月 10 日。在这次朝圣中，住在数英里之遥的许多农民和工匠习惯将竹制品、篮子和其他工艺品带来售卖，以支付朝圣的费用。源起于那时的庙会发展到现在，如今几乎是彻底的商业活动。

阅读南京西路

著者：乔争月

摄影：张雪飞　邵　律　乔争月

插图：廖　方

鸣谢：

郑时龄　熊月之　邢建榕　章　明
唐玉恩　李乐曾　常　青　钱宗灏
王　健　陈中伟　李振东　华霞虹
张姚俊　张　生　王浩娱　廖　方
Alvaro Leonardo Perez　　陈　贤

机构：

上海市档案馆
上海市政府新闻办公室
上海市图书馆
上海市徐家汇藏书楼
上海市文化和旅游局
上海市历史博物馆
上海市体育总会
上海市建筑学会
上海市黄浦区人民政府档案馆
上海市静安区住房保障和房屋管理局
上海市静安区文化和旅游局
上海市黄浦区南京东路街道
上海市静安区南京西路街道
上海市静安区石门二路街道
上海市静安区江宁路街道
上海市静安区静安寺街道
上海静安置业（集团）有限公司
静安寺
长征医院
同济大学校史馆
上海日报
匈牙利驻沪总领馆
上海章明建筑设计事务所
墨辰文化传媒有限公司
上海缪诗肖像摄影

The Bubbling Well Road
Author:Michelle Qiao
Photographer: Zhang Xuefei, Shao Lu,
Michelle Qiao
Illustration:Liao Fang

Acknowledgements:
Zheng Shiling, Xiong Yuezhi, Xing Jianrong,
Zhang Ming, Tang Yuen, Li Leceng,
Chang Qing, Qian Zonghao, Wang Jian,
Chen Zhongwei, Li Zhendong,
Hua Xiahong, Zhang YaoJun, Zhang Sheng,
Wang Haoyu, Liao Fang,
Alvaro Leonardo Perez, Chen Xian

Shanghai Municipal Archives Bureau
Information Office of Shanghai Municipality
Shanghai Library
The Xujiahui Library
Shanghai Culture and Tourism Bureau
Shanghai History Museum
Shanghai Sports Club
The Architectural Society of Shanghai,
　China
Shanghai Huangpu District Archives Bureau
Shanghai Jing'an District Housing Guarantee
　and Building Administration Bureau
The Culture and Tourism Bureau of
　Shanghai Jing'an District
The East Nanjing Road Sub-district Office of
　Huangpu District Shanghai Municipality
The West Nanjing Road Sub-district Office
　of Jing'an District Shanghai Municipality
The No.2 Shimen Road Sub-district Office of
　Jing'an District Shanghai Municipality
The Jiangning Road Sub-district Office of
　Jing'an District Shanghai Municipality
The Jing'an Temple Sub-district Office of
　Jing'an District Shanghai Municipality
Shanghai Jing'an Real Estate (Group)
　Co Ltd,
Jing'an Temple
Changzheng Hospital
History Museum of Tongji University
Shanghai Daily
Consulate General of Hungary in Shanghai
Shanghai Zhangming Architectural
　Design Firm
Mochen Culture Media Co., Ltd
MUSEE FOTO

目录

Contents

阅读《阅读南京西路》

记者乔争月女士的名字这几年频频出现在上海的建筑界和文学界，她对上海历史、人文和建筑的研究，从建筑师到建筑和建筑群，从武康路到外滩，从南京东路到南京西路，不仅写文章，也写书，做讲座，传授知识，俨然是上海建筑的无冕形象大使。我在她的《阅读南京路》的序言中说过：乔争月女士的著作不是单纯的历史故事，更是展望未来的启示，为上海这座城市洒落温润的月光。

正如乔争月女士在书中所总结的，南京西路是一片静谧而又繁华的领地，繁华、静谧成为《阅读南京西路》的主题，南京西路的历史在书中就此款款展开。如同《阅读南京路》的文风，作者以第一手文献资料生动地描写了建筑师和当年与这些建筑相交集的风云人物，从独特的时空交错的视角研究上海和上海建筑。

南京西路的繁华是长时间才历练而成的，1862年开始辟筑的静安寺路在当年还是一条私有的道路，可供刚刚出现的马车通行，成为人们星期日下午游玩的去处。1945年才改名为南京西路。长时间以来，这条路是上海最长的一条街道，两边坐落着上海近代早期最优美的住宅、咖啡馆和餐厅。这里有过1904年开业的上海最早的旅馆，有电梯通往各个楼层，提供电话服务和冬季采暖。其实这里当年还是乡村，这家旅馆的旁边甚至还有一家农场。历年来，南京西路汇集了众多公司、时尚的娱乐场所和俱乐部，也聚集了许多画廊和艺术家。作者所描述的南京西路并非仅仅是一条3866米长的线性的街道，而是不断向周边的街道和建筑延伸的社会蒙太奇，读者会发现这片乐土是浓缩的上海史。今天的南京西路已经成为上海的商业中心和文化中心，充满了无限的生机和未来发展的前景，

与南京东路不同的是，南京西路周围的地域更富含历史的积

淀，毛泽东在1920年曾经在安义路以及铜仁路上的民厚南里居住和工作过，革命文物为南京西路增添了红色的色彩。

南京西路这片地域是许多为世人熟悉或陌生的文化名人活跃的大舞台，他们是宋庆龄、史量才、张爱玲、贝润生、徐悲鸿、叶贻铨等，还有德国医生宝隆、意大利诗人邓南遮、美国作家埃德加·斯诺、地产大亨哈同等。南京西路曾经有过闻名遐迩的银行大楼、酒店、电影院、商业建筑、公寓、花园洋房、里弄住宅等。南京西路有过曾经的远东第一高楼——国际饭店，有中国历史上第一座公园——味莼园，有历史上风云一时的涌泉、愚园、申园、爱俪园，书中也记录了今天的静安公园和静安寺，可惜的是有近两千年历史的静安寺已经失去了昔日涌泉旁的淳朴。

这里是中外建筑师各显神通，争奇斗艳的角逐场，也是世界新建筑的展示场。中国建筑师在南京西路正阔步迈向现代建筑，这里有设计了华业大楼的中国建筑师李锦沛、美琪大戏院的建筑师范文照、设计百乐门的杨锡镠、同孚大楼的建筑师陆谦受和吴景奇、贝宅的建筑师中都工程司顾鹏程、设计哈同花园的黄宗仰。参与设计中苏友好大厦的陈植等。

这里有上海的网红建筑师，设计国际饭店、大光明电影院和绿房子的邬达克，还有他的同乡，大华大戏院的匈牙利建筑师鸿达。英国建筑师有张园安垲第的建筑师金斯密，设计德义大楼和爱林登公寓（常德公寓）的英国建筑师甘少明、设计郭乐和郭顺宅的毕士莱、万国体育总会的建筑师公和洋行、设计了大理石大厦的思九圣和嘉咸宾，思九生还设计了规矩堂和拍马总会行政办公楼和马厩，大华公寓的建筑师道达、卡尔登公寓（长江公寓）的凯司、雷士德医学研究院的德和洋行、设计麦特赫斯脱公寓（泰兴大楼）的新瑞和洋行，跑马总会的建筑师马海洋行等。这里还有德国建筑师倍克，加拿大建筑师爱尔德，也有飞星公司的西班牙建筑师乐福德，设计了华安大楼和西侨青年会（体育大厦）的美国建筑师哈沙德等。这里还有1950年代设计了中苏友好大厦的苏联建筑师安德烈耶夫等，这里有改革开放以后参与设计的众多中国建筑师、美国建筑师、新加坡建筑师和法国建筑师等。

乔争月女士不仅是报导上海和上海建筑的专栏作家，也是研究上海建筑的专家，发表了许多文章和专著，她从深藏在汗牛充栋的各种历史档案和外文文献中寻访、探究上海的建筑及其背后的历史和事件，绘声绘色地加以描述，带领我们认知昔日的上海和今天的上海，想象未来的上海，阅读全书的图片也是一场建筑的盛会。

2021 年 6 月 22 日

Reading *The Bubbling Well Road*

In recent years, Ms. Qiao Zhengyue, the historic architecture columnist of *Shanghai Daily*, has been got to known to Shanghai's architectural and literary circles. Her research on Shanghai's history, culture and architecture covers architects, buildings and architectural complexes, and has been published into series from Wukang Road to the Bund, from Nanjing Road East to Nanjing Road West. She not only writes feature articles for the newspaper, but also publishes books, gives lectures to share her knowledge with the public, and has almost become an unofficial image ambassador of Shanghai architecture. I said in the preface of her previous book *Shanghai Nanjing Road*, Ms. Qiao Zhengyue's work is not only about telling history stories, moreover it is an enlightenment to the future like a beam of soothing moonlight for the city of Shanghai.

As Ms. Qiao has summarized in this book, Nanjing Road West is a quiet yet bustling place, which makes prosperity and tranquility the two main themes of *The Bubbling Well Road*. This book tells the stories of Nanjing Road West in the same way as in her previous book *Shanghai Nanjing Road*. Ms. Qiao vividly describes architects and famous people who intersected with these buildings with a lot of first-hand archives and from a unique perspective with an interesting combination of time and space.

The prosperity of Nanjing Road West doesn't come into being in one day. The Bubbling Well Road built in 1862 was initially a private road then for the newly emerged horse-drawn carriages. Gradually it turned out to be a leisure place for people to spend Sunday afternoons. It was renamed Nanjing Road West in 1945. For a long time, this road was the longest street in Shanghai which was flanked with the most beautiful houses, cafes and restaurants of the early period of modern Shanghai. The earliest modern hotel in Shanghai opened here in 1904 to be well equipped with an elevator to all floors, telephone services and heating during winter time. However, the whole area was still country-like back then and there was a farm just next to this hotel. Over the years, the road had gathered numerous companies, fashionable entertainment venues, clubs, as well as many galleries and artists. The Nanjing Road West depicted by the author is not just a 3866-meter-long linear street, but a social montage that continuously extends to the neighboring streets and buildings. Readers would discover that its development is exactly like a condensed history of Shanghai. Today, Nanjing Road West has become a commercial and cultural center of the city, full of vitality and bright prospects for future development.

Different from Nanjing Road East, the area around Nanjing Road seems to contain a richer history with revolutionary and cultural elements. Among the revolutionary sites, the most famous one would be the former Mao Zedong residence in 1920 in the former South Minhou Lane at the cross of today's Anyi and Tongren Roads.

The region of Nanjing Road West is also a big stage for a galaxy of cultural celebrities who are familiar or unfamiliar to many. They are Song Qingling, Shi Liangcai, Zhang Ailing, Bei Runsheng, Xu Beihong, Ye Yiquan, as well as German doctor Erich Paulun, Italian poet Gabriele d'Annunzio, American writer Edgar Snow, real estate tycoon Silas Aaron Hardoon etc. Nanjing Road West was formerly graced by famous bank buildings, hotels, movie theatres, commercial buildings, apartments, garden houses, lane houses, etc. It had the once tallest building in the Far East, the Park Hotel, the first park in Chinese history, the Weichun Garden, the bubbling well, Yuyuan Garden, Shenyuan Garden and Aili Garden, which were all renowned in history. The book also tells the stories of today's Jing'an Park and Jing'an Temple. It is a pity that after renovation the Jing'an Temple which has a history of nearly 2000 years cannot go back to its originality as it was next to the bubbling well in the past.

The road also provided a competition field for Chinese and foreign architects to demonstrate their magical powers to keep up with the world trend by showcasing all kinds of new architecture. Here the readers can easily see how the Chinese architects bravely embraced modern architecture. They included Chinese architect Poy Gum Lee who designed the Cosmopolitan Apartments, Robert Fan, the architect of the Majestic Theater, Yang Xiyu who designed the Paramount Hall, Luke Him Sau and Wu Chauncey K, the architects of the Yates Apartments, Gu Pengcheng of the Cathay Engineering & Building Service who designed the Pei Villa, Huang Zongyang, designer of the Aili Garden and Chen Zhi who participated in the design of Sino-Soviet Friendship Building.

Also great contributions were made by foreign architects including the current Shanghai Internet celebrity architect L. E. Hudec who designed the Park Hotel, the Grand Theatre and the Green House and his fellow Hungarian architect C. H. Gonda who designed the ROXY Cinema. British architects included T. W. Kingsmill, designer of the Arcadia Hall in Zhangyuan Garden, British architect Eric Cumine who designed both the Denis Apartments and the Eddington House (today's Changde Apartments), Percy M. Beesley, who designed Chinese merchant brothers Kwok Lok and Kwok Chuen's villas, Palmer & Turner, designer of the International Recreation Club, Robert Ernest Stewardson and Graham Brown who designed the Marble Hall. Stewardson also designed the Masonic Hall and the administrative office building and stables of Shanghai Race Club. They also included William Dowdall who designed the Majestic Apartments, P. H. Keys, architect of the Carlton Apartments (today's Changjiang Apartments), H. Lester & Co., architect of Henry Lester Institute of Medical Research, Davies and Brooke, who designed the Medhurst Apartments (Taixing Apartments) and Messrs Spence, Robinson and Partners, architect of Shanghai Race Club. There are also German architect Heinrich Becker, Canadian architect Albert Algar, Spanish architect Abelardo Lafuente, architect of the Star Garage Company, American architect Elliott Hazzard who designed the China United Assurance Building and the Foreign YMCA Building (Shanghai Sports Club), the Soviet Union architect Sergei Andreyev who designed the Sino-Soviet Friendship Building in the 1950s. In addition, there are many Chinese, American, Singaporean and French architects who participated in the design projects along the road after China's reform and opening up.

Ms. Qiao Zhengyue is not only a columnist reporting on Shanghai and Shanghai architecture, she has also become an expert of Shanghai architecture by publishing many articles and books after arduous work in finding the most interesting clues from numerous Chinese and English historical archives and a lot of field visits. With her vivid descriptions, she helped us to get a better understanding of Shanghai's past and present, and to better imagine Shanghai's future. Furthermore, pictures of the book present a grand visual architectural show.

Zheng Shiling

June 22, 2021

静谧的繁华

2020年5月,上海崧泽遗址博物馆举办水文化展,展品中有一根雕花栏杆,是上海静安寺涌泉井栏的原物。这根井栏浸润着南京西路的故事。

19世纪中叶,今日的南京东路是一条外侨散步遛马的乡间小路,而南京西路一带还是古庙荒村、河浜纵横的乡野。昔日的乡间小路如何发展为上海的"第五大道"?乡野之地怎样变为繁华精致的静安南京西路?在这条路上,曾经来过哪些改变中国历史的人物?又有哪些中外建筑师留下了令人难忘的经典作品?

带着这些问题,2017年我从外滩出发,从东到西逐个调研南京路沿线的历史建筑,直到静安寺。沿途我穿越了尘土飞扬、城市更新中的南京东路,亲历上海跑马总会改造的上海历史博物馆开幕,又赶在张园项目启动前采访记录了南京西路的最新变化。

南京路一开始被叫作"大马路"。1850年,外侨在今南京东路河南路一带的花园建跑马总会。由于外滩因商业发展向西扩展,跑马总会两次出让土地西迁,1864年在今西藏中路西侧建第三跑马场,其位置就是现在的人民公园和人民广场。

根据《南京西路一百四十年1862–2002》一书,上海跑马总会于1862年越界筑路,辟筑一条长2英里的跑马道,从泥城浜(今西藏中路)直通千年古刹静安寺。这条跑马道以静安寺前著名的涌泉取名Bubbling Well Road,中文名静安寺路(今南京西路)。1890年管理租界的工部局为这条简陋的泥土路铺设石子路面,翌年在马路两侧种植林木,1899年将马路划入公共租界范围,1921年又向西筑至大西路(今延安西路)。

1945年国民政府接收上海市,将静安寺路更名为南京西路。南京路东段后来被称为南京东路。人们习惯将整条南京路叫做

"十里洋场"，这也成为近代上海大都市的象征和代名词。

随着先施、永安、新新和大新"四大公司"陆续开张，南京路东段发展为远东最著名的商业街。而南京路西段也渐渐布满优雅时髦的商店、剧场、公寓楼和花园别墅，别具风情。与热闹繁华的南京东路相比，南京西路虽然商业氛围也很浓厚，但总给人以宁静闲适的感觉，也许这就是静谧的繁华。

在我写的《上海外滩建筑地图》和《阅读南京路》中，外滩建筑群以银行大楼为主，南京东路和人民广场的商业和公共建筑多，而本书所写的南京西路的建筑风貌则更富有多样性，包括影院、舞厅、教堂、寺庙、公寓、石库门、花园别墅、摩天楼等，几乎涵盖了上海历史建筑所有的主要类型，妙趣横生。

上海这座城市最迷人之处，就是19世纪中叶后，中西文化曾在这里相遇、碰撞、竞争并互相学习、吸收，最后水乳交融。这也是南京路，包括南京东路和南京西路，最让人心动的魅力。

南京西路的城市风貌尤其"中西合璧"，曾经位于南京西路黄金地段的两个花园都是典型案例。犹太富商哈同是西人，但他的爱俪园（现址为上海展览中心）由中国僧人黄宗仰设计，小桥流水亭台楼阁，还举办许多中国文化活动。张园主人张叔和是中国商人，却邀请当时的大牌外国设计师——金斯密（Kingsmill）和安景生（Atkinson）在中式花园里打造了一座著名西式建筑——安凯第，在这里举办各种西洋文化活动。

我写《阅读南京路》时，正好经历并记录了南京东路的城市更新。开始写作本书时，南京西路也恰好开启了新一轮的城市更新。静安区在对张园实行保护性征收，计划将其打造为展示石库门里弄建筑的人文地标。而中信泰富、锦沧文华酒店和静安寺下沉广场也在改造升级，预计今年将陆续展露新的风貌。

调研写作的过程中，活跃在南京西路的中外历史人物的故事让我十分着迷。2021年正好是中国共产党建党100周年，1920

年湖南青年毛泽东曾在静安寺路民厚南里寓居，生活虽清苦，但精神充实，在这里他接触到新鲜的思想，思想发生重要的转变，确立了初心。

年轻的田汉、郭沫若、郁达夫和村松梢风等文学青年也在20世纪20年代来到同一片石库门，过着同样清苦而充实的生活，学习、交流、互相启发，都成长为一代名家。此外，热爱公寓生活的作家张爱玲和坚持新闻理想的报业大王史量才也都住在附近。

中外富商哈同、嘉道理、吴同文、贝润生、郭氏兄弟等纷纷选择在这一带建起壮观的宅邸——爱俪园、大理石大厦、绿房子、贝宅、郭宅，都载入了近代建筑史册。

南京西路还是建筑师邬达克的幸运地，在这里他设计建成了三件代表作——国际饭店、大光明电影院和绿房子。他的欧洲同行鸿达、乐福德等也在这条路上设计了不少知名建筑。而陆谦受、范文照、李锦沛、杨锡镠等近代中国的第一代建筑师更是展露了不俗的实力。他们追求现代设计理念，在南京西路留下美观实用的作品，今日仍保留初建时的功能，如同孚大楼、美琪大戏院、华业公寓和百乐门。

在这条路上，还有两位外国侨民的故事深深打动了我。一位是被老百姓亲昵称为"大宝医生"的德国医生宝隆。这位来自德国的孤儿克服巨大困难，在这里为中国穷人建起医院，还创办了医学院，分别发展为今天的同济医院和同济大学。另一位是英国地产大亨雷士德，他终生未婚、生活简朴，拥有南京路的大量地产，却将几乎所有遗产捐给上海的慈善团体、医院、学校，其中就包括南京西路附近的雷士德医学研究所。他们把上海视为新的家园，身后也都葬在静安寺公墓，他们留下的医院、学校、基金会至今仍在运作，惠及今人。

这些南京西路的故事和精神，宛若那根井栏下曾经汩汩的泉水，充满流动的能量，值得永远铭记。

乔争月

2021年3月于上海武康路月亮书房

The Stories of
Bubbling Well Road

Nanjing Road was constructed in 1851 initially as the "Park Lane" — from the Bund to the first race course on today's Henan Road. It was also widely called as "Ta Maloo" which means "Great Horse Road". The Maloo was extended to Zhejiang Road in 1854 and stretched further to Xizang Road in 1862 as the race course was relocated twice — the last one in today's People's Square.

In 1862 the British consul Walter Henry Medhurst suggested that "the settlement road names should be made intelligible to the tens of thousands of natives who had crowded into the limits for safety from the Taiping Rebellion." Thereafter, Park Lane was renamed Nanjing Road after the ancient Chinese capital city.

According to the book *The 140th Anniversary of Nanjing Road West (1862 to 2002)*, Shanghai Race Club constructed a 2-mile-long road from today's Xizang Road M. to the thousand-year-old Jing'an Temple in 1862. They named the extended part Bubbling Well Road after the then renowned bubbling well fronting the temple. Today the well had been filled up and buried underneath.

The muddy road was paved with stones in 1890, planted with plane trees in 1891 and finally included into the international settlement in 1899. In 1921, the road was further expanded to today's Yan'an Road W.

In 1945, Bubbling Well Road was renamed to Nanjing Road W. — and Nanjing Road became Nanjing Road E. The entire stretch came to be known as Nanjing Road that spanned five kilometers. The street became so prominent as to be the symbol of old Shanghai, and was nicknamed "Shi Li Yang Chang" which meant a "10-mile-long foreign street".

Early last century the eastern part of Nanjing Road was upgraded to a world-class shopping street after Chinese merchants built four modern department stores — concrete structures with modern equipment and high towers — along the street.

The western part also flourished with stylish shops, famous theatres and gorgeous garden villas built by foreign and Chinese tycoons.

There was a saying among early Shanghai expatriates that "if the Bund to be taken as a bow, then Nanjing Road is just like a westward-flying arrow which happens to indicate the direction guiding Shanghai's urban development".

After exploring the bow-shaped Bund, I started my journey westward by following this arrow of Shanghai all the way up to Jing'an Temple.

The first part of the journey focused on the former Park Lane, today's Nanjing Road E. (from the Bund to Xizang Road) and the former Race Course area(today's People's Square area), including the former Shanghai race club building(today's Shanghai History Museum).

Then I walked further westward from the People's Square to the Jing'an Temple along Nanjing Road W. Compared with the buzzy and dazzling Nanjing Road E., Nanjing Road W. seems to be more stylish and relaxing.

With the help of Jing'an District Government and five sub-district governments—Nanjing Road E., Nanjing Road W., No. 2 Shimen Road, Jiangning Road and Jing'an Temple sub-districts along the former Bubbling Well Road, I have explored an amazing variety of historical architectures, ranging from clubs, hospitals, theatres, apartments, garden villas to even the former cemetery park, some of which are signature works from China's first-generation modern architects.

During the journey, I also witnessed and recorded the last days of the century-old Zhangyuan Garden before it closed for a large-scale renovation project with its old residents still living there. In addition, several landmarks buildings along Nanjing Road W. including the Jing'an Temple Square are also undergoing a new round of

regeneration. Soon, the western part of Nanjing Road will take on a fresh new look, just as what has happened to Nanjing Road E. after its pedestrian part was extended to the Bund in September 2020.

In my research, I was particularly deeply moved by the stories of two expatriates whose legacies are still along Nanjing Road W..

One is the British millionaire Henry Lester who made a fortune from old Shanghai's real estate business but donated almost all his assets for the education of the local Chinese. A medical institution built with his money still stands a few minutes' walk from Nanjing Road W.. The Lester Foundation sponsors Chinese scholars to study in the U.K until today.

The other is a German doctor named Erich Paulun. This former German navy doctor travelled thousands of miles to Shanghai, later built a charitable hospital to treat poor Chinese patients for free and founded a medical school to give Chinese western medical education, which evolved to be today's Chang Zheng Hospital and Tongji University respectively. Though the old hospital buildings along Nanjing Road W. have been demolished, Paulun's legacy still has a lingering influence in Shanghai, China and Germany.

Both Lester and Paulun had walked along the Bubbling Well Road, worked at their buildings nearby, and been buried in the Bubbling Well Road Cemetery which was relocated later and turned into today's Jing'an Park.

Their spirits and stories, as well as those of others of the stylish Nanjing Road W. are worth telling and remembering.

Michelle Qiao

March 9, 2021

Moon Atelier, Wukang Road, Shanghai

1926年，华安保险公司聘请美国建筑师哈沙德（Elliott Hazzard）设计兴建了意大利文艺复兴风格的新厦，就是如今位于人民广场的金门饭店。上海档案馆研究员张姚俊认为，这是上海历史建筑中一座罕见的"保险大楼"。

当时，保险公司多为银行所办，办公设在银行大楼中，很少兴建一座保险公司大楼。友邦保险创始人史带（Cornelius Vander Starr)也是租用外滩字林西报大楼来开展业务的。更值得一提的是，建造大楼的华安保险是中国第一家纯华资的保险公司，由吕岳泉创办。

张姚俊从上海档案馆馆藏的吕氏后人回忆中勾勒出吕岳泉传奇的发家史。吕岳泉是上海川沙人，儿时家贫，到英商永年人寿公司外籍经理穆勒家当帮佣。他聪明好学，对主人的保险经纪业务耳濡目染，还自学了英语。穆勒偶然发现吕岳泉的才能后请他担任助理，做翻译等工作，又推荐他到公司从事保险代理业务。

因为业绩优异，吕岳泉升任永年人寿南京分公司总经理。后来，他听从两江总督端方等人建议，创业开办了第一家纯华资的保险公司——华安合群（China United Assurance Co. Ltd）。公司还引进加拿大精算师郁次（A. J. Hughes）等一批外籍人才，于1912年7月1日在外滩规矩会堂开业，后来又搬到南京路。

华安公司将一半的资金用于投资上海的地产项目，盈利可观。根据1923年英文《大陆报》报道，因为外籍高管郁次的建议，公司为建造新大楼在原上海跑马场对面选址购地。"很多人批评在那么远的地方做生意简直愚蠢，而在静安寺路（今南京西路）建那么宏伟的一座大楼真是疯狂的主意。"报道提到。不过此后，南京路地价飞涨，事实证明新大楼的选址是一笔非常明智的投资。

华安保险兴建的是一座钢筋混凝土大楼，被誉为"上海最上等的建筑"，一座不计成本的美厦。上海中西合璧的建筑故事多，华安大楼也是一个经典案例。

设计大楼的哈沙德洋行由美国建筑师哈沙德创办，当年是上海颇具影响力的外国建筑事务所。哈

沙德还设计了南京路上其他三座标志性建筑——比邻的西侨青年会、更摩登现代的永安新厦和上海电力公司。在邬达克的代表作国际饭店于1934年竣工之前,哈沙德设计的华安大楼和西侨青年会曾经控制了上海跑马场(今人民广场)的天际线。

这座9层保险大楼高达76米,顶部有一座钟楼,底部两层以花岗岩贴面,其余楼层的混凝土外立面有石材效果。有研究认为华安大楼的灵感来源于费城独立纪念堂,而大楼落成的1926年是中华民国成立15周年,也是中国从封建统治下获得新生的15周年纪念。

大楼建成后,底部两层是商店、图书室和保险公司,其余楼层为公寓。《大陆报》报道评论:"这也许是世界上第一家由人寿保险公司经营的精装修公寓楼。"

这篇1928年的报道还提到:"二楼的办公室用意大利大理石和硬木装饰,会议室和经理室饰有柚木。公寓都非常美丽,装饰奢华,且层高宜人,夏季可以享受不断吹拂的纯净清凉的微风。大楼和餐厅由史达特曼夫人管理。她会在早上6点半前亲自去市场采购食

物，并监督烹饪，以确保完美的餐食和服务。"

大楼里共有68套公寓，145个房间。餐厅不仅为110名公寓租客提供服务，也向附近的客人开放。华安大楼的公寓深受欢迎，十分抢手，有着长长的等候名单，这是因为"在远东地区很难找到这样拥有高品质餐食服务和便利地段的住房"。

华安保险在鼎盛时期分支机构遍布南洋，1937年日军侵华后业务开始走下坡路，后来不得不将大部分楼层租给金门饭店，仅留二层办公使用。金门饭店于1936年由近百位中国企业家合资在香港注册创办，1937年开办上海分公司，1939年租赁华安保险大楼，次年12月30日开业。

1949年后，大楼由中国纺织局租用。1953年吕岳泉在香港病逝后，大楼由上海市政府接管，改为接待归国华侨的华侨饭店。1992年，酒店为吸引海外旅客恢复了金门饭店旧名，而很多客人都是喜欢酒店历史气息的海外游客。2017年上海市推动"建筑可阅读"工作后，金门饭店将位于大堂的商务中心改为一间酒店历史陈列室。

如今，酒店大堂仍矗立着巨大的大理石柱，雕刻繁复精致。陈列室位于一个大堂安静的角落，虽然面积迷你，但历史照片述说了一间华资保险公司曾经的辉煌与骄傲，值得一看。

昨天： 华安联合保险公司大楼　**今天：** 金门饭店　**地址：** 南京西路 108 号　**设计师：** 哈沙德
参观指南： 建议参观位于大堂的历史陈列室。

Designed by American architect Elliott Hazzard, the China United Assurance building is a stately Italian renaissance architecture built in 1926 for a Chinese insurance company run on foreign lines.

"Among Shanghai's galaxy of historical buildings, this is a rare example of a building devoted entirely to insurance. At that time, most insurance companies were operated by banks and located inside a banking house. Even Cornelius Vander Starr, founder of American Asiatic Underwriters and forerunner of AIG, rented an office in *the North China Daily News* building on the Bund instead of building a headquarter," says Zhang Yaojun, a researcher from Shanghai Archives Bureau.

Owner of this edifice, China United Assurance Co. Ltd. was the first full Chinese-capital life insurance company founded by local man Lu Yuequan.

According to Zhang's research, Lu had very humble beginnings, born into to a poor family in Chuansha, Pudong, and working for a foreign manager of China Mutual, a British life insurance company.

Amazed at his young servant's self-taught English and his knowledge of insurance, the manager made Lu his assistant and later recommended him for a post at China Mutual.

"Owing to his remarkable performance, Lu was appointed as general manager to open the company's Nanjing branch. In Nanjing, capital of Jiangsu Province, he made friends with powerful political figures who persuaded him to found China United Assurance Co. Ltd. in 1912, which was the first Chinese life insurance company organized with purely Chinese capital and run by Chinese," Zhang says.

Because of his experience working in a foreign insurance company, Lu intended to run the company on foreign lines. He invited

a few foreigners, including his former Canadian colleague, A.J. Hughes, to be the general manager and train Chinese staff. It was an experiment, but proved a success.

The company opened on July 1, 1912, at the Masonic Hall on the Bund, later moving to Nanjing Road. The company had been fortunate in their investments from the start, and around half their funds were in Shanghai real estate.

According to a report in the China Press, in 1923 the company purchased the present site opposite the former racecourse at Hughes' suggestion, "although many critics thought it almost folly to locate a business so far out, and especially a wild idea to put up so great and fine a building on Bubbling Well Road".

It was a smart investment as land prices along today's Nanjing Road were soaring in the 1920s and early 1930s.

The building was a steel frame and reinforced concrete structure which was reviewed as "the choicest specimen of architecture in Shanghai" and "ranked with the first half dozen in attractive lines irrespective of cost".

Architect Hazzard, who headed an influential architectural office in Shanghai in the late 1920s and early 1930s, designed three other buildings along Nanjing Road, including the Foreign YMCA building and the more modern Wing On Tower and Shanghai Power Company.

The China United Assurance building and the adjacent Foreign YMCA building had dominated the skyline of the former racecourse before the erection of the Park Hotel in 1934.

The nine-floor insurance building was surmounted by a clock tower crowned with a lantern at a height of 250 feet (76 meters). The first two floors are faced with granite with imposing effect. The other floors, with the appearance of plain stone, are in reality concrete.

The offices of Lu's company occupied the first floor and there were two large vaults for books on the ground floor. The remainder of the ground floor was occupied by stores and shops, and all other floors had been furnished and served as apartments. *The China Press* called it "probably the only life insurance company in the world running a furnished apartment building".

Its 1928 report said: "The offices on the first floor are finished

in Italian marble and hardwoods, the boardroom and the manager's room in teak. The apartments are also beautifully finished and luxuriously furnished, and the height above ground gives a constant pure, cool breeze in summer. The management of the building itself is in the hands of Mrs M. Stadtmann, who also runs the dining room, making all purchases herself at the market before 6:30am. She superintends the cooking and in general sees to it that perfect meals are served and perfect service given."

There were up to 68 apartments and a total of 145 rooms in the building. The restaurant served not only the 110 tenants of the apartments, but also guests from nearby. There was always a waiting list for the rooms and apartments in the building as "it was not easy to duplicate the quality of the food, convenience and fine appointments of the rooms anywhere in the Far East".

The heyday of China United Assurance came to an end when the Japanese army invaded China in 1937. Their business all over the country almost came to a halt and branches were closing down. The company had to rent out the lobby and other floors to the Pacific Hotel, maintaining only the second floor as its office.

The Pacific Hotel Co. Ltd. was launched and invested by more than 100 Chinese entrepreneurs. The company was registered in Hong Kong in 1936, opened a Shanghai branch in 1937, rented the China United Assurance building in 1939 and opened the Pacific Hotel on December 30, 1940.

After 1949, the building was lent to the East China Textile Administration as its office. It was taken over by the Shanghai government after Lu died in Hong Kong in 1953 and since then reopened as the Huaqiao Hotel to host Chinese who returned from overseas. In 1992, the hotel reverted to its old name, the Pacific Hotel, to attract more overseas tourists.

Now around 40 percent of guests are foreigners who like the historical ambience of the hotel which now belongs to the Shanghai Jin Jiang International Hotels (Group) Ltd.. In 2017 the hotel transformed the former business center on the ground floor into an exhibition room of history.

The exhibition room sits in a quiet corner of the hotel's lobby graced by tall marble columns and exquisite sculptures. The room is not big, but precious old photos and silver tableware showcase the history of a fine building built by a Chinese insurance company that is well worth a read.

Yesterday: China United Assurance Building   **Today:** The Pacific Hotel
Address: 108 Nanjing Rd W.   **Architect:** Elliott Hazzard
Architectural style: Italian Renaissance style
Tips: Please visit the history exhibition room with a bilingual introduction to the hotel's history.

华安大楼开幕仪式
Finished Work 'Speaks for Itself'

周日，华安联合保险公司位于静安寺路34号的新总部大楼在举行正式开幕仪式。大楼为此特别布置装饰，众多来宾出席了仪式。

当天主持活动是徐固卿将军，他用中文概述了华安公司的历史。他说，1925年底，公司的有效业务达1170万两白银，资产有176万两白银，去年偿付了176万两理赔，到期款项有43.9万两。

华安公司总经理兼名誉董事郁次在介绍上海工部局总董费信惇（Stirling Fessenden）时说："在实现华安保险公司的宗旨的历程中，这座大楼的竣工是又一个里程碑。华安保险成立于1912年，就在中华民国成立后不久，而今天是中华民国成立15周年纪念。我们期望在新的秩序下做一些真正具有建设性价值的事情。

"很自然地，我们都为这座大楼感到自豪。我谨代表公司全体董事和管理层，借此机会郑重地表达我们对建筑师哈沙德先生的欣赏。他的作品本身就展示了他的专业技能。我们特别请哈沙德来设计这个项目，是因为他曾在纽约设计类似的建筑，有丰富而宝贵的经验。在整个设计和建造过程中，这种经验的好处非常明显。

"我还想借此机会就大楼所在土地的产权情况辟谣。它不是租赁产权，而是永久产权，我们永久拥有这块地。这块地产包括一块近12亩地的方形方块，其中大楼和后方车库占地约3亩。这块土地于1923年11月以远低于现在市场价的价格购入。当时我们预期商业区将向西快速扩张，投资收益会高于中央区，目前这些预期已经实现。"

The formal opening took place on Sunday of the new head office building of the China United Assurance Co. Ltd. at 34 Bubbling Well Road. The building was specially decorated for the occasion and a large number of guests attended.

The chairman of the day was Gen. Hsu Ko-ching who outlined in Chinese the history of the company, and said that, at the end of 1925, the society had Tls. 11,700,000 business in force and Tls. 1,760,000 in assets. It paid Tls. 1,713,000 in claims and Tls. 439,000 on maturity last year.

Mr A. J. Hughes, the general manager and honorary director, in introducing Mr Stirling Fessenden, Chairman of the Shanghai Municipal Council, said: "The completion of this building is another mile-stone on the road  to the fulfillment of the aims of the promoters of the China United Assurance Society. The Society was started in 1912, just after the inauguration of the Chinese Republic, of which today is the 15th anniversary, in the hope of doing something of real constructive value for the new order of things.

"Naturally we are all very proud of this building and on behalf of the Directors and Executive staff I wish to take this opportunity of expressing in a more public manner than has hitherto been possible our appreciation of our architect, Mr Elliott Hazzard, whose finished work speaks for itself of his professional skill. He was specially selected as having had a wide and valuable experience in the erection of similar buildings in New York and the benefit of that experience has been very much in evidence during the whole course of designing and construction.

"I take this opportunity of disposing of a rumor which has reached us in regard to the land on which this building is erected. It is not leasehold but freehold property, our own in perpetuity. The whole consists of a square block of nearly 12 mow of which this building and the garages in rear occupy about three mow. It was purchased in November, 1923, at a figure very considerably less than the present market value in anticipation of a very rapid expansion of the commercial district westward and a much more profitable investment than the Central District afforded. Both these anticipations have been realized."

摘自 1926 年 10 月 16 日《北华捷报》
Excerpt from *the North-China Herald,* on October 16, 1926

哈沙德的菱形图案
Elliott Hazzard's Patterns

1928年夏天，美国建筑师哈沙德设计的西侨青年会在上海跑马场对面开业。西侨青年会是为旅沪外侨青年设计的住所，融娱乐设施和宿舍为一体，还有一座上海较早的温水游泳池。

1844年，基督教青年会由英国人乔治·威廉姆斯（George Williams）创办。1900年，中国基督教青年会在上海创办，1931年在附近的西藏路兴建了一座融合中国元素的现代建筑。而建造这座西侨青年会大楼的想法则源于1920年上海外侨精英的一次会议。

1928年3月24日英文《密勒氏评论报》（*The China Weekly Review*）透露，西侨青年会时任秘书长乔治·费奇(George Fitch)提到与会人员认为要"给远离故乡的男士们一个家"，让"来自不同西方国家的男青年们互相认识，在健康的友谊中互相融入，在有吸引力的环境中舒适生活，而所需花费要在能够承受的范围内"。

这个想法后来获得来自纽约和上海的捐赠支持，变为现实。西侨青年会大楼由美国建筑师哈沙德设计，高达10层，呈现意大利文艺复兴风格。大楼的现代化让前来采访的记者感到惊叹，认为是科学和金钱所能做到的极致。

"南立面的粗糙墙面装饰有棕色、米色和奶油色砖拼成的菱形图案，这是一种让人印象深刻的宜人设计。底部三层的米色和棕色和谐融合，与土褐色的建筑形成好看的对比。"1928年6月30日的英文《大陆报》报道。

在这家英文报纸记者看来，大楼诸多建筑细节中，位于静安寺路（今南京西路）上的入口表现了这座建筑的重要性。入口有三座大门，门的上方设计有三扇高而缩进的窗，由两对修长优雅的柱式分隔。

美国密歇根大学研究员梁庄爱伦（Ellen Johnston Laing）发现，哈沙德为大楼立面设计了威尼斯主题的装饰。"底部数层用不同颜色的砖拼出菱形方块的图案覆盖整个立面，这一处理手法源于威尼斯总督府。把彩色砖呈几何图样地铺设在建筑表面，将其从一个平淡无奇的墙面转化为令人激动的、

精致的、蕾丝状的结构，”她在一篇关于哈沙德的论文中写道。两年后，哈沙德将这种装饰手法运用到上海新光大戏院的立面上。

哈沙德是老上海最重要的建筑师之一，1879年出生于南卡罗来纳州一个大米种植园家庭，在格鲁吉亚技术学院学习建筑。他毕业后在纽约知名的建筑事务所工作，1905年就在第五大道成立了自己的事务所。在纽约的建筑活动为哈沙德日后在上海的成就埋下伏笔。他1921年来到上海后，将当时风靡美国的布扎美术风格、意大利文艺复兴风格和英式风格等移植到了上海的建筑风貌中。

1923年上海英文报纸的广告里提到，上海只有三位“真正的美国建筑师”，他们分别是哈沙德、邬达克早期的合伙人克利（R. A. Curry）和后来设计北大、清华校园的茂飞（Henry Murphy）。

有趣的是哈沙德初到上海时曾与茂飞共事，还居住在茂飞位于外滩3号顶楼的公寓里。1923年茂飞关闭上海办事处后，哈沙德留在上海独立执业，设计了很多留存至

今的著名建筑，如金门饭店（华安大楼）、枕流公寓、静安宾馆和淮海西路富兰克林住宅。

哈沙德设计的西侨青年会和华安大楼落成后，成为现代上海摩天楼的标志性建筑。两座大楼雄踞在跑马场的一侧，控制着上海跑马厅一带的天际线。不过南京路的地段升值太快，两座建筑的霸主地位并未保持很久，1934年邬达克设计的国际饭店作为中国最高建筑改变了上海的城市天际线，成为新的视觉中心。而今天再看，国际饭店的高度又被一次次超越，棕褐色颀长的低调身影隐没在摩天巨厦的海洋里。

在近年网红的“上生·新所”城市更新项目中，哈沙德设计的哥伦比亚乡村俱乐部又与邬达

克作品孙科故居相距不远，被一些媒体混淆为邬达克作品。

对比哈沙德和邬达克的人生轨迹，也有一点"既生瑜，何生亮"的味道。他们年龄相差十几岁，在三年间先后到沪发展。从职业资历看，哈沙德曾在纽约等大都市有建筑设计经验，比大学刚毕业就应征入伍的邬达克更胜一筹。两人到上海后都幸运地赶上了一段城市发展的"黄金时代"，留下很多经典作品。二战期间他们都选择留在上海，但红火的事务所都变得门可罗雀，1943年哈沙德在日军集中营里病逝，而邬达克1947年离开上海后去美国定居。两人都活了60多岁。

当年的英文报纸提到，西侨青年会大楼的室内设计与外立面一样，美观实用。大楼中央供暖，装修精美的房间光线充足、空气新鲜，健身房、游泳池、跑道、保龄球道、俱乐部和更衣室一应俱全。西侨青年会还提供优质餐饮、学习课程、研究设施和拓展讲座。所有房间的龙头都提供过滤水。炎炎夏日里，饮用水通过冷却装置冰镇，而健身房角落里也有汽水桶随时提供可口饮料。

抗战时期，大楼被日军占领，1950年由上海市政府接管。在时任上海市长陈毅的建议下，西侨青年会大楼改为上海体育俱乐部，1957年开始对儿童和青少年开展游泳、围棋和国际象棋的业余训练，从中发现培养体育人才。从那时起，西侨青年会变成一座"冠军的摇篮"，许多上海籍的世界冠军，如游泳选手杨文意和围棋选手常昊都是从体育俱乐部开始启蒙训练的。

如今，已改名为"体育大厦"的大楼开设了上海体育博物馆，展示中国参与奥运会的历史。一块块奥运金牌和成长于"体育摇篮"的冠军照片，与哈沙德设计的华丽天花板相映生辉。

上海体育俱乐部原主任梁立刚认为，这座楼保护得比较好，因为1949年后一直是体育局使用，没有更换过单位。"从局领导到每个员工，都对这座设计精美的历史建筑很有感情。有些老员工回忆，大楼夏天可以不用空调，因为对流特别好，到处回响着风吹关门的声音。"他说。

体育大厦的很多室内细节，也保持着90多年前开幕时的旧貌——如入口处的三座门、深木装饰的图书馆、温水游泳池，还有哈沙德的菱形图案。

昨天： 西侨青年会大楼　**今天：** 体育大厦　**建造时间：** 1928 年　**建筑师：** 哈沙德
建筑风格： 意大利文艺复兴风格
参观指南： 建议参观位于二楼的上海体育博物馆，每周二到周日上午 9 点 30 分到 11 点，下午 2 点到 5 点对外开放。体育大厦的门厅和二楼博物馆大厅都有大量哈沙德设计的建筑细节。

The former Foreign YMCA building opened in the summer of 1928 opposite Shanghai Race Course, today's People Square. Since then the building has always been linked with sporting activities and later became "a cradle of world champions".

The building was constructed to provide accommodation and recreation for foreign young men in Shanghai. The idea of building this magnificent building originated in 1920 when a group of leading men in the city discussed the formation of a Foreign Young Men's Christian Association in Shanghai.

The history of the YMCA dates back to 1844 when Englishman George Williams founded the international organization. In 1900 a Chinese YMCA was found in Shanghai and a modern building with Chinese elements was also built on the People's Square.

In an article in *The China Weekly Review* on March 24, 1928, the then Foreign YMCA general secretary George Fitch recalled it was to provide "a home for men away from home" and "a place where young men of various Western nations could meet and mingle in wholesome fellowship and where they could live comfortably in at-tractive surroundings at a cost of what would be within the reach of all".

With generous contributions from both New York and Shanghai, the idea turned into reality — a fire-proof building designed by American architect Elliott Hazzard.

Heading an influential architectural office in Shanghai in the late 1920s and early 1930s, Hazzard designed three other buildings along Nanjing Road, including the Wing On Tower, Shanghai Power Company and the adjacent China United Assurance Building. The latter and the Foreign YMCA building had dominated the skyline of the former Race Course before the erection of the Park Hotel in 1934.

The 10-floor Foreign YMCA Building in Italian Renaissance style was described by local media as a wonder building "as modern as science and money can make it".

"The rusticated walls of the lower story on the southern facade were in a diaper pattern of brown and rich buff and cream brick set to an effective and pleasing design. These three lower stories blend well with the buffs and the browns and form a pleasing

contrast to buildings of drab coloring. The walls have been broken up by bringing out piers between windows and at the corners which carried right up to the red-tile caps. The piers at the corners are buttressed slightly and the effect secured adds greatly to the charm of the building," *the China Press* reported on June 30, 1928.

In the eyes of this reporter from the American newspaper, it was the triple entrance on Bubbling Well Road (today's Nanjing Road W.) with its three tall and deeply recessed windows above

separated by two pairs of slender and graceful columns that gave significance to the architecture of the building among the many details.

Ellen Johnston Laing, a researcher from Michigan State University, noted the drape pattern was a treatment formerly used on the famous Palazzo Ducale di Venezia. In a study about architect Elliott Hazzard, she wrote that this decorative, very special treatment on the facade was rarely seen in Shanghai. Hazzard used it again in the Xinguang Theater on Ningbo Road two years later.

And the interior of the building was in keeping with its exterior which was not only attractive but

also rather functional. Although an institution with a religious background, both the Chinese YMCA and the Foreign YMCA carried out various activities focusing on young people including sports activities and informative lectures.

The building provided centrally heated, fully furnished rooms with plenty of light and air, a gymnasium, a swimming pool, running track, bowling alley, good meals, club rooms, dressing rooms, special courses of study, facilities for research work, extension lectures and the like.

In all rooms, filtered water from the faucet was available. During the heat of summer the

water was first sent through a large cooling coil. Fountains in the corners of the gymnasium provided refreshment for athletes.

During World War II, the building was occupied by the Japanese army and in 1950 it was taken over by the Shanghai government. The then mayor, Chen Yi, assigned the building to Shanghai Sports Bureau, which opened the Shanghai Sports Club here in 1957 to organize start-up sports classes to select and train future athletes from local children and youngsters.

Since then it became "a cradle of world champions". A galaxy of Chinese stars, including swimmer Yang Wenyi and the go player Chang Hao, started their careers as amateurs at the Shanghai Sports Club.

Now part of the second floor is open to the public as an exhibition room of Shanghai Sports Museum. The history of the Olympic Games and Chinese participation is showcased. Olympic gold medals and huge pictures of smiling Chinese champions who had their first training here glisten under the gorgeous ceiling of this well-designed building.

"The building was well preserved because it has always been used by Shanghai Sports Bureau since 1950. From the bureau leaders to every staff member, we have deep feelings for this well-designed historical building. Some old staff recalled the ventilation was so good that air conditioners were not necessary in hot days. There was constantly the sound of wind blowing doors to close," says Liang Ligang, club director.

It's true that much of the original exterior and interior has remained as on the opening day 90 years ago, such as the triple entrance, the beautiful arches, the dark-wood library, the swimming pool still with warm water in winter and Elliott Harzzard's signature diaper patterns on the facade.

Yesterday: Foreign YMCA Building   **Today:** Shanghai Sports Club   **Built in** 1928
Architect: Elliott Hazzard   **Architectural style:** Italian Renaissance style
Tips: The exhibition room of Shanghai Sports Museum on the second floor is open to the public at 9:30am to 11am, 2pm to 5pm from Tuesdays to Sundays. The exhibition hall as well as the lobby feature abundant original architectural details.

赖斯上校在开幕式上的讲话
Colonel G. R. Rice's Speech at the Opening Ceremony

我想提醒您，三角形是三边形的，代表了人格的三位一体——精神、灵魂和身体。建造这座建筑的目的明确，就是要照顾上海年轻人的这三重需求。这里有一个可供举办演讲和类似活动的高级大厅，为满足年轻人的精神和智力需求做好准备。其实不仅是年轻人，一些年长的人也强烈希望能受邀参加这里的活动。对于年轻人和年长者来说，这座建筑的演讲厅都可以成为传播一切美好事物的中心。那么，大楼为社交活动提供了哪些优质的设施呢？我敢肯定，在健康的氛围中，没有什么地方更适合为那些精神上和智力上有全面需求的人提供服务了。

我还需要讲"三角形"的那第三条边吗？身体的舒适感在这里并没有被忽略，体育馆、游泳池、餐厅、休息室、起居室等设施，可以满足身体的需求。

沃洛普将军希望引起注意的一点，是基督教青年会工作的国际性。尽管这座特殊的建筑是专门为外国人建造的，但基督教青年会在各个种族间开展工作，强调全人类的兄弟情谊。在中国的年轻人也做了大量的工作，而中国基督教青年会在为那些真正善良的中国人提供了一个聚集的地方。这座大楼也将为不同种族和国家的外国年轻人提供相遇的机会，可以讨论问题。在社交时间，不同国家的人可以一起喝杯茶，以友好的方式交流，解决他们脑海中所困扰的问题。而并且随着不同观点的出现，人们能够通过他人的眼睛和视角来看待事物。为了人类共同的利益，他们将会取得进步。而彼此了解得越多，我们越有能力看到问题的两个方面。通过基督教青年会和此类机构建立的国际友谊具有真正的价值，我们有责任尽力协助执行"彼此相爱"的宗旨。

May I remind you, that the triangle is three-sided and it represents the trinity of the human personality — spirit, soul and body. This building has been put up with the express purpose of ministering to the three-fold needs of the young men of Shanghai. There is the fine hall which is available for lectures and the like, and it is here that provision is made for meeting the spiritual and intellectual needs of Shanghai's youth; and not only the youth, for it is the fervent hope of some of the older ones among us that we shall be invited to attend such addresses, and that the lecture hall of this building may be a center for the dissemination of all that is best for young and old...

Then what fine facilities are afforded for social intercourse! There is this side for which provision is required as well as the spiritual and intellectual side and I am sure that no place is better fitted for ministering in a healthy atmosphere to those necessities of a full-orbed existence than the building in which we now find ourselves.

Need I refer to the third side of the triangle? The comfort of the body has not been overlooked. Inspect the gymnasium, the swimming pool, the dining hall, the lounge, the living apartments, and see how admirably the needs of the body have been catered for.

There is one more point to which Gen. Wardrop wished to draw attention and that is the international character of the work of the YMCA. Although this particular building is specially for foreigners, I suppose we are aware that the YMCA carries on its work among all races and does all in its power to emphasize the brotherhood of man. There is a large work among the young men of China and the Chinese YMCA has done much to form a rallying point for those who have the real good of China at heart.

In this building, too, there will be given a common ground for foreign young men, not all of the same race, to meet and discuss questions which affect them. It will be possible during the social hour, over a cup of tea, for men of different nationalities to ventilate, in a friendly way, the problems that occupy their minds, and, as the different points of view are brought to light, and a man is enabled to see matters through the other man's spectacles, definite progress will be made in the interest of humanity, for the more we know one another, the more we understand one another, the better able are we to see that there are two sides to every question and that all the right is not on our own side. International friendships, brought about through the agency of the YMCA and such institutions, have a real value, and it is our duty to do all in our power to assist in the carrying out of the command of the Mater — "Love one another".

摘自 1928 年 7 月 7 日《北华捷报》
Excerpt from *The North-China Herald*, on July 7, 1928

1934年12月1日国际饭店开业，英文《大陆报》制作了一份厚厚的特刊。

这座中国第一座摩天大楼的巨幅照片气势逼人，占据了几乎整个头版，其余20多个版面的报道从不同角度介绍了这座位于上海市中心跑马场的大楼。这是一幢22层高、由四行储蓄会出资建造的大酒店，83.8米的高度堪称当时的亚洲最高楼。来自各国的建材设备供应商，如德国品牌西门子和国产的泰山面砖也纷纷刊登广告，骄傲地宣布这座堪称"上海历史上最有雄心的建筑冒险"的巨厦使用了自家产品。

其中有一篇报道透露，国际饭店能建这么高，与斯裔匈籍设计师邬达克（Laszlo Hudec）有关。如果不是这位东欧建筑师坚韧智慧的"斗争"，国际饭店就不会成为"远东第一高楼"。

邬达克在上海居住了将近30年，为这座城市留下近百个建筑作品，至今仍然熠熠生辉。

1914年邬达克毕业于布达佩斯的匈牙利皇家约瑟夫技术大学建筑系，但一战的爆发让美好前途成

为泡影。年仅21岁的他应征入伍成为一名奥匈军队的炮兵，1916年不幸被俄军俘虏。1918年辗转逃跑至上海。

当时的上海是全世界少数几个不需要护照就能居住的城市，对邬达克来说是一个理想的避难地。他身无分文、腿伤糟糕，口袋里只有一张用假冒俄国护照换来的安全通行证，唯一的资产就是作为建筑师的技能，而这在上海这座经济腾飞人口剧增的城市正好派上用场。功底扎实的邬达克从绘图员做起，迅速崭露头角，几年后就当上了美商克利洋行的合伙人，1925年在外滩创办了自己的事务所。

20世纪30年代是邬达克职业生涯的黄金时期，而南京路又是他的幸运地。1931年到1938年间，邬达克在南京路沿线设计建成了代表作——远东第一高楼国际饭

店、远东第一影院大光明电影院和俗称"绿房子"的远东第一豪宅铜仁路吴同文住宅。其中国际饭店一项足以让他名垂青史。这座装饰艺术派风格的摩天楼，在中国保持建筑高度纪录近半个世纪，一直被视为上海的城市地标。

据《大陆报》报道，由于上海的土地由江海淤积的泥沙形成，大多数建筑都会发生沉降，所以监管租界工程的工部局在国际饭店之前从来没有批准过建造这么高的大楼。他们提出如沉降风险、火灾隐患等种种借口，而业主对这个高度也有顾虑。

邬达克竭尽所能，他先让储蓄会的业主相信，建造摩天楼不仅是可行的，而且在地价昂贵的上海是非常明智的决定。得到业主的认可后，他又与工部局展开周旋，承诺从技术上消除各类安全隐患，如增加消防喷头和使用高质量的钢材，最终让方案通过审批，国际饭店得以顺利建成。

"对于建筑师邬达克来说，这是一场长期而艰难的战斗，但最终他获得了胜利。看看这个漂亮的堪称技术典范的工程，谁不会为邬达克先生这开拓性的工作而喝彩？毫无疑问其他人会接着去建造一座座摩天楼，而他们肯定也会回头看看国际饭店这个最好的'鼻祖'。"报道写道。

邬达克用400根33米长的美国松木桩来夯实国际饭店的地基，又克服了大量技术困难，终于在土质松软的上海第一次建成了这么高的建筑。但是，开工前的这场"战斗"的难度，恐怕不亚于这复杂的地基工程。

国际饭店轮廓修长，顶部层层收进，楼顶好似去掉顶端的金字塔，雄心勃勃地指向天空。建筑的造型是纽约摩天楼惯用的手法，强调垂直线条。立面是防霜的深棕色耐火砖，塑造了国际饭店深色而高雅的经典形象。

四行储蓄会壮丽的营业大厅位于底层，柱子由黑色玻璃包裹，楼上休息厅的墙面镶板则是乌木和黑色大理石制成，天花板呈现抛光的橙黄色。在这里客人们可以坐在愉悦的空调环境里，一边享用饮料，一边观看赛马比赛。

客房的家具均用进口核桃木和柚木制成。14层有举办庆典和

私人派对用的沙龙和烧烤屋，通往一个巨大的景观露台。15到19层都是为贵宾客人设计的套房，储蓄会主任吴鼎昌的套房就在19层。这些套房所用家具陈设极尽奢华，足以满足到访上海的名流们的需要。

上海要建摩天大楼是受到美国影响。据同济大学建筑与城市规划学院刘刚教授介绍，1929年大萧条之前全世界都洋溢着乐观情绪，上海的经济很蓬勃，中国政治也暂时稳定，这一时期的财富积累和文化繁荣都是上海摩天的动力。从20世纪20年代末到30年代初，上海有一种长高的氛围，一批著名高层建筑纷纷涌现，如峻岭公寓（现锦江饭店贵宾楼）、毕卡第公寓（现衡山宾馆）和沙逊大厦（现和平饭店），国际饭店也是其中之一。

邬达克设计国际饭店的灵感很可能缘于1929年大萧条前夕的美国之行。他是一个勤奋认真的人，从年轻时代起每到一地旅游都要记大量笔记和建筑素描，以积累设计素材。在美国访学期间，刘刚教授发现邬达克灵感的来源很可能是位于纽约暖炉大厦（American Radiator Building）的布赖恩特公园酒店（Bryant Park Hotel）。位于美国公共图书馆附近的这家酒店，无论是建筑风格还是褐色面砖饰面这样的细节特征，都与上海国际饭店有着亲切的姐妹关系，只是规模略小而已。

"邬达克所看到的20世纪20年代纽约大都市景象是一种巨大的视觉冲击和心理冲击。他会感觉到一种力量、一种雄心，对未来有更多的一份自信。这份对于未来和城市的崇拜，对于普通人都是自然而然地发生的。"刘教授说。

但他认为，聪明的邬达克把纽约酒店的形体进行简化以适应国际饭店位于上海跑马场的基地，他对于纽约大都市风不是简单拷贝，而是捕捉此类建筑精华后的一种文化移植。

《邬达克》传记作者、意大利建筑历史学者卢卡·彭切里尼（Luca Poncellini）认为国际饭店凝聚了邬达克的各种天赋，是其建筑师生涯的巅峰之作，而国际饭店的落成让上海渴望摩天大楼的梦想成为现实。

"在20世纪二三十年代之交（就像现在一样）摩天大楼是现代化的标志，象征了一个城市在国际舞台上的权势与成功。国际饭店楼顶飘扬的旗帜不仅标志着上海城市的最高点，同时表明这座城市开始以令人震惊的速度，去征服新的荣耀的高点……几十年来的梦想将由这座新近落成的壮美建筑来实现了。建筑大胆的高度及各处的配置显然反映了这个摩登时代……虽然与纽约、华盛顿和其他美国城市的摩天楼相比，国际饭店只有其几分之一的高度，但却是东半球——从伦敦到巴黎，建造过的最高的大楼，确实值得称道。"彭切里尼在书中写道。

1934年《大陆报》的报道也认为国际饭店是将上海由一座普通城市向"领先城市"提升的第一步。

"今天一座摩天大楼是真正的现代化的标志，因为它需要多种最新的技术设备来实现。打个比方，建造它所需的20世纪技术和工艺，就好像2500年前埃及造金字塔和2000年前中国造长城所需要的一样。"报道写道。

当代著名建筑师贝聿铭（Ieoh Ming Pei 1917-2019）曾在一次采访中承认，他对建筑的热爱缘于童年时一次骑车路过静安寺路（现南京西路）。他看见工人们正在为国际饭店挖地基，以建造这幢高达22层的建筑。

继国际饭店之后，邬达克接到几个摩天楼设计项目，包括一个拟为轮船招商局在外滩建造的40层巨厦，但因为1935年银元危机和1937年淞沪抗战爆发等原因最终无一付诸实施。

而由于战乱、政治动乱和经济等原因，国际饭店建成后近半个世纪上海再未建这么高的大楼。国际饭店作为上海的"第一高度"一直持续到1983年上海宾馆建成。此后，高楼大厦像雨后春笋一样在这座昔日的摩登之都拔地而起。"国际饭店连接了我们的过去与未来，摩天楼激励我们努力奋斗。但看到上海中心城区高楼密布，出现大面积像插花一样建高层建筑的城市景观，对于未来的城市和生活环境有什么影响？"刘刚说。

1947年时局动荡，邬达克

Hostelry Of Far East Opens To World Public Here

It Commands The Skies Of Asia

Determine Foundation
les Best; Sheet-Pilings
Displacement Of Soil;
m Columns To Piles

B. S. C. E.

At J.S.S. Building

Building, facing the Race
d-Park Road corner, is the
ave the street level in rise
grade outlook and 200 feet
rrounds 18 feet down
int of the lowest pob
. There are, then, 500

rip From Top
f Hotel Down
s Described

riter Takes "Tour" Of
Building ; Impressed
y Comfort Motif

By LO KEI SAN

Chinese farmer gazing at the
top of Park Hotel from the street
corked to his friend that the
nilling is a "foreign temple".
robably people who have never
skyscrapers will agree with
farmer for anyone making a
through this giant structure
stands so imposingly above
the thousands of buildings in
nghai will gasp at the many
ders" which have never been
ssed before in the Orient.
foreign tourists who pay their
visit to the old temples in Pel-
g, and marvel at the Age of
construction, the historical
ground and the unique de-
. the Park Hotel visitor will
have the same feeling of ad-
ation; only it is for the new
modern and the most up-to-
thoughts and equipment of wes-
construction transplanted on
nese soil.

Max Schiller, quiet, polite
ever-obliging manager of the
Hotel, acted as official guide
I made a "tour" through the
ting. Ushered into one of the
. 600-feet-per-minute elevator
ound ourselves on top of the
ing in 18 seconds! Measuring
ther flagpole to the level of
street we were 300 feet nearer
the clouds than the rikisha
who was pulling his human
up Bubbling Well Road. In-
of making the "tour" from
bottom up we reversed the
by starting from the tower
the 22nd floor, which is exclu-
reserved for the Fire Brigade
Shanghai Municipal Council
went. Going down two
by a narrow concrete stair-
we passed the water-tanks, the
generators and elevator-
es in special enclosures. Here
the Visitors Gallery which is
of like a (photon deck of a
sel. No one can forget the
of Shanghai and the vici-
rom this point.

Excellent View Provided

ting around this gallery, dur-
daytime one can get an ex-
view of the Frenchtown, the
national Settlement, the
hoo, Pooting, and on a clear
ne can see as far as Woo-
and the famous Shanghai Hill
hundred and one big and
vessels and the vast terri-
Pootung. Looking around at
the Race Course is a black
le with the millions of light
ing in all directions, includ-
hint above. The view down
r Road, with the powerful
htful and flashing advertise-
It is scene that will always
emembered.

h, floor has been reserved
D. C. Wu general manager
Yien Yieh Commercial and
gs Savings Society. This
r is probably the highest
the Far East and the lo-
romost ambition that the
ness position that the
his "tophole hi" at

Fit For A King

Mayor Wu Te-chen To Offic
On Bubbling Well Road;
Follow; Day's Events To
ning With Grand Banquet

in Social Shanghai will focus its
Joint Savings Society Building as
structures of the world between 1
e doors of the bank as well as
etting opening to the public at
10 o'clock this morning.

The facilities will extend thre
up tonight with a grand din
the 14th floor of the 22-story

J.S.S. Building
Makes Shanghai
"Leading" City

Joint Savings Society,
Builders, Congratulated
For Courageous Task

To the directors of the Joint Savings Society at Shanghai must go
the credit for building the Park
Hotel. Many others assisted and
many others gave valuable advice,
but it is the owners who have the
sentiments. They passed on the
plans of the architect, they de-
termined what they wanted and they
made their selections accordingly.

We not wish the directors of the
Joint Savings Society to congratu-
lations for undertaking to build this
new hotel but that they have done
so in the face of a world-wide depression makes a doubly more significant.

Shanghai has reason to be proud
of the attainment of the Yangtze,
Kincheng, Continental, and China
South-Sea Banks who are the four
members of the Joint Savings Society and owners of the Park Hotel.

The J.S.S. Building is the first
step towards raising Shanghai from
the level of a common city to a
"leading" city. A skyscraper today
is the first sign of real moderniza-
tion.

because it has required all the most
up-to-date mechanical devices that
must be perfect in the later event,
it is the culmination of 18th century engineering and skill just as
the Pyramids were in Egypt 3,000
years ago and the Great Wall was
in China 2,000 years ago.

The International Hotel Company,
Limited, was formed to erect and
maintain the Park Hotel. The officers and directors were Dr. W. W.
Yen, ambassador to the U.S.S.R.,
Dr. T. Z. Wong, former minister to
foreign affairs; Mr. K. P. Chen,
general manager of the Shanghai
Commercial Savings Bank; Mr.
P. Keel, manager of the realty department of the National Commercial Bank; Dr. T. C. Wu, gene-
manager of the Yien Yieh Co-
mercial Bank and the Joint Sav-
Society; Mr. W. M. Chow, gene-
manager of the Kincheng Bank
Corporation; Mr. Y. Hao, gene-
manager of the China & South A
Bank; Mr. P. H. Hsu general ma-
ger of the Continental Bank; Dr
M. Chien, assistant general mana
of the Joint Savings Society;
Foh, sub-manager of the
Savings Society; Mr. Jent Z
Foh, sub-manager of the
Savings Society; Mr. Sheng Z S
manager of the credit and
department of the Joint
Society; and Mr. Z. L. Lee, ch
manager of fifth division.

Out of the 13 members
Board of Directors, his wer
ed to serve as the managing
tors. They were Dr. T. C.
Chairman, and Messrs. Pan
Juan Z. Y. Hsen, Sheng Z
and Y. Fu Director

This serve as the di
tors they were Dr. T.
as well they were Dr. T
e was an effort to
Municipal Council as a
their 4 five acres of
has on a two bargain
it is one with it.
train hardly overcome
haired in grant 5 he
in the 53rd story and to
ramate spreaders contem
throughout the lawsui
anderg and colonate

The head office of the Joint Savings Society Bank and the Park Hotel as it looks today.

When People Travel, They Want To Stay In A

离开上海，先赴瑞士，晚年移居美国，1958年在加州因心脏病去世。他再也没有回到这座城市，在美国加州伯克利大学谋到教职，安静地从事一直热爱的宗教与考古研究，就这么挥一挥衣袖，仿佛上海的一切都是过眼云烟。

邬达克的名字渐渐被这座城市遗忘了，直到近年关注历史建筑的人越来越多，邬达克重新"热"了起来，甚至成为家喻户晓的"网红"人物。在上海邬达克的两个故居，番禺路别墅和延安西路达华宾馆，都设立了邬达克纪念室。

1949年，国际饭店收归国有，如今是锦江集团旗下的一家四星级酒店。1950年，上海市测绘

部门以国际饭店楼顶旗杆为原点，确立了上海城市平面坐标系。如今，酒店在大堂用一个美丽的装置将原点位置标出，供人欣赏。也许这座昔日中国第一摩天楼是一个新的原点，让人思考上海这座城市的历史与未来。

昨天： 国际饭店　**今天：** 国际饭店　**建筑师：** 邬达克　**建筑风格：** 装饰艺术风格
参观指南： 酒店大堂可供参观，大堂夹层的走廊展示着加拿大学者提供的珍贵历史照片。

In a 1933 cartoon by famous artist Zhang Guangyu, two country bumpkins were speaking against the backdrop of the Park Hotel, then still under construction. Bumpkin A asked, "Wow! Such a tall building, what's it for?" Bumpkin B replied, "You sure know nothing, it's for when the water in the Huangpu River swells up!"

The 83.8-meter, 22-story hotel dominated the city's skyline from 1934 to 1983. It is also architect Laszlo Hudec's most famous work.

In 1930, the Joint Savings Society, founded by four Chinese

banks, decided to invest in a tall modern hotel fronting the former race course. Hudec won the project after an open competition largely due to his previous work on the society's Union Building near the Bund.

"In the early 1930s, at the peak of his career, Laszlo Hudec became the protagonist of the most ambitious and important architectural adventure in the history of Shanghai — the construction of the city's first skyscraper," Italian architectural historian Luca Poncellini wrote in his book *Laszlo Hudec*.

The Park Hotel, or J.S.S. Building, was the first step toward raising Shanghai from the level of a common city to a "leading" city, reported English paper *the China Press* upon the hotel's grand opening in 1934.

"A skyscraper today is the first sign of real modernity because it requires all the most up-to-date mechanical devices of man to perfect it. In other words, it is the quintessence of 20th century engineering and skill just as the Pyramids were to Egypt 2,500 years ago and the Great Wall was to China 2,000 years ago," the paper reported.

Tongji University professor Liu

Gang says Shanghai was in an atmosphere to grow higher since the 1920s under the influence of American skyscrapers and worldwide optimism before the 1929 Great Depression.

"Shanghai's booming economy, China's temporary political stability and cultural prosperity were all forces to push the city higher and higher. Some tall buildings had been erected since the late 1920s, such as the Sassoon House and Broadway Mansion. Park Hotel was one of them," he says.

During a US trip in 1929, Hudec witnessed the architectural upheaval that left leading American cities dotted with skyscrapers and grand hotels.

"He spent a long time in New York, Chicago and other cities and made drawings of many skyscrapers and their decorative details. His trip to America must have had a decisive influence on the designs he later drew for the J.S.S. Building," says architectural historian Poncellini.

Professor Liu says New York in the 1920s had a huge visual and psychological impact on newcomers, who would naturally feel a kind of power and ambition.

The facade of the Park Hotel is emphasized with vertical stripes, which shrink layer upon layer until the top, a typical American modern Art Deco style. Today its imposing but stable silhouette, as well as the staircase-like tower above the 15th floor provide a unique elegant look compared to the surrounding modern skyscrapers.

As a visiting scholar from University of Pennsylvania in the US years ago, professor Liu says Hudec may have been inspired by the Bryant Park Hotel in New York.

"Located close to the Public Library, the Bryant Park Hotel closely resembles Shanghai Park Hotel, from the architectural features to the unique facade covered by dark-brown tiles. New York's version was a bit smaller in scale," Liu says.

"But Hudec was so brilliant that he simplified the shape of the New York hotel to suit Shanghai's context. His design highlighted architectural grandeur in a more intense way," he adds.

"He captured the essence of this architectural form and made a cultural transplantation. I don't think it was a copy. He was not obedient, instead he joined this trend with unprecedented confidence. Remember it was an era of internationalism rather than globalization."

It's widely known that Park Hotel sits on a reinforced concrete raft base of 400 33-meter-long piles of Oregon pine, which is topped by light-weight alloy with great strength to prevent it from sinkage, a problem Shanghai architects had struggled with for decades.

Compared with the efforts to solve the foundations problem, Hudec expended more energy just to get approval to build the hotel.

According to a 1934 article in *the China Press*, the then Shanghai Municipal Council had not allowed buildings over the height of the J.S.S. Building. Various excuses were offered such as fire hazards or danger of sinking.

"In addition to the opposition from the government, Mr. Hudec had to convince the owners of the bank that a skyscraper was not only reasonable but highly advisable. At first they were disinclined to accept the reasoning but in the end Mr. Hudec was able to convince the owners that a skyscraper on Bubbling Well Road would not only be most practical but one of the most unique ventures that have been undertaken in the Far East. With the consent of the owners in his pocket, Mr. Hudec returned to the fray with the Council authorities."

This took considerably more time. With promises of a fire lookout on the 22nd story and other guarantees with regard to fire sprinklers, the quality of steel and general structural materials, permission was finally given for the new skyscraper.

"It was a long and hard fight waged by architect Hudec, but eventually he won. Looking at this beautiful example of engineering skill, who today will not extend a hearty applause for the pioneering work of Mr. Hudec in fostering the first real skyscraper in the Far East? No doubt others will follow and when they do they must look back upon the Joint Savings Building as their rightful forebearer," the report said.

On the morning of Decem-

ber 1, 1934, then Shanghai Mayor Wu Te-chen cut the ribbons at the entrance and officially opened the Park Hotel. From the opening day, the hotel became a major venue of modern life and the first choice of international VIPs while in Shanghai. Renowned Chinese-American architect I.M. Pei has admitted it was the Park Hotel that greatly attracted him to architecture.

It's noteworthy that the hotel was built by main contractor Voh Kee Co. with various Chinese suppliers providing everything from black polished granite on the plinth of the external walls to dark brown Taishan tiles on the facades.

Hudec and his team enjoyed the highest honor of their career from this skyscraper. He received commissions for other skyscrapers one after another. Even the China Merchants Steam Navigation Company planned to erect a

40-story building on the Bund.

However within a year the 1935 world silver crisis had a devastating effect on Shanghai. The financial center of China fell into a depression, which was exacerbated after Japan invaded Shanghai in 1937. Construction came to an abrupt halt in the city.

After 1949, the Park Hotel became state-owned and now serves as a 4-star hotel of the Jinjiang Group.

The Park Hotel remained the city's only skyscraper for decades, until it was surpassed by the 26-story, 91.5-meter Shanghai Hotel in 1983.

Once Shanghai Hotel was built, high-rise buildings began mushrooming around Shanghai, especially in the 1990s.

The Chinese term for skyscrapers, mo tian lou, literally means magical building that reaches the sky. In his famous book *Shanghai Modern: The Flowering of a New Urban Culture in China 1930-1945*, Harvard University professor Ou-fan Lee describes skyscrapers as a visible sign of the rise of industrial capitalism and the most intrusive addition to the Shanghai landscape, which offered a sharp contrast to the general principles of low-rise Chinese architecture.

No wonder skyscrapers had elicited such heightened emotions about socioeconomic inequality — the high and the low, the rich and the poor — in 1930s cartoons and films such as the two country bumpkins talking about the Park Hotel.

"The Park Hotel connects our past to the future. Skyscrapers encourage us to strive for more, but now our city is filled with them like massive flower arrangements planted in a casual way," says professor Liu.

In a 1950 municipal survey, the flagpole of the Park Hotel was referred to as "Zero Center Point of Shanghai" because of its central location and height. Upon its 80th anniversary, perhaps the Park Hotel will once again become a starting point for us to ponder the city's past and its future development.

Yesterday: the Park Hotel   **Today:** the Park Hotel   **Built in** 1934
Architect: L. E. Hudec   **Architectural Style:** Art Deco
Tips: I'd suggest visit the informative archival showroom at the second floor of the hotel.

螺蛳壳里做电影院

Hudec's Most Difficult Job

2010年上海世博会期间，一部关于建筑师邬达克的斯洛伐克纪录片在大光明电影院举行全球首映，片名为"改变上海的男人"。这位东欧建筑师留给上海的百件建筑作品中，大光明电影院被业界认为是最有挑战的设计。

"这是我最喜欢的邬达克作品。因为基地狭长且不规则，邬达克的设计几易其稿才最终确定，真正体现了'螺蛳壳里做道场'的功力。他的建筑图纸最终为英国皇家建筑师学会所收藏。"《上海邬达克建筑地图》作者、同济大学教授华霞虹说。

这个后来被誉为"远东第一影院"的建筑其实是个改建项目。初建于1928年的老大光明影戏院是一座古典风格的影院，由邬达克的东欧老乡——匈牙利建筑师鸿达（C. H. Gonda）的鸿达洋行设计，因放映辱华电影《不怕死》（Welcome Danger）影响声誉而停止营业。1932年，英籍广东人卢根与美商组建联合电影公司拆除旧楼，邀请邬达克在原址设计一座新影院。

曾担任大光明电影院修缮建筑师的林沄研究历史图纸发现，改建后的大光明大戏院用地条件极差：整个地块形状狭长而不规整，仅内部腹地稍宽，沿南京西路的街面被夹在店铺之间。在这样的地块上要设计一座豪华影剧院，观众厅还要容纳2000个座位，是相当困难的。

邬达克的解决方案非常巧妙。他在老大光明大戏院的椭圆平面基础上，将观众厅与门厅轴线做了30度扭转。两层的休息厅设计成腰果形，与流线形的门厅浑然一体，休息厅中央还点缀着灯光喷水池。走进大光明，两部气派的大楼梯直通二楼，让人完全感觉不到基地狭长的不足。

邬达克用装饰艺术手法设计了影院进厅与休息厅的楼梯栏杆和暖气外罩等细部，还使用了当时时髦的不锈钢材料，打造了充满金色和银色金属光泽的墙面和天花板。他设计的水磨石地坪还不断出现装饰性符号图案，仿佛引领观众一步步进入影厅，成为大光明电影院很吸引人的装饰特色之一。

林沄还提到，当时国泰大戏院和兰心剧院等剧场都位于街道转角处，地理位置显著，而大光明大戏院的主入口在高楼林立的南京西路，三层高的建筑很难"脱颖而出"。为此，邬达克又想出妙招，在大光明南立面上增加了一个高达 30.5 米的玻璃灯塔，在夜晚明亮夺目，成为点睛之笔。建筑外观呈现装饰艺术风格，立面横竖线条形成对比，中间升起的高耸灯塔成为所有竖线条的高潮，错落有致，一气呵成，为这座娱乐建筑塑造了活泼动人的形象。

1931 年，邬达克的设计方案发布后，英文《大陆报》进行了详细报道。

"上海就像世界上任何一个如此规模的城市一样，为电影而疯狂。中国的其他地区都不了解好莱坞的活力，但这座大都会每年都乐于付出高昂代价，以大饱眼福地欣赏在银幕上演的滑稽动作。上海剧院的发展最近才开始跟上大众对电影的兴趣。今天，上海刚宣布建设第一个'电影圣殿'的计划，新的大光明大戏院位于静安寺路。"报道写道。

1933 年 6 月 14 日，更名为大光明大戏院的新影院开幕，首映好莱坞电影《热血雄心》（*Hell Below*），开启了一个辉煌时代。1949年前，大光明主要放映美国福克斯、米高梅等公司的原版影片，也是工部局音乐会的常驻地。这里也是第一家使用译意风(Earphone，类似同声翻译)的影院。除了放映电影，大戏院里还设有舞厅、咖啡馆和弹子房等娱乐设施。著名建筑师贝聿铭少时常去大光明电影院看电影、打撞球。在那里，他深受美国电影的影响，也被邬达克另一件代表作——国际饭店深深吸引，从此开始了做一名建筑师的梦想。

《邬达克》传记作者、意大利学者卢卡·彭切里尼提到，邬达克设计大光明时正值他建筑师生涯的鼎盛时期。随着国际新建筑风格的出现，邬达克的设计风格也发生了重大转变，成为上海新风格建筑最引人注目的大力推动者。他的设计风格的转变最初出现在1932年建成的的真光大楼上，这座表现主义风格的办公建筑造型简洁，有哥特式尖券的造型和褐色面砖。

"具有强烈时代感的大光明大戏院于1933年6月的落成，标志着邬达克设计风格完成了彻底的转变，他的新潮设计立刻受到建筑界的广泛关注，并由此奠定了他作为上海最有影响的现代建筑师的地位。"彭切里尼写道。而一年半后高达83.8米的国际饭店落成，进一步确立了他在上海建筑史上的先锋地位。位于南京路沿线的大光明大戏院、国际饭店和1938年建成的更现代的"绿房子"（吴同文住宅），成为邬达克三件最著名的代表作。

1949年后，大光明大戏院更名为大光明电影院。2007年，林沄任职的上海章明建筑设计事务所负责修缮影院，恢复了不少历史原貌，同时升级了观影设施。2017年，章明事务所将这个项目收入《我在上海修历史建筑》一书中。

在修缮中，因为只有黑白历史照片，调查建筑细部的原始色彩是最困难的。入口大厅的天花板有三层颜色——浅黄、浅绿和金色，观众厅的天花板也有七层不同时期的颜色，从银色到各种

林晓 2019.02.11.
大光明彩笔

深浅的绿色都有。

最终，修缮团队根据上海建筑史学家罗小未先生、建筑师章明和影院老员工的回忆，为大厅天花板选用"阳光氛围"的金色箔纸，为观众厅挑选了淡雅别致的浅灰绿色，营造温暖沉稳的氛围。

2009年1月19日，大光明电影院重新开业，金色大厅和灰绿色观众厅都受到好评。大光明再次成为一家明亮夺目的电影院。

昨天： 大光明大戏院　　**今天：** 大光明电影院　　**地址：** 南京西路 216 号　　**建造时间：** 1933 年
建筑风格： 装饰艺术风格
参观指南： 建筑室对外开放，放映厅需购票进入。请留意 1928 年大光明大戏院的历史遗迹——位于二楼的砖砌柱，也可以欣赏大厅地面上的"邬达克密码"。

Architect Laszlo Hudec's most difficult project in Shanghai has to be the Grand Theatre.

"Hudec showed the ultimate skills in handling this project, which almost seems impossible — to design a spacious, stylish cinema on a very unusual shaped plot of land. The draft was later added to the collection of the Royal Institute of British Architects," says Tongji University professor Hua Xiahong, author of *Shanghai Hudec Architecture*.

In 1928, a cinema was built on the plot. It earned notoriety after screening the film *Welcome Danger*, a movie that humiliated Chinese by portraying them as drug dealers and robbers. The cinema was forced to close down in 1931 because the movie ignited anger among locals.

Chinese-British Lu Geng, co-founder of United Movies Co., demolished the cinema and hired Hudec to design a new one.

Lin Yun of Shanghai Zhang Ming Architectural Design Firm and chief architect of the theater's 2007 renovation project says the plot was long, narrow and irregular, which made it extremely difficult to design a luxurious 2,000-seat cinema.

He says Hudec's solution was ingenious. Graced by fancy fountains, the lobbies on the first and second floors were shaped like cashews to fit with the shape of the land plot.

Two grand staircases led people from the entrance to the second floor. The artful use of a variety of curves created a free-flowing effect inside.

"Some famous cinemas built in that era like Nanking Theatre or the Cathay Theatre were on street corners, which were prominent locations. But the Nanjing Road facade of Grand Theatre was unfortunately sandwiched between tall shops," Lin adds. "Therefore, Hudec designed a 30.5-meter-high glass lighting pillar atop the 3-story cinema, which immediately stood out from a line of shops. The cubic glass lighting pillar was

particularly eye-catching at night as it contrasted with the vertical and horizontal lines on the facade — very modern."

Hudec's style changed significantly in the 1930s as new trends swept across the city. He first experimented with this change on the True Light Buildings on Yuanmingyuan Road in 1932. The Grand Theatre marked a complete transformation, which made him the most noticeable architect in Shanghai's new architectural movement.

As soon as Hudec's tentative plan was released in 1931, English newspaper China Press gave a detailed report:

"Shanghai is as movie-mad as any city of its size in the world. The rest of China is oblivious to

the energies of Hollywood, but this metropolis pays a huge annual toll cheerfully to feast its eyes on the antics of the silver screen. The theaters in Shanghai have improved in proportion to the interest shown in them, until today plans have just been announced for Shanghai's first 'Cathedral of the Moving Picture' — the new Grand Theatre on Bubbling Well Road."

The Grand Theatre opened its doors to the public on June 14, 1933, with the Hollywood movie *Hell Below*. It immediately became one of the most popular entertainment venues in town, going on to screen movies produced by 20th Century Fox and Metro-Goldwyn-Mayer, as well as staging concerts. It was also the first cinema to offer simultaneous translation when foreign films were screened.

The building also had a dance hall, cafe and billiard rooms. The main auditorium was shaped like a big bell and seated nearly 2,000 people on two floors — the biggest capacity of any cinema in China at the time.

Grand Theatre was renamed Grand Cinema in 1949 and continued screening movies through the 1990s (the name was changed back after the renovation). By this time, moviegoers started going to newer facilities with modern comforts and conveniences. Thus the 2007 renovation project was not just about reviving its original look, but also upgrading the facilities. Five small halls, a roof garden and a restaurant were added during the renovation project.

Architects used one of Hudec's draft plans for the cinema to help with the restoration. Archival photos also helped. Lin says getting the original colors just right was the toughest task since they had to work with black-and-white photos. His team discovered seven layers of historical fragments from the ceiling of the main auditorium — silver in the innermost layer to various shades of green.

They chose a light green tone for the ceiling after speaking with former cinema employees and Shanghai architectural historian Luo Xiaowei.

The entrance hall's ceiling had three layers of colors, buff, gentle green and gold. The restoration team finally decided to use a golden foil based on architect Zhang Ming's impression that the theater had a "golden sunny atmosphere".

"Hudec has depended largely upon a combination of lighting

effects and beautiful materials to get the desired result," Lin says. "In the old days the Grand Theatre looked even more 'shiny' than today because it was designed for the city's 'modern era' — the 1930s."

The team's hard work has paid dividends. Since reopening on January 19, 2009, moviegoers have returned to the cinema in droves. It is once again one of the city's top theaters — and also happens to be the most unique.

Yesterday: The Grand Theatre   **Today:** The Grand Theatre   **Address:** 216 Nanjing Rd W.
Built in 1933   **Architectural style:** Art Deco
Tips: Relics of the 1928 cinema have been preserved by both Hudec and architects in charge of the 2007 renovation, including exterior brick columns on the second floor (fronting No. 2 Cinema hall) and creamy white terrazzo staircase on the western side. It's interesting to find them or decode the mysterious "Hudec symbols" used extensively on the floor. Tickets are required to enter the auditorium.

跑马总会的新时代

A New Era for Shanghai Race Club Building

1933年的一个春日，上海跑马总会董事长伯克尔先生（A. W. Burkill）在来宾见证下，以夫人的名义为总会新楼和新看台安放奠基石。"1933年5月21日，奠基石由凯瑟琳·伯克尔夫人（Mrs Katherine Burkill）安放，以纪念新楼的崛起，也纪念1863年的老看台被拆除。"奠基石上写着。

今天，这块奠基石依然镶嵌在上海历史博物馆北立面的左下角。2018年3月，昔日跑马总会俱乐部历经多年修缮，改造为上海历史博物馆对公众开放。博物馆从11万件馆藏里精选了1000件文物展示，但主持修缮的著名建筑师唐玉恩认为，"上海历史博物馆最大的展品，就是这座建筑本身。"

她认为，这座总会建筑蕴含了丰富的历史。20世纪50年代开始，它历经变迁，先后做过上海图书馆、上海博物馆和上海美术馆，建筑本身映射了上海的历史。

1934年大楼竣工时，英文《大陆报》称这是"远东地区最好最奢华的的俱乐部"。

同济大学郑时龄院士在《上海近代建筑风格》新版中写道，跑马总会大楼由擅长古典主义风格的英国建筑事务所马海洋行设计，立面比例严谨。由于面对南京西路的面比较窄，建筑师设计了一座高49米的钟塔，形成一条南北向的轴线。

他提到，马海洋行由英国土木工程师学会准会员马矿司（Robert Bradshaw Moorhead）于1900年创立，其名称历经从马矿司洋行（Moorhead, R. B）到马海洋行（Moorhead & Halse, Moorhead, Halse & Robinson）再到新马海洋行（Spence, Robinson & Partners）的变化，代表作还有外滩1号麦边大楼、拉结会堂和中南银行。

唐玉恩研究发现，大楼是一座典型的总会建筑。总会建筑是为满足租界外籍人士聚会社交的需求而建的一种特殊建筑类型，也是西方文化和城市生活传播到远东的体现。在老上海，各国都建造了富有本国特色的总会建筑，如外滩的英国上海总会和德国总会、福州路的美国花旗总会，还有两家法国总会——分别是今天的科学会堂和花园饭店。总会建筑的设计与商业建筑不同，倾向于使用轻松的乡村风格或类似该国民间建筑的形式。

"上海中心城区有数量众多的总会建筑，这在我国其他城市是不多见的。这些总会以会员制为主，提供酒吧、餐厅、阅览室、滚球房等设施，空间非常丰富，功能多样，是高端的交际场所。"唐玉恩介绍。

而上海跑马总会的功能与其他总会建筑也很相似。《大陆报》报道介绍，一楼有为会员和客人计算赌金的设备，二楼有休闲室、阅览室、会员咖啡屋、客人休息室和纸牌屋。楼上还有两座羽毛球场、两条英式和四条美式保龄球道、几个壁球场和公寓房。看台可以容纳大量观众。

如今，昔日跑马总会俱乐部被称为"东楼"，以区别于历史博物馆院落中的"西楼"——一座建于20世纪20年代的马厩。在这次修缮中，"马厩"也被改造为博物馆的展陈空间。

"俱乐部"与"马厩"虽然建于不同年代，比例都很优美，反映了当时正流行的英国新古典主义建筑风格。与华丽的外滩银行建筑相比，跑马总会的两座楼很简约。

"建筑师并没有用大量石材，而是使用红砖与水刷石相结合。上海工匠的高超技艺令人惊叹，他们用水刷石做出很多漂亮的细部，仿石水平非常高，铁饰也很精致。东楼的轮廓线如此美丽，已经成为上海的城市地标。"唐玉恩评价道。

她认为这座造型优美的建筑作为文化建筑很合适，无论作为图书馆、美术馆还是历史博物馆，市民都很喜欢。不过，为上海历史博物馆找到这个合适的"新家"，却花费了原馆长张岚和团队数年的时间。

"我们做过好几个方案，包括汉口路原工部局大楼、外滩原汇丰银行大楼、大世界、杨浦水厂和上海世博会城市足迹馆等。这些备选建筑由于面积、停车和安置费用等问题都不适合。"张岚回忆道。

上海历史博物馆源于20世纪30年代上海市博物馆的历史文献展厅和上海通志馆。1954年，上海市政府学习苏联模式筹建上海历史与建设博物馆，将老上海市博物馆的部分文物和上海通志馆的文献组成了这样一个馆。长期以来，上海历史博物馆并无固定展陈空间，曾在文化广场、农展馆和东方明珠等地设展。2010上海世博会举办后，上海美术馆迁往中华艺术宫，空置下来的昔日跑马总会大楼成为

历博的"新家"。

张岚认为2016年启动的改造工程非同一般，"是在一个保护建筑里建博物馆"。在满足功能的前提下，最重要的是保护好历史建筑。而工程的亮点是露出原来封闭的历史细部，如砖墙和藻井，展陈设计的线条也尽量与新古典主义线条吻合，做到与老建筑完美结合。

唐玉恩提到，木雕、石雕和跑马主题特色的马头雕饰等细节都根据历史照片进行修复。工程进行中不断有新的历史细节被发现，设计方案也相应做了多次修改。

"经过修缮，东楼塔楼的大钟正常运行，给南京路沿线提供报时。我们对于历史建筑的保护和使用常怀敬畏之心，精心保护并科学使用，真正让历史建筑有尊严地走向未来。"她说。

虽然坐落于一座历史建筑里，上海历史博物馆却是按照现代博物馆的要求设计的，有恒温恒湿系统、流通的展线和自动扶梯。舒适照明和展柜的低散射玻璃都让参观变成愉快的享受。

如今，东楼和西楼由地下连廊连接，两楼之间的空间设计为一个内院，保留着几棵历史悠久的大树。

"上海历史博物馆不是以专家作为参观主体，它为每一个对上海这座城市感兴趣的人而设计。观众们可以得到不同的享受，这是个让青年人受教育、让中年人休闲和让老年人怀旧的地方。"张岚说。

1933年的那个春天，伯克尔主席致辞时讲到，安放奠基石标志了上海总会新纪元的开始。如今，这座建筑已经开启了上海城市历史的新时代。

昨天： 上海跑马总会俱乐部　**今天：** 上海历史博物馆（上海革命历史博物馆）
地址： 南京西路 325 号　**建造时间：** 1934 年　**建筑师：** 马海洋行
参观指南： 周二到周日全天 9 点到 5 点开馆，建议欣赏建筑内的历史细节，如楼梯栏杆的马头雕饰。这里的展览也生动展示了上海这座城市独特的历史，展品包括曾用来铺设南京路的铁藜木砖。

On a spring day 85 years ago, A.W. Burkill, chairman of Shanghai Race Club, laid on behalf of his wife the cornerstone of the new stands and clubhouse at the Bubbling Well racecourse.

A large gathering witnessed the ceremony, and lines on the stone read: "This foundation stone was laid on 21st May, 1933, by Mrs. Katherine Burkill and commemorates the demolition of the original grandstand erected in 1863 and the erection of this building."

The stone can still be seen on the facade of the building which reopened in 2018 as Shanghai History Museum after years of preparation and restoration.

The new museum displayed 1,000 exhibits handpicked from its rich collection of some 110,000 antiques and documents on the history of Shanghai. However, Tang Yu'en, chief architect of the restoration, says "the largest exhibit is the building itself".

"The building was built as

Shanghai Race Club, which underwent changes and was used as Shanghai Museum, Shanghai Library and Shanghai Art Museum. This is a monument that mirrors the history of Shanghai." Tang says.

When completed in 1934, the structure was described as "the finest and most luxurious in the Far East" by *the China Press* newspaper.

Tang says it is a typical club building, a unique genre of architecture in old Shanghai, which served as a social center for expatriates and showcased Western culture's spread to the Far East.

Several countries established their own clubs in Shanghai at that time, including Britain's Shanghai club and Germany's Club Concordia on the Bund, an American club on Fuzhou Road and two French clubs which are today's Science Hall and Okura Garden Hotel.

"It was rare for a Chinese city like Shanghai to have such a congregation of foreign club buildings in the downtown area. With a variety of inner spaces for multiple functions, these clubs served as high-end social centers, offering their members different services—from bars, restaurants, bil-

liard rooms to reading rooms," Tang says.

The racecourse club was no exception according to *the China Press*:

"On the ground floor are betting facilities for members and guests. On the first floor are recreation rooms, reading rooms, members' coffee room, guest rooms and card rooms. The upper floors contain two badminton courts, two English and four American-style bowling alleys, several squash courts and residential flats. The pavilion is made to accommodate a large number of spectators under one roof."

Tang says foreign club buildings, which differed from commercial architecture, were often designed in a more relaxed country style or in a style similar to the nation's traditional architecture.

Today, the race club is called the "east building" because the museum compound has a "west building", a former stable built in the 1920s which has been restored as an exhibition hall.

Both buildings have beautiful proportions and feature the British neoclassical style popular at the time. Unlike the sumptuous financial buildings on the Bund, the two race club buildings are in a more simple style. Instead of using a lot of stones, the architect combined red bricks with Shanghai plaster which was more economic.

"I was amazed at the superb skills of Shanghai craftsmen who created many beautiful details with plaster and imitated stone effects successfully. There are also delicate cast iron decorations. The east building has such a beautiful, lively shape whose silhouette has become a landmark of Shanghai,"

Tang adds.

She says the building is ideal for a cultural venue popular with Shanghai citizens no matter if it was as a library, an art museum or the soon-to-be history museum. But it took years for former curator Zhang Lan and his team to secure the historic building which became vacant only after Shanghai Art Museum moved to the China Pavilion after World Expo. Shanghai 2010.

"Before this building was available, we had several plans and choices for the museum's new home—from the former Shanghai Municipal Council building on Hankou Road, the old Shanghai Natural History Museum on Yan'an Road to the former HSBC

building on the Bund, Yangpu Water Plant and the Urban Footprint Pavilion of Shanghai Expo.. These plans all failed due to various reasons such as building size, parking places or relocation costs. Finally the art museum became vacant," recalls Zhang.

The history of the race club building dates back to an exhibition hall of historical documents of Shanghai Museum in the 1930s and later a Shanghai history section organized by the city's cultural relics management committee. Without a permanent display space for decades, the museum had to host exhibitions in various places including the Oriental Pearl TV Tower in the Pudong New Area. The restoration project for the new home kicked off in 2016.

"It's a unique project because we built a museum inside a historical building, so preservation came first. It took great efforts to fit new functions of the museum into an old building," Zhang says.

The highlight of the restoration is the display of some hidden original parts, such as the exquisite caisson ceilings and brick walls. A galaxy of architectural details, from decorative sculptures on the verandas and wooden dados to ornaments shaped like horses' heads have all been carefully restored according to historical and field surveys.

"The restored bell on the tower top will work and give time to the Nanjing Road area, just like the bell tower of Custom House on the Bund. The principle of my work is to first respect old buildings which contain historical and artistic values, and then use them in a scientific way. So that they can be sustainably used and live in a new era with dignity," Tang says.

Though in a historical building, Shanghai History Museum is equipped with modern facilities such as temperature-and-humidity-control systems, escalators, comfortable lighting and anti-reflective glass to ensure a pleasant visit. Most of the exhibition content is child-friendly and interactive.

The east and west buildings are now linked by an underground corridor while the space between them will be turned into a garden with the original tall trees preserved.

"This museum is not only for experts and researchers, but for everyone interested in Shanghai. I hope it will be a place where young people can learn, the middle-aged can relax and more elderly visitors can enjoy some nostalgia," says Zhang.

In 1933, Burkill said the laying of the foundation stone marked

a new epoch in the history of Shanghai Race Club. In the spring of 2018, the building marked the beginning of another new epoch in the city's history.

Yesterday: Shanghai Race Club Building
Today: Shanghai History Museum/Shanghai Revolution Museum
Address: 325 Nanjing Rd W.   **Date of construction:** 1934
Architect: Messrs Spence, Robinson and Partners
Tips: The museum opens daily, except for Mondays, from 9am to 5pm (no admission after 4pm).

同舟共济的德国医院
The Story of Tung Chee Hospital

2020年的抗疫新闻几乎每天都有关于武汉同济医院的报道。武汉的同济医院，全称是华中科技大学同济医学院附属同济医院，其官网写着"长江之滨，黄鹤楼下，有一所海内外闻名遐迩的医院……同济医院1900年由德国医师埃里希·宝隆创建于上海，1955年迁至武汉"。医院介绍还配了一张这位大胡子德国医生的照片。

这位曾被上海人亲切称为"大宝医生"的宝隆（Erich Paulun）1862年3月4日出生于德国，2岁时父母患肺结核双双去世，他不幸成为孤儿。由亲戚抚养长大的宝隆选择参军，1882年在基尔的皇家弗里德希·威廉外科医学学院学习，后成为一名德国海军的上尉随舰医生。

1891年，他在德国海军服役期间随军舰，第一次到访上海，亲眼所见老城里卫生条件不佳，流行病和瘟疫肆虐，穷人缺医少药深受疾病之苦。宝隆深受触动，想用自己所学改变这些悲剧。他后来写信给常驻上海的德国医生策德里乌斯（Carl Zedelius），表达了自己的强烈愿望：希望用自己所有的力量和知识为中国的穷人办一家医院。这位精力充沛的德国医生是个行动主义者。为了实现自己的想法，他开始认真地做准备工作，先回国进修学习，到两家医院工作提升外科医术，并继续到大学进修，同时也为筹建医院积攒资金。

19世纪90年代初，宝隆再次来到上海，先担任策德里乌斯的助理。1899年，策德里乌斯去世后，宝隆接替了他的工作。同年，他与另一位德国医生冯沙伯（Oscar von Schab）成立了上海德医公会，起初在德国驻沪领事馆行医，随后在后来的白克路、静安寺路（今凤阳路、南京西路）买了一块地，终于实现多年的心愿——开办了收治中国穷人的"同济医院"（Tung Chi Hospital），并担任院长。

同济近似上海话里"德国"的发音"Deutsche"，也有"同舟共济"的寓意。根据1909年4月3日英文《北华捷报》报道，这家成立于1900年的医院开始只有几座从德国军方购买的白铁皮房子，仅有20张床位，十分简陋。同年，宝隆和策德里乌斯的女儿结婚，在上海正式安家落户。

到了1901年，医院用来自中德人士的捐款在原址建起一座红砖建筑。一份1909年关于医院的新闻报道写道："一楼有一间药房、几个储藏室、门诊室、仪器室和手术室。主要的手术室有三张手术台，并配有消毒器、器械箱、洗手池，实际上配备了现代无菌手术所需的所有条件。手术室外面有一个设备充沛的仪器室，外面是一个装有电灯浴的小房间，用于治疗风湿病人。此外，还有其他电气设备。大楼另一端的主药房与门诊室相连，德国医生每晚在这里慈善义诊50到70位病人。楼上有12间供中国付费病人使用的房间，男女病人各6间。"

同济医院对病人"区别对待"——穷苦华人可享受免费治疗，而德国公司的中方雇员看病需要支付费用。医院得到时任德国总领事克奈佩（Wilhelm Knappe）、上海道台和一些华商

的捐助，包括叶澄衷、朱葆三和虞洽卿。

在上海，宝隆实现了自己的另一个心愿：在同济医院的基础上建一所培养中国医生的同济德文医学堂。1907年10月1日，这家得到中德两国政府支持的医学堂举行了开学典礼，宝隆担任首任校长，德国领事和上海道台都出席了仪式。医学堂在白克路同济医院对面的房屋中启动，随后于1908年在今复兴中路、陕西南路购地，邀请德国建筑师Carl Baedecker设计新校区，1912年又增建了工学堂。在动荡岁月里，这所学堂历经多次起伏变迁，最终发展为一所综合性的大学，就是今天的同济大学。

不过世事难料，1909年3月5日，宝隆医生染病英年早逝，年仅47岁。

宝隆医生去世后，"同济医院"改名为"宝隆医院"，以示纪念。1927年，国际饭店设计师邬达克曾负责医院新楼的设计。

巧合的是，在接手宝隆医院项目一年前的1926年，邬达克在上海设计了另一家外侨捐建的医院：宏恩医院（The Country Hospital，今华东医院一号楼）。在落成时，匿名出资的美国富商用两名外国医生的名字为宏恩医院的两间病房命名，以表达他"最崇高的敬意"，其中一位就是宝隆。

1946年抗战胜利后，宝隆医院更名为中美医院，1951年又更名为同济大学附属同济医院。1951年到1955年，同济医院分批迁往湖北武汉，更名为"武汉医学院附属第二医院"。1955年10月1日，国防部颁令在汉口路515号建立第二军医大学急症外科医院，对外称上海急症外科医院。1959年，上海急症外科医院与同济医院合并，改名为第二军医大学附属第二附属医院，使用"上海同济医院"的名字，后更名为上海长征医院。凤阳路上留下的院址，成为今天长征医院所在地。如今，长征医院在院史中也专门介绍宝隆和同济医院的悠久历史。

宝隆创办的同济德文医学堂，位于复兴中路陕西南路，校园里，德国建筑师设计的红砖古典建筑犹存，如今是上海理工大学的校园。校门口的陕西南路也一度被命名为宝隆路。

而在位于四平路同济大学校园内的校史馆里，宝隆医生的雕像就在入口处，仿佛仍在散发着他的热力、生命力和阳光，迎接对这段历史感兴趣的人们。2000年，同济大学合并上海铁道大学，将铁道大学附属甘泉医院更名为同济大学附属同济医院。

迁往武汉的同济医学院和同济医院发展为华中科技大学同济医学院和其附属同济医院。2020年2月20日新华社刊登的战疫报道里提到，武汉同济医院的院训"与国家同舟，与人民共济"，也是全国医务人员驰援武汉，战胜疫魔坚定信念的写照。来自国内顶级医院的医疗队纷纷驰援武汉，同济医院成为武汉市收治新冠肺炎重症患者最多的医院之一。这些前往武汉驰援的医疗队伍中也有来自同济医院创办地上海的医疗队，他们与武汉同济医生一起真正地"同舟共济"。

昨天： 宝隆医院　**今天：** 上海长征医院　**地址：** 凤阳路 415 号　**设计师：** 邬达克

German doctor Erich Paulun was orphaned at the age of 2 but he had a loving heart of determinations. Today, both Shanghai Changzheng Hospital and Tongji University originated from the charitable "Tung Chee Hospital" Paulun founded in the heart of Shanghai for poor Chinese patients.

The name "Tung Chee" or "Tong Ji" represents the transcription of the word "German" or "Deutsche" pronounced in Shanghai dialect. This name not only indicated the charitable hospital for Chinese was initiated by Germans, but also referred to the Chinese idiom "tong zhou gong ji" meaning "on the same boat".

Born in Pasewalk of Germany in 1862, Paulun had studied in the Friedrich Wilhelm University in Berlin, an army medical institution, and served on Germany navy ships S. M. S. Wolf and Iltis in Asia in the late 1880s and early 1890s.

In a letter to a Shanghai-based German doctor Carl Zedelius, whom he knew during navy times, Paulun shared his idea to found a charitable hospital for poor Chinese patients who were suffering from illness and without access to medicine in old Shanghai.

To realize this hospital dream, he left the navy, worked in two hospitals in Germany to improve his surgeon skills and began raising funds. In 1895 he returned to Shanghai to work as assistant to

Zedelius and became his successor after he died in 1899.

The same year Paulun and German doctor Oscar von Schab founded the Shanghai German doctors' guild and purchased a land in Burkill Road (today's Fengyang Road) across Bubbling Well Road to build the Tung Chee Hospital.

According to *the North-China Herald* on April 3, 1909, the hospital founded in 1900 "at first consisted only of a few corrugated iron buildings purchased from the German military authorities." In 1901 a brick building was erected by funds contributed by both German and Chinese residents.

"On the ground floor there are a dispensary, store-rooms, out-patients' rooms, instrument rooms and operating theatres," the 1909 news report documents.

"The main operating theatre has three tables and is equipped with sterilizers, instrument cases, washbasins and in fact with every requisite for a modern aseptic surgery.

"A well-stocked instrument-room opens out of this theatre, and beyond is a small chamber fitted with a Sanitas electric light bath for rheumatic patients, and other electrical apparatus.

"The main dispensary, at the other end of the building, connects with the out-patients' room, where the German doctors see between 50 and 70 charity patients every evening. Upstairs are 12 rooms for Chinese paying patients — six for men and the same number for women."

Professor Li says the hospital treated two kinds of patients — poor Chinese in the International Settlement were treated for free while Chinese employees working for German firms were charged fees.

The hospital was founded with the support of the then German Consul General Wilhelm Knappe who wanted to increase German influence in China through education and medical services. The hospital also received funds from Shanghai Taotai (the circuit intendant for foreign affairs in Qing Dynasty), and prominent Chinese merchants including Ye Chengzhong, Zhu Baosan and Yu Yaching.

The hospital was renamed Paulun Hospital after the German doctor died of disease a day after his 47th birthday in 1909. In the news story regarding the change of hospital name, *The North-China Herald* says a few foreign residents, besides Germans, knew of the existence of the hospital which had become well-known to the Chinese.

"No more fitting memorial could be found to the name of one who gave up so much for others than to establish the institute for ever as the Paulun Hospital," *The North-China Herald* reported.

Unfortunately the old buildings of the Paulun Hospital do not remain today. It's possible that the huge extension part, designed in 1927 by Park Hotel architect Laszlo Hudec, is wrapped inside a modern surface added during a 1980s renovation.

When Hudec's other hospital, the Country Hospital (the No.1 building of today's Huadong Hospital), was unveiled in 1926, the anonymous donor endowed two wards each in memory of Shanghai's departed philanthropists— the late Dr MeLeod and the late Dr Paulun "for whom the donor had the greatest respect," according to a report in *the China Press* on June 9, 1926.

In the 1950s Tongji Hospital was moved to Wuhan of Hubei Province and the site since then has been used by the Shanghai Changzheng Hospital which was attached to the Second Military Medical University.

During the last few years of his life, Dr Paulun founded Tongji German Medical School in Burkill Road hospital with support from both German and Chinese governments. The school hosted a grand opening ceremony on October 1, 1907, which was attended by representatives of German consulates and Shanghai Taotai.

Owing to tight space within the hospital, the school purchased land in today's Fuxing Road M. in 1908 and commissioned German architect Carl Baedecker to design a new campus.

In 1912 the school was expanded to include engineering in its programs and got its new name as Tongji Medical and Engineering

School. In the following turbulent years, the school endured many changes and moves and eventually grew to be a comprehensive university specializing in engineering which is today's Tongji University.

In 1978, the then Tongji University president Li Guohao restored the university's relationship with Germany.

Though the Paulun Hospital buildings, along the Bubbling Well Road, have been demolished, Changzheng Hospital introduces history and heritage left by this pioneering hospital in its own hospital history today.

At the Fuxing Road campus, red-brick buildings designed by a German architect are largely preserved and used by the University of Shanghai for Science and Technology.

In the Tongji University History Museum situated in a quiet corner of its Siping Road campus, a statue of Dr. Paulun welcomes visitors at the entrance.

The Tongji Medical College and Tongji Hospital that moved to Wuhan of Hubei Province developed into Tongji Medical College

of Huazhong University of Science and Technology and its affiliated Tongji Hospital.

During the COVIC-19 pandemic in early 2020, the Tongji Hospital in Wuhan received the most critically ill patients and was fortunately aided by medical teams from China's top hospitals. Among these medical teams was one from Shanghai, where Tongji Hospital was founded in 1900. The Shanghai doctors and their Wuhan colleagues performed a real story of working on the same boat some 120 years after Dr. Paulun named the hospital "Tung Chee".

Yesterday: Paulun Hospital   **Today:** Shanghai Changzheng Hospital
Address: 415 Fengyang Road   **Architect:** L. E. Hudec

宝隆医生逝世
Shanghai in Mourning after Philanthropic Doctor Dies

　　大家都非常遗憾地得知宝隆医生去世的消息。他几天前因感染伤寒被送医，因为肾脏并发症，他于昨天凌晨4点死于尿毒症。几年前，他创立了一家面向中国人的慈善医院，后来又创办位于白克路（今凤阳路）的中德医学院。对于上海这座城市来说，他首先是一名外科医生。众所周知，宝隆医生的昵称"大宝医生"是对他的医术和勇气的称赞。宝隆医生的敏捷和决断力挽救了很多人的生命。无论天气好坏，无论白天黑夜，他总是为了病人而随时待命，对待免费病人和有钱病人一视同仁。许多他的穷苦病人都能说出宝隆医生所做的善事，他会为病人急需的假期资助费用，对病人耐心照顾。就在他去世前不久，宝隆医生还说希望再活20年，以便继续从事他所奉献的职业。

The news of the death of Dr. E. H. Paulun will be learnt with extreme regret by the whole community. Dr. Paulun was taken to the General Hospital only a few days ago, suffering from typhoid fever. Kidney complications set in, and he died at 4 o'clock yesterday morning from uraemia.

Dr. Paulun was one of the best known Germans in Shanghai, not only to his fellow-countrymen, but throughout the entire community.

He founded a charitable hospital for Chinese, the natural corollary to which was the German Medical School for Chinese in Burkill Road. He was a Governor of the General Hospital, member of the German School committee and a committee member of the Club Concordia, in which capacity he rendered invaluable service with his suggestions regarding hygiene in the new building.

To all Shanghai, however, he was, first and foremost, a surgeon. The nickname by which he was familiarly known was a compliment alike to his skill and nerve. Many persons owe their lives to his promptness and decision.

In good or bad weather, at any hour of the day or night, he was always

at the disposal of his patients, and he treats those from whom he knew he could receive no fee with the same consideration as the wealthy. Many of his poor patients can tell of kindly acts, of money unostentatiously given them for a much needed holiday, of his care and patience during their illnesses.

Only a short time before his death Dr. Paulun said that he would have liked to live for another 20 years to carry on the profession of which he was so devoted an exponent. Though honors fell thick upon him during his career the most lasting monument of his work will be tender regard in which his memory will be held by many who had every reason to appreciate his services.

摘自 1909 年 3 月 6 日《北华捷报》
Excerpt from *the North-China Herald*, on March 6 1909

伊斯兰风情的飞星公司
Star Garage in Islamic Style

2019年10月26日，南京西路702号改造为时尚空间"L'art 702"，隆重开业。

这座历史建筑的外立面与众不同，有一行马蹄形的连续拱柱廊，带着伊斯兰风情。1917年，西班牙建筑师乐福德（Abelardo Lafuente 1871-1931）在此将伊斯兰西班牙式风格带到上海，也开启了一段辉煌的职业生涯。

同济大学郑时龄院士在《上海近代建筑风格》新版中提到，

南京西路702号是一幢伊斯兰西班牙式与新古典主义的混合建筑，由乐福德与伍腾组成的赉丰洋行（Lafuente & Wooten）为西班牙商人雷玛斯（A. Ramos）作为住宅设计，后来被美商飞星公司（Star Garage Company）租用。

曾在上海工作的西班牙建筑师佩雷斯（Alvaro Leonardo Perez）研究乐福德档案发现，他是近代上海唯一正式注册从业的西班牙建筑师。自学成才的乐福德虽然没有正规地学习过建筑学，但他的父亲曾在菲律宾首都马尼拉担任市政建筑师，耳濡目染的他在马尼拉建筑行业工作了13年。1913年，乐福德来到上海。

飞星公司这座楼是乐福德在上海的早期项目之一。根据《静安历史文化图录》，飞星公司主营汽车整车销售、维修、兼营汽车配件，并代理上海多家汽车公司的售后服务，堪称百年前的4S店。因为业主科亨（Albert Cohen）是犹太商人，这个项目也为建筑师打开了犹太商界的大门，后来为犹太富商嘉道理（Sir Elly Kadoorie）设计了多个项目。

在上海，乐福德成立了自己的建筑师事务所，自主设计各类项目的同时，也与美国建筑师伍腾（G. O. Wootten）和俄国建筑师协隆（A. J. Yaron）在不同时期合作设计。

1913年到1931年间，他在中国设计建成了大量重要的建筑案例，包括为雷玛斯设计的数家影院，还有俱乐部、教堂、清真寺、车库、别墅、公寓、办公楼及医院。其中，最著名的项目是礼查饭店（Astor Hotel）孔雀厅。璀璨的孔雀厅悬挂着水晶吊灯，墙面镶嵌着无数面镜子，厅内矗立着大理石柱，镶木地板设计为巨大的螺旋图案。

在今日的南京西路沿线，这位西班牙建筑师设计了夏令配克电影院（Olympic Theatre）、中央公寓（Central Apartments 或 Lafuente Building）和犹太俱乐部（Jewish Club，遭遇火灾后被改为嘉道理公馆）。1923年，他还将麦边住宅改造为惊艳的大华饭店（Majestic Hotel），四年后蒋介石和宋美龄的盛大婚礼就在这家酒店举行。如今，这四座建筑都已不存，只有飞星公司基本保留历史旧貌。

根据上海章明建筑设计事务所修缮南京西路702号时所做的调研，这座建筑面积达3113.55平

方米，是一座钢筋混凝土建筑，后来被美国海军士兵俱乐部（US Navy Enlistedmen's Club）、黄河皮鞋厂、上海皮革公司商厦等单位使用。2017年，静安置业从黄河皮鞋厂购入物业，费时半年进行消防抗震的土建改造，对外立面等重要历史部位进行保护修缮后，马蹄形拱柱廊的光彩重现。

郑时龄院士认为，飞星公司的马蹄形拱柱廊是西班牙穆迪扎尔风格（Mudejar style）的特征之一。他解释，穆迪扎尔人是基督教徒收复伊比利亚半岛后仍留在西班牙的穆斯林，而穆迪扎尔建筑风格是融合西班牙风格与阿拉伯风格的建筑风格，特点是圆顶、尖塔、马蹄形拱饰檐部、螺旋形圆柱、石造花窗格、黑白相间的条纹和釉面砖镶嵌。1917年，乐福德在静安寺路这个项目中首次将西班牙穆迪扎尔风格引入上海近代建筑中，他对推动上海的西班牙建筑风格具有重要的影响。飞星公司项目完成后，乐福德还在上海设计了两个类似风格的建筑，分别是建于1918年的长阳路弗兰契宅（Residence for Mr. French）和建于1924年的多伦路250号雷玛斯宅（Casa Ramos）。

虽然同样才华过人、作品众多，乐福德与1918年到沪发展、已经称为"上海符号"的东欧建筑师邬达克相比，他的名字对上海市民显得相当陌生。这与他职业发展的际遇有关。

1928年，乐福德到美国加州开设了建筑师事务所，在好莱坞和洛杉矶设计了多个电影院和别墅项目。但他不幸遭遇1929年美国"大萧条"，耗尽积蓄，1931年回到上海。

1931年10月19日，英文《大陆报》刊文，报道这位"曾设计礼查饭店和大华饭店舞厅、著名娱乐场所和上海最美丽建筑的建筑师"刚刚回到上海。

"乐福德先生在好莱坞执业四年，他设计了该市和洛杉矶一些最漂亮的电影院，还有好莱坞、比佛利山庄和周边城市一些最好的私宅。在美国的岁月里，乐福德先生想念上海。他昨晚告诉大陆报代表，他一生中最快乐的时光都在这里度过，所设计的建筑是他的骄傲和喜悦。"报道提到。

乐福德在美国度过四年，正是上海近代史上城市发展最快的

"黄金时代"，更现代摩登的建筑纷纷建成。在此期间，他留在魔都的外国建筑师同行都发展得不错：1929年公和洋行威尔逊（George Wilson）在外滩设计建成了沙逊大厦（今费尔蒙特和平饭店），不仅成为外滩地标，更将上海全面推向了装饰艺术时代。一年后，邬达克在圆明园路的真光大楼也竣工了，他将事务所搬入这座邻近外滩的大楼，开始设计后来成为自己代表作的两个建筑——大光明电影院和国际饭店。

回到上海的乐福德也计划再次大展宏图，无奈造化弄人，当年

12月3日他在上海公济医院（the General Hospital，现上海市第一人民医院）病逝，终年60岁，安葬在虹桥路外国公墓。

佩雷斯提到，1917年，乐福德还曾赢得苏州河畔美国领事馆的设计竞赛，可惜后来没有建成。乐福德的建筑作品现存不多，但华丽璀璨的孔雀厅和伊斯兰风情的飞星公司，仍在展示一个西班牙建筑师的骄傲和喜悦。

昨天：飞星公司　**今天：**L'art 702　**建筑师：**乐福德（1871-1931）
参观指南：建筑作为时尚艺术空间对公众开放，建议欣赏伊斯兰风情的建筑立面。

The building at 702 Nanjing Road W. has been renovated to "L'art 702", a space of life-style & fashion. It opened with a grand ceremony on October 26,2019.

The facade of this historical building is unique, adorned by a row of horseshoe-shaped continuous arcades in an Islamic style. In 1917, Spanish architect Abelardo Lafuente (1871-1931) introduced the Islamic Spanish style to Shanghai on this building. Since then he also started a brilliant career in the city.

In the new edition of *The Evolution of Shanghai Architecture in Modern Times*, Tongji University professor Zheng Shiling notes that the building displays a mixed Islamic Spanish and neoclassic styles. It is a work of Lafuente & Wooten,

a firm Lafuente cooperated with American architect G. O. Wooten. Initially the building was designed as the residence for Spanish businessman A. Ramos but later rented by the Star Garage Company.

After researching the Lafuente archives, Spanish architect Alvaro Leonardo Perez found that he was the only Spanish architect officially registered in modern Shanghai. Although Lafuente was a self-taught architect who had not studied architecture in educational institutions, his father worked as a municipal architect in Manila, the capital of the Philippines and he himself had also worked in the construction industry in Manila for 13 years. In 1913, Lafuente came to Shanghai.

This Star Garage building was

one of his early projects in Shanghai. According to *Jing'an History and Culture Catalogue*, Star Garage Company was mainly engaged in the sales and maintenance of automobiles. It also dealt in auto parts and acted as an agent for the after-sales services of many automobile companies in Shanghai, pretty much like a 4S store today.

Because Albert Cohen, the owner of Star Garage, was a Jewish businessman, this project probably opened the door to the Jewish business community for Lafuente. Later on he designed several projects for Sir Elly Kadoorie, a famous Jewish tycoon.

In Shanghai, Lafuente established his own firm and designed various projects on his own. But he also cooperated with the American architect G. O. Wootten and the Russian architect A. J. Yaron in different periods.

From 1913 to 1931, he designed and built a large number of important architectural projects in China, including several theaters for A. Ramos, as well as clubs, churches, mosques, garages, villas, apartments, office buildings and hospitals. Among them, the most famous project is the ballroom of the Astor Hotel, which was hung with crystal chandeliers and graced by marble columns. The walls were inlaid with countless mirrors and the parquet dancing floor was designed in a huge spiral pattern.

Perez finds that the Spanish architect had designed several buildings along today's Nanjing Road W.—the Olympic Theatre, the Central Apartments (or Lafuente Building) and Jewish Club (later changed to Kadoorie's residence. In 1923, he also transformed the Mcbain residence into the stunning Majestic Hotel. Four years later, the grand wedding of Chiang Kai-shek and Soong Meiling was held in this hotel. Today, these buildings no longer existed, only the Star Garage retains its historical appearance.

According to the research of Shanghai Zhangming Architects and Design Office responsible for the renovation of No. 702, this building is a reinforced concrete structure covering an area of 3113.55 square meters. It was later used by the US Navy Enlistedmen's Club, the Yellow River Leather Shoe Factory, and Shanghai Leather Store. In 2017, Jing'an District Land Company purchased the property from the Yellow River Leather Shoe Factory and spent half a year on the renovation to improve fire-fighting and earth-quake-resistant functions. After the protection and repair of important historical parts such as the facade, the horseshoe-shaped arcades reappeared.

Professor Zheng Shiling believes that the horseshoe-shaped arcades of the Star Garage is one of the characteristics of the Spanish Mudejar style. He explains that the Mudejars were Muslims who remained in Spain after the Christians regained the Iberian Peninsula, and the Mudejar architectural style is a fusion of Spanish and Arabic styles, characterized by domes, spires, horseshoe-shaped arched eaves, spiral columns, stone flower panes, black-and-white stripes and inlaid glazed bricks.

In 1917, Lafuente introduced the Spanish Mudejar style into modern Shanghai architecture for the first time in the project on the former Bubbling Well Road. He had an important influence on the promotion of the Spanish architectural style in Shanghai.

After the completion of the Star Garage project, Lafuente also designed two buildings of similar style in Shanghai, namely the Residence for Mr. French on Chang-yang Road built in 1918 and Casa Ramos on 250 Duolun Road built in 1924.

Lafuente's name, compared with Hungarian-Slovakian architect Laszlo Hudec who is known as a "Shanghai Symbol", is quite unfamiliar to the public today. This is due to his career development.

In 1928, Lafuente opened an architect's office in California, USA. He designed several movie theaters and villa projects in Hollywood and Los Angeles. But he lost his savings during the "Great Depression" in 1929 and had to return to Shanghai in 1931.

On October 19, 1931, the English-language newspaper *the China Press* published an article reporting that the architect "who designed the ballrooms of the Astor Hotel, the Majestic and other noted places of amusement, as well as some of the finest buildings in Shanghai" had just returned to Shanghai.

"Mr. Lafuente has spent the past four years in Hollywood practicing his profession. He has designed buildings of some of the most beautiful cinemas in that city and Los Angeles, as well as some of the finest private homes in Hollywood, Beverly Hills and other nearby cities. Through the years in America Mr. Lafuente has longed for Shanghai, he told a China Press representative last evening. The happiest years of his life were spent here, he said, and the buildings he designed were his pride and joy," the report says.

The four years that Lafuente spent in the United States happened to be during the "golden age" of Shanghai when the city developed at the fastest speed in modern history. Modern buildings were mushrooming and the city became a paradise for architects.

During this period, foreign architects who stayed in the "magic city" all developed well. In 1929, British architect George Wilson from Palmer & Turner designed and built the Sassoon House (now the Fairmont Peace Hotel), which not only became a landmark on the Bund but also brought Shanghai architecture to an era of Art Deco style. One year later, Hungarian-Slovakian architect Laszlo Hudec's twin buildings on today's Waitanyuan were also completed. Hudec moved his firm into one of the buildings and started design-ing two important projects that later became his masterpieces—the Grand Theatre and the Park Hotel both on the Bubbling Well Road.

After returning to Shanghai, Lafuente planned to make a big show again. Unfortunately he died in the Shanghai General Hospital on December 3 of that year at the age of 60. He was buried in the International Cemetery on Hongqiao Road.

Perez adds that in 1917, Lafuente had won the design competition for the new American Consulate on the bank of Suzhou River, but it was not built. Today, not many of Lafuente's works remained. However the gorgeous ballroom of the former Astor Hotel and the Islamic-Spanish Star Garage are showing the pride and joy of a Spanish architect in Shanghai.

Yesterday: Star Garage   **Today:** L'art 702   **Architect:** Abelardo Lafuente（1871-1931）
Tips: The building is open to the public as a fashion & art space. Please admire the unique facade in Islamic style.

上海建筑未来的警告
A Warning Note from Architect Lafuente

昨天，礼查饭店和大华饭店舞厅设计师乐福德先生（A. Lafuente）就上海建筑的未来发出警告。他在加利福尼亚旅居四年后于本周回到中国。乐福德是这座城市最资深、最知名的建筑师之一，他的名字在过去几年与上海一些最好的建筑联系在一起。如今，他已回到这里执业。离开上海四年让

他对这里建筑的问题有了清晰的认识。

"上海必须为未来做好计划，" 乐福德先生说，"否则，未来几年这座城市将陷入困境。"

他强调了上海的营造商在建筑工程中采用最佳材料的必要性。"否则，这些建筑物将不会很持久。"他说，提到一些建筑处于破败的状态，就是因为营造商对建筑师太过吝啬。"美国证明了建筑业是有钱人的冒险。" 乐福德说。

"对造价太小气是结构性的自杀，因为许多本地建筑师都被迫压低预算。如果上海希望成为一个清洁、明亮、现代化的城市，那么所有新建摩天楼都必须使用最好质量的砖块、石头和钢铁。"

他指出，世界上几乎每个大城市都有分区规划的法规，而上海则没有。而他肯定，除洛杉矶外，上海的发展速度可能比其他任何大都市都要快。

他描述了目前正在南加州进行的生气勃勃的建筑活动。他说："尽管商业萧条在某种程度上限制了这些工作，但我认为，加州南部地区在建筑规划方面是世界上最活跃的地方。洛杉矶的新公寓楼和摩天楼体现了每一项新发明和建筑的完美度。一个星期还没有过完，但是建成的一些新建筑，已经超越了前一周竣工的建筑。

A warning note concerning the architectural future of the city of Shanghai was struck yesterday by Mr. A. Lafuente, designer of the Astor Hotel and Majestic Hotel ballrooms, who returned to China this week after an absence of four years in California. One of the oldest and best-known architects in this city, M. Lafuente's name has been associated in former years with some of the best buildings in Shanghai. Now he has returned here to practise his profession in this city. His four-years absence has given him the advantage of a clear insight on the building problem here.

"Shanghai must plan for the future," Mr. Lafuente stated. "Otherwise the city will be in a bad tangle in years to come."

He emphasized the necessity of builders in Shanghai employing the best types of material in construction work. "Otherwise the buildings will not last," he said. He named one or two buildings already in a state of disrepair because the builders were stingy with the architects. "America has proven that the building business is a rich man's adventure," Mr. Lafuente stated.

It is constructional suicide to stint on costs, as so many local architects are forced to do. If Shanghai hopes to be a clean, bright, modern city, the brick, stone and steel in all the new skyscrapers must be of the best quality, "he said.

Almost every big city in the world has zoning laws, he pointed out, while Shanghai has none. Yet Shanghai is growing faster than probably any other metropolis with the exception of Los Angeles, he asserted.

He described the animated building activities taking place in Southern California at the present time. "Although the business depression has curtailed the work somewhat," he stated, "the Southern part of California is, I believe, the most active in the world in regard to building plans. Every new invention and perfection of architecture is embodied in the new Los Angeles apartment houses and skyscrapers. A week doesn't pass but some new building is opened which surpasses the one finished the week before.

摘自 1931 年 10 月 22 日《大陆报》
Excerpt from *The China Press*, on Oct. 22, 1931

总会大楼的辉煌历史

Honesty Lays Foundation of a "Tudor style" Shanghai Building

    1929年5月1日，一把金色钥匙开启了静安寺路万国体育会（International Recreation Club）的大门。如今，这座古典建筑座落于南京西路722号的院落内，低调地隐藏着昔日辉煌。

    南京西路722号的故事缘起于1909年。百年前的上海，位于今天人民广场的英商上海跑马总会实行会员制服务。宁波富商叶澄衷之子叶贻铨（T. U. Yih）因为曾被拒之门外，决心成立一家中国人自己的跑马会。1909年，这家名为"万国体育会"的跑马会开张，会所设在722号的花园洋房里，跑马场建在江湾。

    在近代上海史中，叶澄衷的

故事也是一个传奇。他出生于浙江宁波的一个贫困家庭，后来到上海谋生，用一条小舢板将食品贩卖给外国水手。1862年，一位美国商人雇佣叶澄衷的舢板后，不慎留下一个装满现金和贵重物品的公文包。叶澄衷苦等良久后将公文包归还失主。这位年轻人的诚实打动了美国商人，在他的帮助下叶澄衷开设了五金杂货店，事业蓬勃发展，到1899年去世前涉足金融、工业和航运等多个领域。

根据陈洋阳的论文"老上海体育建筑遗存：江湾跑马厅民国时期面貌考"，叶贻铨于1908年在上海北部江湾镇购置了一个农场建造万国体育会跑马场，面积有80万平方米。体育会俱乐部接受中国会员，而外资的上海体育基金（Shanghai Recreation Fund）也是主要股东之一。叶贻铨还在赛马场附近建了一个十分美丽的中式花园，供会员休闲放松。后来在他的老师、著名医学教育家颜福庆的建议下，叶氏将花园捐赠并改造为一家肺病疗养院，1933年对外开放。

研究上海建筑历史的同济大学教授钱宗灏认为，叶贻铨应该在1908年后不久就建造了南京西路722号会所大楼。他收藏的一张1913年上海老地图显示，会所座落于现在南京西路靠近凤阳路的位置。

"地图显示1913年时会所已经存在，但无论房型布局还是位于基地西北角的位置，都与南京西路722号的建筑有差异。"他说。

不过，老上海英文报纸的一则报道解释了他的疑问：1913年地图所示的会所老楼于1928年被拆除，又建的新楼就是今天的南京西路722号。

1928年3月31日，英文《北华捷报》的这篇报道称静安寺路"老会所"拆除工作已经完成，公和洋行设计的新会所方案展现了万国体育会的"坚实发展"。

"万国体育会成立于1908年，当时由布罗迪·克拉克先生（Mr. Brodie Clarke）和叶贻铨先生赞助了这项事业。体育会一开始有100名成员，现在的记录显示有各国会员1400名。江湾赛马场也许是万国体育会最大的荣耀，经常被称为是远东最好的赛马场。

每年在那里举行20天的比赛，每次比赛都证明是深受欢迎的。"《北华捷报》报道写道。

报道还回顾了万国体育会在江湾镇的建设项目。1921年，体育会建造了比赛看台，1924年在江湾建起新会所，1925年建成马球场和高尔夫球场。到1928年时，体育会的中国籍会员占百分之六十，英籍会员占百分之三十，其他国籍为百分之十。会员名单透露还有30位女性会员。

1929年，万国体育会位于静安寺路的会所新楼开幕，这座新建筑给来宾们带来震撼的感受。5月4日《北华捷报》刊登的报道形容新楼"在上海无可匹敌"。

"他们说这是'都铎式风格'：对于要享受舒适的一般人来说，这是'一个很小的地方'——整齐的红砖，在如今充斥着浓厚商业气息的静安寺路显得独特而令人着迷。会所的室内是一个坚固而舒适的地方。女士有单独的房间，她们忘记打牌的王牌花色时可以在那里讨论帽子话题。"报道描述道。

此外，会所新楼还有宽阔的阳台、开阔的大厅和很多大房间。每个房间都用柚木护墙板装饰，显得既厚重又舒服。由美艺公司（Arts＆Crafts）制作的经典俱乐部家具在风格和品质上都与建筑保持一致。在老上海制售西式家具

的外商中，成立于1904—1905年间的美艺公司名气最大，其总部位于南京路44号，在上海营业长达半个多世纪，直到1954年。

会所一楼设有宽敞的行政办公套房，"这在上海最雄伟的商业建筑里是无与伦比的"。此外，会所还有一间酒吧、一间极好的公寓、阅览室和吸烟室等。楼上有"上海最好的台球室"和"公共租界最棒的舞厅"。这里的舞厅是一个光彩夺目的场所，21米乘12米见方，带有星光玻璃屋顶和弹簧地板。

这座新楼竣工后的一个多世纪里，历经多次变迁，但幸运地基本保持历史旧貌。

叶贻铨的江湾跑马场后来经营不善，淞沪抗战后损失惨重，在炮火中损毁。

静安寺路会所后来曾被上海商团（the International Club of Shanghai）和美国海军俱乐部（US. Navy Enlistedmens' Club）等单位使用。也有文章指出建筑曾用作犹太俱乐部。

1949年后，南京西路722号长期作为上海市委统战部和上海市宗教局的办公地，后来为来自江苏省的春兰集团使用。

20世纪90年代，春兰集团曾是中国最大的空调生产商。春兰集团上海办公室的工作人员介绍，集团曾对这座历史建筑进行整体修缮。此外，每年也会检查修缮，近年还更换了部分朽烂的屋顶瓦片，更换的新瓦片根据原样定制。"最棒的舞厅"仍保留着星光玻璃屋顶和弹簧地板，如今722号是春兰集团上海办公室和投资公司所在地。

1929年5月1日，静安寺路会所举行隆重的开幕仪式，时任上海特别市市长张群在致辞中说，这座吸引人的壮美的新楼预兆了万国体育会的光明未来。

叶贻铨将金钥匙交给了俱乐部主席布罗迪·克拉克，后者用钥匙打开了会所的前大门。随后，参加仪式的各国来宾进入大楼，热心地参观这座新建筑。

虽然这座"无与伦比"的建筑并未给万国体育会带来光明的前景，但它直到今天仍然保存完整，成为南京西路沿线的历史风景。而体育会位于江湾的花园也保留至今，如今是上海肺科医院怡人的花园。

这些绵延一个多世纪的辉煌动人的传奇，都源自一个年轻人诚实的心。

昨天：万国体育会俱乐部　**今天：**春兰集团　**地址：**南京西路 722 号　**建筑师：**公和洋行
建筑风格：古典主义风格
参观指南：建筑不对外开放，但可以从门口欣赏优雅的立面、宁静的院落和中央的一棵古树。

上海萬國體育會
International Recreation Club
第廿七期春季大會
27th ANNUAL RACE MEETING
民國廿八年四月十五日(星期六)開獎
SATURDAY, 15th APRIL 1939.

萬國大香賓得獎號碼單
Result of the Drawing of the I. R. C. Champions Sweep

頭彩	1st Prize	Magic Circle	...	14616
二彩	2nd „	Ryehampton	...	26727
三彩	3rd „	Gold Vase	...	16193

Pony Name		Chance No.	Pony Name		Chance No.
Night Raider	...	13009	Fruitylight	...	13820
Florin	...	10019	Alberto	...	14149
Fancylight	...	10268	Special Delivery	...	14312
High Power	...	10276	Duke of Cornwall	...	14372
Neville	...	10313	Second Thoughts	...	14377
Lora-Fela	...	10506	Danbury	...	14620
Toodle-do	...	10695	Corps Cavalry	...	14802
Ancient Ensign	...	10804	Little Joe	...	14889
White Willie	...	10812	Brown Bomber	...	25263
Night Express	...	11454	Cordon Rouge	...	25339
Spicylight	...	11724	Joylight	...	25890
Rain	...	11864	Mr. Deeds	...	25669
Blenheim	...	11988	New General	...	25705
Anything Goes	...	12156	Hindhead	...	25721
Andy	...	12788	Rye	...	25815
Spotted Sand	...	12882	Winner of Race 8	...	26184
Spring Tide	...	13607	Merrylight	...	27079

本大香賓票共售出七千壹百金磅除開支二成另
撥助上海難民救濟協會慈善款一成外淨計國幣
四萬九千七百元獎款分配如下

頭獎 1st Prize	...	...	...	磅得 $27,832.00	每磅得 $2,530.18
二獎 2nd „	...	...	...	每件 $7,952.00	„ $722.90
三獎 3rd „	...	...	...	每件 $3,976.00	„ $361.45
小獎 Unplaced Entered Ponies				磅得 $292.00	„ $26.54

A golden key opened the new clubhouse of International Recreation Club on the Bubbling Well Road on May 1, 1929. This imposing edifice, now at today's 722 Nanjing Road W., reveals intriguing stories of a former racecourse and a garden that was turned into a sanatorium.

"It was Chinese merchant Ye Yiquan (T. U. Yih) who founded the International Recreation Club which operated the former Jiangwan (Kiangwan) Racecourse in today's Yangpu District. He opened a head office on Bubbling Well Road for selling tickets and attracting members," says Tongji University professor Qian Zong-hao, an expert of Shanghai architectural history.

Ye Yiquan inherited wealth from his father, Ye Chengzhong (Yih Ching-chong), a legendary Chinese tycoon who earned the first bucket of gold by doing a good deed.

According to the book *The Century-Old Famous Factories and Stores in Shanghai*, Ye Chengzhong, who was born to a poor family in Ningbo of Zhejiang Province, had a humble beginning in Shanghai by selling food to foreign sailors on a small boat.

In 1862 an American businessman hired Ye's boat for a ride but left behind a briefcase full of cash and valuables. Ye Chengzhong waited for a long time for the owner to return for the briefcase, who was greatly touched by the young man's honesty and helped him open the city's first hardware shop. As Ye's hardware business boomed, he further expanded into areas of finance, industry and shipping before he died in 1899.

According to researcher Chen Yangyang's thesis "Kiangwan Racecourse during the Republic of China (1912-1949)," Ye Yiquan bought an 800,000-square-meter farm in Jiangwan Town of north Shanghai to build a racecourse in 1908, which allowed the Chinese to be club members. The foreign-owned Shanghai Recreation Fund became a major shareholder. Near the racecourse, Ye built a breathtakingly beautiful Chinese garden for the members to rest and relax, which he later donated to open a pulmonary sanatorium in 1933 at the advice of his teacher, famous medical educator Yan Fuqing.

Professor Qian believed Ye built the IRC clubhouse on the Bubbling Well Road not long after 1908. On a 1913 map of Shanghai from his archival collections, the International Recreation Club perched on the site was juxtaposed between today's Nanjing Road W. and Fengyang Road.

"The map showed the clubhouse already existed in 1913. But both the layout and the building's specific location at the northwest corner of the site differed from the current building on 722 Nanjing Road W.," he said.

Reports in an old English newspaper answered his quests. The old clubhouse premises on the 1913 map had been demolished to build a new clubhouse in 1928, which is today's 722 Nanjing Road W.

A North-China Herald piece on March 31, 1928 said demolition work had been completed on the grounds at Bubbling Well Road, formerly occupied by "the old clubhouse." And the "steady growth" of the International Recreation Club was well illustrated in the plans of the new quarters drawn by Messrs. Palmer & Turner.

"The IRC was established in 1908 when Mr. Brodie Clarke and Mr. T. U. Yih sponsored the undertaking. At the start there were 100 members. At the present time, the records show 1,400 members of all nationalities. The Kiangwan Racecourse is perhaps the IRC's chief claim to glory, being as it has been frequently called the finest racecourse in the Far East. Twenty racing days are held there annually, and the popularity of the course is attested to at each meet," the report said.

The report also recounted IRC's building activities in Kiangwan Town, which built the concert stand of the course in 1921, the new clubhouse at Kiangwan in 1924 and the polo section with a golf course in 1925. By 1928, Chinese members had composed 60 percent, British 30 percent and other nationalities about 10 percent of IRC. The roll also revealed 30 lady members.

When the new clubhouse on the Bubbling Well Road was final-

ly unveiled, the building "over-whelmed" visitors and was described "beyond compare in Shanghai" by *the North-China Herald* on May 4, 1929.

"'Tudor style' they say it is: to the ordinary man who is going to enjoy its comforts it is 'a mighty pretty little place' — something unique and distinctly attractive in its red brick neatness amongst the heavy commercial stuff which now is defiling Bubbling Well Road. Within, it is a place of solid comfort, even as regards the rooms, which are set apart for the ladies, and wherein they may discuss hats what time they are forgetting the trump suit," the report stated.

There were wide verandas, spacious halls and commodious rooms. Each room was heavi-ly and comfortably paneled in teak, suggestive of mugs, punch-bowls and rollicking choruses. The typical club furniture by Arts & Crafts was in keeping with the building, both in style and quality.

The ground floor featured a commodious suite of administrative offices "unequalled in the most princely of Shanghai's commercial houses," a bar, a magnificent apartment, reading and smoking rooms. On the upper floor there was "the finest billiard room in Shanghai" and "the finest ball-room in the settlement". The ballroom was a glorious place of 21 meters by 12 meters, with a starlit glass roof and a spring floor.

In the following 90 years the building endured many changes but remained largely the same as this opening day.

Ye's racecourse in Kiangwan ceased operations and was later destroyed by bombing during the war in the late 1930s.

The new clubhouse on the Bubbling Well Road was subsequently used by the International Club of Shanghai and US. Navy Enlistedmens' Club. Some articles say it was also used by a Jewish club.

After 1949 it served as a friendship club attached to The Chinese People's Political Consultative Conference Shanghai Committee and later was used by Shanghai Municipal Bureau of Religious Affairs.

The building was then purchased by Chunlan Group, an enterprise from Jiangsu Province, when it was China's largest air conditioner producer in the 1990s.

"We restored the building before we moved in. And we replaced deteriorated roof tiles with new ones tailor-made according to historical look," says Wang Yongchun from Chunlan's Shanghai office.

"The ballroom still had the starlit glass roof and the spring floor. Now it served as Chunlan's Shanghai headquarter and investment company."

During the grand opening ceremony of the building on May 1, 1929, General Zhang Qun, the then Mayor of Greater Shanghai, said "the magnificence of the new building appealed to me as a bright augury of the club's future".

Ye Yiquan handed to Brodie Clarke, president of the club a golden key, with which he unlocked the front doors. The large company "which was thoroughly representative of all nationalities in the Shanghai area then entered to inspect and enthuse over the new building".

Though the magnificence of the new building did not bring a bright augury of the club's future, it survived almost intact until today as well as Yih's Garden which now houses Shanghai Pulmonary Hospital.

All these incredible building stories originated from a young man's good heart.

Yesterday: International Recreation Club   **Today:** Shanghai Headquarter of Chunlan Group
Address: 722 Nanjing Road W.   **Architects:** Messrs, Palmer & Turner
Architectural style: Classical style

Tips: The building is not open to the public but the graceful facade, tranquil yard and a lush period tree can be admired from its gateway.

慈善家捐赠医院以治疗遭受病痛和苦难的市民
Philanthropic Benefactor Donates Hospital to Care For City's Suffering

昨天，上海著名的江湾叶家花园主人、本地著名商人叶贻铨进行了捐赠。这是一项关乎上海市民福祉的重要而值得赞扬的慈善事业。叶先生将在花园里建一家最新式的医院，该医院将特别治疗患有肺结核和神经疾病的病人，以及康复患者。

叶家花园靠近江湾赛马场，被公认为是上海最美丽的中式花园。花园占地80余亩，面积广阔，价值约有100万美元。

捐赠者叶贻铨先生是上海一位富有的商人。他是著名的慈善家和体育爱好者，还是万国体育会的创始人之一。他是宁波富商叶澄衷的儿子。叶澄衷是老一代典型的华商，他的承诺据说比书面合同更可靠。几年前去世的叶澄衷先生是一所中学的创办人，如今学校以他的名字命名。

为了纪念父亲，叶贻铨将花园里建造的新医院命名为"澄衷医院"。在上海城市发展的早期，他的父亲曾为这座城市发展为重要的商业都市而做出了贡献。

新医院将由三个部门组成，分别是结核病疗养院、精神和神经疾病医院以及一般疾病的康复疗养院。这三个部门都很适合这座花园地产的环境，而这些治疗服务也是大众非常需要的。

迄今为止，还没有一家专门用于治疗肺结核病人的疗养院。一般而言，普通医院并非治疗肺部疾病的理想场所。对于肺结核患者来说，他们有特殊的需求，例如新鲜的空气、良好的环境和充足的阳光，而普通医院不容易具备这些条件。位于乡村地区的叶家花园却是结核病疗养院的理想地。

目前已经对疗养院的第一单元病房进行翻新并配备有40张病床，

其中至少20张病床将免费提供给贫困患者。洛克菲勒基金会已经捐赠了1500两白银，用于购置一套X射线设备。而其他必要的设备（如透热疗法、气胸等）由卫生部和上海国立医学院等机构出借。

　　花园中众多的凉亭和建筑物现已变成病房，每个建筑自成一个单元，配有卧室、浴室、卫生间，都享有优美的风景。现在正在推进翻新工程，计划在6月15日开始为第一个科室接待所有类型的结核病患者，包括肺结核、颗粒状结核和骨结核。

An important and praiseworthy piece of philanthropy for the welfare of citizens in Shanghai was revealed here yesterday in the donation of the famous Yih's Garden in Kiangwan by its owner. Mr T. U. Yih, prominent local businessman, for the purpose of an up-to-date hospital which will soon be erected in the garden to take special care of invalids suffering from tuberculosis and nerve diseases as well as convalescents recovering from illness.

The garden, which is near the Kiangwan Racecourse, is recognized as the most beautiful Chinese garden in Shanghai. It occupies a spacious ground of more than 80 mow and is worth about US$1,000,000.

Mr. T. U. Yih, the donor, is a wealthy businessman in Shanghai. He is also a well-known philanthropist and sports enthusiast, being one of the founders of the International Recreation Club. He is the son of Mr. Yih Ching-chong, wealthy merchant from Ningpo, who was noted in his day as a typical Chinese merchant with his word of promise more reliable than a written contract. Mr. Yih Ching-chong, who died years ago, was the founder of a middle school now bearing his name.

The new hospital to be built in Mr. T. U. Yih's garden will be known as the Ching Chong Medical Hospital in memory of his father who, in the early days of Shanghai, helped to make this city an important commercial metropolis.

The new hospital will be composed of three units, namely, a tuberculosis sanitarium, a mental and nerve disease hospital and a convalescent home for general cases, for all of which the garden property is not only admirably fitted, but of which the community is in great need.

Up to present, there is not a single sanitarium specially devoted to the treatment of tuberculosis patients and generally the ordinary hospitals are not the ideal places for curing lung diseases. For sufferers from tuberculosis have their special needs, such as fresh air, good environment, and plenty of sunshine, which the ordinary hospitals do not find it easy to provide. The Yih's Garden, being in the rural district is therefore an ideal place for a tuberculosis sanitarium.

Steps have already been taken to renovate and equip the first unit of the sanitarium with 40 beds, 20 of which at least will be free for poor patients. The Rockefeller Foundation has already donated a sum of Tls 1,500 for the purchase of a set of X-ray apparatus, while other necessary equipment such as diathermy, pneumothorax, etc., have been loaned by such organizations as the National Health Administration and the National Medical College of Shanghai.

The numerous pavilions and buildings in the garden have now been turned into wards, each forming a unit by itself and equipped with bedroom, bath, toilet and commanding fine views. Renovation work is now

being pushed and it is scheduled that this first unit will be ready to receive all types of tubercular patients, including pulmonary, granular and bone tuberculosis, on June 15.

摘自 1933 年 6 月 8 日《大陆报》
Excerpt from *The China Press*, on June 8, 1933

宁静的现代公寓
Apartments Stand Testament to a Millionaire's Passion for Sports

　　德义大楼位于南京西路石门二路转角处，地段显赫。大楼建于1930年，英文名为"Denis Apartments"，源自一位热衷体育活动的富商。

　　"德义大楼与对面的同孚大楼，跟20世纪30年代纽约曼哈顿的公寓一样，都使用了咖啡色面砖。"同济大学钱宗灏教授说。

　　上海西洋建筑权威罗小未先生也在《上海建筑指南》中写到此楼："这座高达9层的近代公寓临南京路一面平面呈较长的曲尺形，转角处作弧形转折。底层为商店，楼层由3个内廊式住宅单元和1个内廊式宿舍和单元组成。"

　　她评价，这是上海较早设有单身宿舍的公寓，形式属装饰艺术派，内部装修标准较高。外墙镶贴的褐色面砖拼成图案，底层上部饰横向线条，二层墙面有挑出的雕花座，其中4座有立雕人像，可惜毁于1966年。

　　如今，大楼底层仍为店铺，包括1932年就在此营业的南京美发厅，上层是不同房型和大小的公寓。

　　1928年，英文报纸《大陆报》（the China Press）报道了这座有防火设计的公寓楼的建造情况。

　　"长度为88英尺的桩基将被

784
南京西路

德義大樓

打入有潜在危险的上海的软土层，以确保不会发生沉降。该公寓将配备所有最舒适和最新式的照明、暖气和卫生设施。所有的饰面都将做得很出色。"1928年8月28日的报道写到。

报道提到，大楼由英商锦明洋行（Messrs. Cumine and Co.）的甘少明（Eric Byron Cumin）设计。设计大楼时，建筑师刚从欧洲来到上海。他在欧洲完成学业后曾到"现代建筑的诞生地"——意大利游览。

同济大学郑时龄院士在新版《上海近代建筑风格》中提到，克明洋行由亨利·克明（Henry Monsel Cumin）于1903年建立，1925年改组为锦明洋行。亨利·克明于1882年出生于上海，1899年起在上海工部局公共工程司工作。德义大楼设计师甘少明是老克明之子。克明洋行的作品还包括贵州路239号北京大戏院（Peking Theatre）、福州路89号的中兴银行（Cheng Foung Kung Sze）和位于南京西路另一端的爱林登公寓（Eddington House，今常德公寓）。

"建筑师摒弃了建筑上的繁文缛节和古典母题，外立面呈现一种建筑设计的新意。立面设计的基础是考虑功能与建造，而非通常那种考古或者'引用'著名建筑元素的做法。整座大楼的基调是都市性与宁静感，与现代设计精神一致。"1928年的报道写到。

1930年1月，报纸又刊文预告，德义大楼计划在5月开幕时"成为上海公共租界西区最高的建筑"。

郑时龄院士曾在上海市杨浦区图书馆一场讲座中提到，20世纪30年代是上海建筑的繁盛时期。这段"摩登时代"源于经济活动的发展、房价迅速攀升和建筑技术的推动。

"20世纪30年代的上海是全国工商业经济教育文化中心，也是工业中心、金融中心、商业中心、对外贸易中心、交通运输中心、航运中心和通讯中心。 1933年上海工业总产值几乎占全国工业总产值的一半。我们叫它摩登时代。摩登是现代的意思，上海的摩登又不同于现代，有很多商业化的成分在里面。这个时期也可以成为摩登建筑的时期，既有现代建筑的因素，也有商业化的因素。"他说。

德义大楼便是"摩登时代"建筑的经典之一。这座钢筋混凝土结构的大楼高达120英尺（约36.6米），填充以空心砖，可以隔绝极端温度与噪音，减轻建筑物的负荷。地基的梁架由带有木质延伸的混凝土桩承载，总长度约为80英尺（24.4米）。

1930年德义大楼落成时，包含有80套大小不同的公寓，从带浴室和大衣橱的一室公寓到六室套房都有。大楼安装了四台奥的斯（Otis）电梯，除一室公寓外，所有公寓均配备有电冰箱。大楼底层还有一排很吸引人的现代商铺，这些店"将会加速上海下一个商业中心的发展"。

1930年的报道还提到，德义大楼由Denis Land Investment Ltd.投资兴建，大楼的英文名（Denis Apartments）因公司的灵魂人物——程贻泽（Denis Cheng）而得名。

程贻泽酷爱体育运动事业，而德义大楼恰好位于上海多家体育俱乐部的中心。万国总会（the International Recreation Club）、乡村俱乐部、上海跑马总会、华人曲棍球会、西侨青年会和各类体育运动会所，都在附近，大楼距离法国总会也不远。

根据《静安历史文化图录》，程贻泽为提高中国体育的地位，出资设立以其名字命名的足球比赛——"台尼斯杯"（Denis Cup），计划用德义大楼来接待前来参赛的十几支球队的运动员。不料程家因经营失利出现资金困难，大楼建成后即被拍卖。

程贻泽是上海巨富程谨轩的孙子。作为程谨轩长子的后代，程贻泽与程谨轩次子程霖生共同继承了巨额遗产和大量房地产。

"程贻泽为人豪爽，喜欢体育，组织运动会，养足球队，一掷千金毫不吝啬，对经商却全无兴趣，一应事务任由程霖生处理，程霖生因此也成为房地产巨子。20世纪20年代末，程霖生转战金融市场，用房地产做抵押向银行借款，做标金投机，不久因投标失败损失惨重，宣告破产。其名下所有的房地产均被银行扣押抵债，连程贻泽的住房都被程霖生拿去抵债，为此叔侄闹得不可开交。"上海金融史专家邢建榕说。

德义大楼的造价约为50万两银子，对于这座建筑的体量和质量而言算是经济。建筑师在设计时善于控制建造成本，去掉多余的装饰以避免不必要的花费。大楼设计有简洁的垂直线条，这是富有现代主义的表达。此外，这座公寓楼没有设计阳台，原因是建筑师观察发现，人们除了抽烟不太会使用阳台。虽然外廊的设计很流行，但却大幅增加了建造成本，而业主希望公寓租金保持在合理的范围内。为

了弥补阳台缺失，建筑师设计了一个屋顶花园。

1930年的报道还指出，这座建筑不会因为塔楼和强有力的中心线而显得不友善。建筑师考虑到，它应该是一座街道建筑，对周边建筑物"要有礼貌的态度"。

20世纪40年代，程贻泽资助的足球队也因为缺乏资金而解散了。1982年，他在上海去世。

但这座因他而命名的大楼仍矗立在南京西路，宁静而雄伟，默默注视摩登都市的变迁。

昨天：德义大楼　**今日：**德义大厦　**地址：**南京西路 778 号　**建筑师：**锦明洋行
建筑风格：装饰艺术风格

The Denis Apartment perches around a prominent corner of the former Carter and Bubbling Well roads (Shimen Rd No. 2 and Nanjing Rd W.). Completed in 1930, it is named after a Chinese millionaire who was passionate about sports.

"Both Denis Apartments and the Yates Apartments opposite Nanjing Road W. mirrored those 1930s apartments built in New York's Manhattan in many ways, such as the use of brown face tiles," says Tongji University professor Qian Zonghao.

According to Shanghai architectural historian Luo Xiaowei's book *A guide to Shanghai Architec-* *ture*, this nine-story reinforced concrete structure was "an austere looking, Art-Deco-like apartment building faced with brown facing bricks laid in a diagonal pattern. There were four figure sculptures in art modern style standing on platforms by the wall, but were, unfortunately, knocked down in 1966".

The ground floor featured a line of shops including the famous Nanjing Hair Salon which opened in 1932 and is still there today. The upper floors were various sizes of apartments.

English language newspaper *The China Press* carried an article on the construction of the fire-proof building in 1928.

"Piles of 88 feet in length will be driven into the treacherous Shanghai soil to ensure practical: no settlement. The apartment will be fitted out with all the most comfortable and up-to-date lighting, heating and sanitary installations. The decorative finish will be excellent in all branches," it reported on August 28, 1928.

According to the report, the architectural design was by Eric Cumine of Messrs. Cumine and Co., Ltd., who had just returned from Europe. The architect had completed his studies there and traveled in Italy — "the birthplace of modern architecture".

"The architect has forgone the use of architectural cliches and classical motifs, and the facades will present something new in architectural design. Expression of purpose and construction have been made the basis of the design on the facades, and not as has been generally the case, archeology and 'quotations' from famous buildings. In compliance with the modern spirit and feeling in design, urbanity and serenity have been made the keynotes of the work throughout the whole building," the 1928 report said.

In January 1930, another report in the newspaper predicted that "it will be the tallest building in the western district of Shanghai's International Settlement" when it was scheduled to complete in May of 1930.

In a lecture at Yangpu Library, Tongji University professor Zheng Shiling said the 1930s saw a "modern era" of Shanghai and prosperity of architectural activities.

"Shanghai was the industrial, financial, commercial, trade, transportation, shipping and communication center of China in the early 1930s while the city's GDP composed nearly half of that of the whole country," he says.

"We called the period the 'modern era' and it was also a period of 'modern architecture.' Buildings of that era contained elements of both modern architecture and commercialization," he said.

He added that this prosperous period of architecture was the result of a growing economy, soaring house prices and the advancement of architectural technology.

The Denis Apartments was such an example of modern 1930s architecture. The 120-foot-high building covers a total floor area of 24 acres. The framework of the building was of reinforced concrete while the infill was hollow brick to insulate against any extreme temperatures and noise and to lighten the load of building. The foundation beams were carried on concrete piles with wooden extensions, the total length of which was about 80 feet. The apartments building was installed with four Otis lifts and electric refrigerators were equipped in every apartment except one-roomed ones.

When completed in 1930, the building contained around 80 apartments varying in size from one room with bath and large closets to six-room suites. The ground floor featured a row of modern shops attractively finished and arranged and "these will accelerate the development of Shanghai's next shopping center".

According to the 1930 report, the apartment building was constructed for the Denis Land Investment Co. Ltd. and Denis Cheng was "the moving spirit of that land enterprise".

Probably due to Cheng's renowned passion for sports, the building was situated in the heart of "clubland" — "the International Recreation Club, the Country Club, the Race Club, the Chinese Jockey Club, the YMCA and various sporting clubs, the Race

Course itself is adjacent and the distance is not too great to the French Club".

According to the *Jing'an History and Culture Catalogue*, in order to improve the status of Chinese sports, Denis Cheng established a football game named after himself, the "Denis Cup" and planned to receive athletes of participating football teams in the Denis Apartments. Unexpectedly, the Cheng family encountered financial difficulties due to business failures and the building was auctioned off after it was completed.

Denis Cheng, or Cheng Yize, was grandson of Shanghai tycoon Cheng Jinxuan. As the son of Cheng's eldest son, Denis inherited a fortune left by his grandfather along with his uncle Cheng Linsheng, the tycoon's second son.

"Denis Cheng was a generous man who loved sports and was enthusiastic in organizing sporting matches and even had a football team of his own. He spent a lot of money on this hobby. Not so keen on business, he left the family business to be managed by his uncle Cheng Linsheng," says Xin Jianrong of the Shanghai Archives Bureau.

"Afterward, though the uncle

became a tycoon in Shanghai real estate, he failed in financial investment. The pair of uncle and nephew ended up bankrupt and lost many of their properties," he adds.

The cost for building the Denis Apartments was around half a million taels, "which considering the size and quality of finish is remarkably low," according to the 1930 report. A strict watch had been kept on the financial side of the design by the architects. Unnecessary expenditure on over-elaborate decoration had been eliminated.

The report also introduced the "modern expression" of the building with simple verticals.

There were no balconies as it had been observed that nobody used balconies except for cigarette ends. Verandahs were popular but these added enormously to the cost. They had been omitted to keep rents reasonable. A roof garden was constructed instead.

On the second floor there were "setbacks" of a few feet to provide positions for the introduction of sculptural relief in the form of four figures representing comfort, progress, etc. .

"Another point which has been before the designer's mind is that this building will not shout in an unneighborly manner of its presence with tower and strong center lines. It is meant to be street architecture with an air of polite consideration for the buildings in the district. Towers and other landmarks are really meant for civic and monumental and ecclesiastical buildings, but sometimes such features are insisted upon and can be mitigated when they are treated as advertising factors," the report noted.

Denis Cheng passed away in Shanghai in 1982. His football team had dissolved in the 1940s due to lack of funds.

But this nicely designed building named after him stands on Nanjing Road today as a witness to the city's modern era.

Yesterday: Denis Apartments   **Today:** Deyi Building   **Address:** 778 Nanjing Road W.
Architect: Messrs. Cumine and Co., Ltd.   **Architectural style:** Art Deco

又一场警察突袭赌博场所
Yet Another Police Raid on Gambling Den

　　昨天晚上，上海工部局警察对公共租界内赌博窝点的打击继续进行，警方在静安寺路（Bubbling Well Road）和卡德路（Carter Road）转角的德义大楼突袭了一间公寓。

　　警察应该已经对这里观察了一段时间，得知一些外国人正在该场所秘密地操纵轮盘游戏。另据了解，该窝点在上海的赌博界是众所周知的。

　　昨日在公寓外看到两辆警探们乘坐的面包车。但当警察闯入公寓时，所有赌博用品都已被拿走了。据报道，所有用品已经被转移到位于法租界西区的另一个外国人的住所。

当警察突袭公寓时，几个在场的外国人和中国人感到惊讶。警察没收了很多文件和帐目报表，据信这足以给窝点的主人定罪。

据报道，这名外国人在德义大楼公寓内进行秘密赌博活动，在警察到来之前转移走赌博用品。这些东西已经从房子后面被带出，并用卡车运到了法租界。

The war waged by the Shanghai Municipal Police on gambling dens within the International Settlement was continued yesterday evening when a Police party raided a flat in the Denis Apartments, at the corner of Bubbling Well and Carter Roads.

The police, it is believed, had watched the place for some time, having learned that some foreigners were secretly operating a roulette wheel on the premises. It was also learned that the den was well-known to the gambling community of Shanghai.

Two vans with detectives were seen outside the apartments yesterday, but when the police broke into the flat, all gambling devices had been removed. It was reported that the whole paraphernalia had been taken to another foreigner's place in the western part of the French Concession.

The Police party surprised several foreigners and Chinese on the premises when they raided the den, and seized many documents, and statements of accounts, which, it is believed, are enough to convict the owners of the den.

The foreigner, conducting secret gambling in Denis Apartments, was reported to have removed the gambling devices just before the arrival of the police. It was believed that the stuff had been taken out by the rear of the house and taken to the French Concession in a truck.

摘自 1941 年 1 月 15 日《北华捷报》
Excerpt from *the North-China Herald,* on January 15, 1941

一座奇怪的大楼

A Strange House

同孚大楼是南京西路上一座新月型的建筑，设计师陆谦受称这是一所"奇怪的房子"。

"这是一所奇怪的房子。畸形的地盘，使平面的布置非常困难。最低两层，银行留作自用，其余俱属出租的公寓。这样的需要，增加了不少我们的困难。第一，银行的进口和公寓的进口要分开。第二，公寓住客的入口和工人的入口也要分开。一块这样畸形和狭小的地皮，请问如何办法？"陆谦受在1936年出版的期刊《中国建筑》上撰文写到。

作为中国银行建筑科科长，同孚大楼是陆谦受为中国银行设计的第二家上海分行。他此前设计的中国银行虹口分行也是一项类似的建筑挑战。两座建筑均建在一块细长型的不规则土地上，都要求设计为底层是对外营业的银行，楼上为居住公寓。

"这两座建筑都显示了建筑师对土地的正确利用。中国银行建筑部负责人陆谦受在仅有100平方米的狭窄基地上，创造了高达1000平方米的使用空间。"同济大学郑时龄院士曾在讲座中评价

孚大楼。

他介绍，因为当时上海土地价格十分昂贵，所以建造了好几座类似的高层建筑。

当年因为高昂的土地售价，中国银行购买同孚路（Yates Road，今泰兴路）这块基地也成为英文《北华捷报》报道的一则地产交易新闻。

"赫德路（Hart Road，今常德路）的地皮卖家售价更高。有些地块要价在每亩3万两银子。但是，这个数字与静安寺路（Bubbling Well Road，今南京西路）和同孚路西角的土地价格相比，就显得微不足道了。那块土地毗邻天主教会女校，面积只有半亩不到，不过是位于一个拐角处。最

后买家支付了6万3千两银子。"1930年5月13日的《北华捷报》报道。

上海建筑史学家罗小未先生在《上海建筑指南》（1996年）中也提到了同孚大楼。

"大楼连地下室共10层，平面结合道路转角呈南北长的半月形，西面墙面平直，东面南北两端呈弧形转折。底层和地下室为银行使用，余为出租公寓。建筑外貌以横线条处理，深褐色面砖墙面，呈近代高层建筑风格。"

而英国建筑历史学家爱德华·丹尼森（Edward Denison）研究发现，陆谦受在同孚大楼和中国银行虹口分行使用了相似的设计手法——功能的区分在立面上显而易见。底部两层用作银行，外立面用石材覆盖，而大楼其余部分的立面则使用砖砌装饰。

"在大楼南端，他将立面弯曲成一条紧密的曲线，仿佛中国画卷轴一般，其核心形成了一个不高的圆柱塔，从檐口上方突出。银行大楼的两个入口之一就位于这个弯角的底部。入口装饰有铁格栅、金属照明支架和环绕门口的圆形钢制图案。在北端，建筑师对立面的处理更为显著，也透露了建筑错综复杂的内部格局。水平窗户的线条被一对颀长的垂直玻璃条带打断。玻璃条带照亮了上部七层私人公寓的楼梯间和升降井。" 丹尼森在其著作《陆谦受——被遗忘的中国现代建筑师》（*Luke Him Sau Architect—China's Missing Modern*）中写道。

根据陆谦受1936年的文章，同孚大楼每层有三种面积大小不等的公寓：分别带有四间、三间和两间卧室。虽然后来有人批评这些公寓的空间太狭小，但是陆谦受用狭窄的地块为自己辩护，并且认为房间实际使用起来并不算小。

陆谦受（1904—1992）是近代中国第一代建筑师中的代表人物，祖籍广东新会，出生于香港，幼年曾随父赴英国，1930年毕业于伦敦英国建筑学会建筑学院，成为英国皇家建筑学会会员（A.R.I.B.A）。1929年，时任中国银行副行长的张嘉璈旅欧考察时，将这位年仅25岁的建筑师从伦敦请回国担任银行建筑科科长。年轻的建筑师答应了邀约。他没有按照父亲的要求回港继承家业，而是选择前往上海开创事业，从此改变了自己的人生。

此后几十年间，陆谦受负责建设中国银行的各类项目，从银行、办公楼、住宅到仓库，成了"银行设计专业户"。外滩中国银行大楼项目开工前他已完成中国银行多家分行和行员宿舍等的设计任务，包括同孚大楼。

而他最值得一提的作品当然还是中国银行位于外滩23号的总部大楼，那是一座他与公和洋行共同设计的带有中国元素的装饰艺术建筑。这是外滩唯一一幢有华人参与设计的临江大楼。1937年竣工的西式摩天楼高达17层，用琳琅满目的中式元素装饰，如四方攒尖屋顶、铜绿色琉璃瓦、镂空花格窗和石质斗拱。同济大学常青院士幽默地将23号的风格定义为"Shanghai Deco"（上海装饰艺术派），认为这件作品是将中国古典装饰几何化的一次成功尝试。

在《陆谦受——被遗忘的中国现代建筑师》一书中，英国建筑历史学家爱德华·丹尼森认为这位中国银行的"御用"建筑师非常幸运。业主保持不变让陆谦受的建筑风格得到延续，也让他在动荡岁月里无生计之忧，不用参与竞争来满足不同业主的需求。而陆谦受恰好是那种能将一种风格和类型发挥到极致的设计师，十分擅长利用简单经济的材料营造最佳的视觉效果。这与为满足不同业主而设计风格变幻多样的斯裔匈籍建筑师邬达克形成了对比。

郑时龄院士提到，上海的很多历史建筑都是包括陆谦受在内的中国近代建筑师的作品。在南京西路上，杨锡镠设计的百乐门舞厅和范文照的美琪大戏院都是中国建筑师的经典案例。

中国传统文化中没有名为"建筑师"的职业，只有工匠。20世纪10年代，这种情况发生了改变。一批中国学生在海外学习建筑学回国后，他们或加入外国建筑设计公司，或像后来的华盖事务所一样开设了自己的事务所。陆谦受是其中的佼佼者之一，他成为中国银行的专职建筑师。他与曾在美国宾夕法尼亚大学学习的中国建筑师吴景奇（Wu Chauncey K.）在中国银行共事多年，共同设计了包括同孚大楼在内的多个建筑项目。

20世纪40年代后期，陆谦受回到香港，面临再次从零开始创业。抗战期间，陆家在香港的祖宅被毁，父亲也去世了。

"尽管如此，陆谦受告诉自己的儿子，他从不后悔在大陆工作的那段岁月。当时他年纪轻轻就设计了很多项目，参与上海的城市规划工作，甚至还有一些国家级的项目。尽管他回港后设计了很多医院、教堂和高层建筑，但他更珍视自己在大陆的时光。陆谦受为孙辈的名字都加上了中华的'华'字。"研究中国近代建筑师的上海交通大学讲师王浩娱提到。

1936年同孚大楼竣工两年时，陆谦受和吴景奇在《中国建筑》杂志联合发表了一篇著名的文章，题为《我们的主张》。

"我们以为派别是无关重要的。一件成功的建筑作品，第一，不能离开实用的需要；第二，不能离开时代的背景；第三，不能离开美术的原理；第四，不能离开文化的精神。"

昨天：同孚大楼　**今日：**吴江大厦（底层为中国工商银行分行）　**地址：**南京西路 801 号
建筑师：陆谦受（Luke Him Sau）和吴景奇（Wu Chauncey K）　**建筑风格：**现代风格。
提示：欣赏建筑师对狭窄场地的精准利用。位于南京西路的绿色铁门是上层公寓的入口，透过铁门可以欣赏富有设计感的楼梯。

Architect Luke Him Sau (Lu Qianshou) called the crescent-shaped Yates Apartments on Nanjing Road W. "a strange house".

"This is a strange house built on a deformed site which made it very hard to arrange the layout," Luke wrote in an article in the 1936 journal *The Chinese Architect*.

It was the second Shanghai branch the Hong Kong-born architect designed for the Bank of China. The first one, the Hongkou branch, was a similar architectural challenge. The two buildings were both built on a slender, irregular strip of land and had to accommodate banks on the ground floor and apartments above.

"Both buildings demonstrated the architect's accurate use of the land. On the narrow 100 square meters' site, Luke, who headed the Bank of China's architectural department, created a space of up to 1,000 square meters for use," said Tongji University professor Zheng Shiling in a lecture about the city's 1930s buildings.

He explained that several similar high-rises were built in that era because land prices were so expensive. The purchase of the Yates Road site was big news for *the North-China Herald* because of the site's cost.

"Property in Hart Road (today's Changde Road) shows a higher figure, taken at sellers' values. Offers to sell certain parcels here have been made at Tls. 30,000 per mow. These figures, however, pale into insignificance when the price for the site at the western corner of Bubbling Well Road and Yates Road is mentioned. Situated next to the Cathedral School for Girls, the piece of ground is only half a mow in extent, but, as stated, it is a corner site. And a sum of Tls. 63,000 was paid for it," *the North-China Herald* reported on May 13, 1930.

Shanghai architectural historian Luo Xiaowei also mentioned

the Yates Apartments in her book — *A guide to Shanghai Architecture* (1996).

"The Yates Apartments building with banking space on the ground floor was built on a narrow land on the corner of Yates Road, so was called Yates Apartments," Luo wrote.

"The bank opens to Nanjing Road, and the apartments on the upper eight stories can be seen from the other side. The main facade of pale ochre tiles, follows the line of roads, forming an interesting curved wall with strong horizontal lines."

British architectural historian Edward Denison discovered a similar style used by Luke in the Yates and Hongkou branches. In both buildings, the separation of function is apparent in the facade. The ground and first floors used as banks are faced in stone, while bricks are used throughout the rest of the facade.

"At the southern end he coiled the facade into a tight curve, like a Chinese scroll, the core of which forms a short cylindrical tower projecting above the cornice. One of the bank's two entrances stands at the base of this coiled corner, decorated with iron grilles, metal lighting brackets and circular

steel motifs framing the doorway. At the north end the treatment of the facade is more prominent and reveals the building's intricate interior arrangements. The lines of horizontal windows half abruptly at a pair of slender vertical glazed strips that light the stairwell and lift shaft for the seven storeys of private apartments," Denison wrote in his co-authored book *Luke Him Sau Architect—China's Missing Modern*.

According to Luke's 1936 article, each of the upper floors contained three sizes of apartments: four, three and two bedrooms. These apartments were later criticized for their small space. But Luke defended himself by pointing to the narrow plot and stated "the rooms were actually not so small for use".

Luke was one of the first-generation architects in modern China. Born in Hong Kong, he had studied at the Architectural Association School of Architecture in the United Kingdom. In 1929 Zhang Jia'ao (Chang Kia-ngau), the then Bank of China's Vice President, met Luke in London and offered the 25-year-old architect the post of heading the bank's architectural department.

Luke then denied his father's request to return to Hong Kong to inherit the family business and headed to Shanghai.

In the following decades, Luke was responsible for building a variety of Bank of China projects, ranging from banks, offices, residences to warehouses all over China. Among them, the most noteworthy was the Bank of China building on the Bund, a modern Art Deco structure with strong Chinese elements which he co-designed with Palmer & Turner.

Professor Zheng Shiling said many of Shanghai's historical buildings are the work of China's remarkable first-generation architects, including Luke. Other examples on the former Bubbling Well Road included the Paramount Dance Hall by Yang Xiliu and the Majestic Theater by Fan Wenzhao, which will be introduced later in this column.

He explains that traditionally the profession of "architect" did not exist in China — only craftsman. But things changed after several Chinese students studied architecture overseas and returned around 1910 and kick-started a building boom.

When Chinese students returned with overseas architectural degrees, they joined foreign architectural enterprises or later opened their own companies like the Allied Architects. But Luke was exceptional among them as he became a full-time architect employed by a Chinese bank.

Luke co-designed a large amount of architectural projects with his long-time Bank of China partner, Wu Chauncey K. (Wu Jingqi), a Chinese architect who had studied in the University of Pennsylvania.

In the late 1940s Luke returned to Hong Kong, where his old family house was demolished during World War II and his father had passed away. He had to start a career all over again.

"Despite this, Luke told his son he never regretted his years working in China's mainland. As a young man, he designed many projects and participated in Shanghai's urban planning work and even some state-level projects. Though he designed quite a few hospitals, churches and high-rises later in Hong Kong, he valued his career more in the mainland from 1929 to 1949," says Wang Haoyu, a PhD researcher and lecturer from Shanghai Jiao Tong University who had interviewed Luke's descendants and wrote a research paper about this architect.

"Luke added 'Hua,' an abbreviation for China, in his grandchildren's names."

In 1936, two years after the completion of Yates Apartments, Luke and Wu co-authored a famous article in the journal *The Chinese Architect* named "Our Proclamation".

"We think styles are of little importance. A good building calls for, first, practical needs, second, contemporary background, third, aesthetic principles, fourth, cultural spirit," Luke and Wu wrote.

Yesterday: Yates Apartments
Today: Wujiang Building (ground floors used as an ICBC branch)
Address: 801 Nanjing Road W.   **Architects:** Luke Him Sau and Wu Chauncey K.
Architectural style: Modern
Tips: Admire the building's accurate use of the narrow site. Through a green iron gate on Nanjing Road W., which serves as the entrance to the apartments, you can appreciate a stylish staircase.

一个 19 世纪花园的命运
The Story of Zhangyuan Garden

2019年春节，红灯笼点亮了张园的灰砖墙与黑木门。居民们隆重庆祝在这里的最后一个春节后，陆续搬离这片夹在吴江路和威海路之间的石库门里弄。

张园居民邢建民希望未来的新家离这里不要太远，最好还在静安区，因为他会非常想念从小长大的张园。邢建民的家位于一幢张园别墅二楼的一个房间。这座别墅楼道蒙尘，堆满杂物，仍能看出原本开阔的公共空间、大楼梯和精致雕花，比传统石库门里弄房气派很多。邢建民回忆，儿时在二楼宽敞的走廊打羽毛球，把大楼梯扶手当成滑梯玩。

2019年1月，张园地块旧城区改建项目征收生效，这里计划改造为融休闲、商业和时尚文化为一体的新地标。项目竣工后，地铁2号线、12号线和13号线也将在地下连通一体，便利换乘。张园的历史建筑会得到保护，居民们也拿到了动迁安置补偿。

同济大学教授钱宗灏认为张园堪称"石库门博物馆"，极具研究和保护价值。"张园原来是西人格农的花园，初为20亩，历

史可以追溯到19世纪60年代。"钱宗灏说。

格农（Groom Francis）是英国商人，在南京路经营一家名为Glover & Co. 的公司，居住在圆明园路的一座公寓楼里，后来搬到静安寺路（今南京西路）的花园。

钱教授提到，清末著名实业家张叔和买下了这座西人花园，作为"味莼园"供母亲居住养老。张叔和是江苏无锡人，原在轮船招商局任职，因亏款被革职，又因商务航行台湾地区途中遭遇沉船事件，爬上桅杆才幸存，此后决定远离官场。母亲过世后，张叔和本

来要卖掉花园，在友人劝说下于1885年将花园对外开放。19世纪时，管理公共租界的上海工部局不允许华人进入公园，许多像张园一样的私家园林销售门票对公众开放游园。为了让花园更加吸引人，张叔和不仅添置娱乐设施，还将花园面积从20亩扩充到70亩。

张园有丰富的中式园林元素——假山、花卉、柳树和竹林。但1893年张叔和却邀请两位英国人——金斯密（Thomas William Kingsmill又译作景斯美1837—1910）和艾特金森（Brenan Atkinson又译作庵景生 1866—1907）在园内打造了一座西式建筑——安凯第（Arcadia Hall）。

这座西式建筑后来成为张园的标志，也给这座名园带来中西合璧的风貌。1923年出版的《上海游客和居民指南》（*Shanghai: A Handbook for Travelers and Residents to the Chief Objects of Interest in and Around the Foreign Settlements and Native City*）在介绍这座海上名园时就提到安凯第。

"会堂（指安凯第）是上海最漂亮的建筑之一，花园也不错。每年夏季都会有烟花表演，效果很像西式烟火，还有点心供应。张园经营团队增加了许多诱人项目，包括水滑道和自行车赛道。"

根据同济大学郑时龄院士的《上海近代建筑风格》新版，金斯密是英国土木与建筑工程师，曾被《字林西报》誉为土木建筑界巨星。他1848年前经香港来华，1958年在汉口建立事务所，1860年与英国建筑师怀特菲尔德在上海建立有恒洋行（Whitfield & Kingmill），1863年后在沪定居。金斯密的设计作品表现出明显的新文艺复兴风格，细部处理也采用正统的西方建筑手法。金斯密的有恒洋行是上海最早的建筑师事务所，有恒洋行在上海的设计作品还包括外白渡桥和福州路总巡捕房。上海许多著名的外国建筑师都来自该行，其中包括共同设计安凯第的艾特金森。1894年，艾特金森创立了近代上海最重要的建筑事务所之一——通和洋行（Atkinson & Dallas）。

1893年当安凯第还在建造

时，《北华捷报》就刊文报道这个建筑实质上是一座中式娱乐花园"新的起点"。

"从外观欣赏，建筑的总体效果非常悦目。建筑是意大利文艺复兴风格的，建造材料使用了熟悉的红砖。在大楼东北角有一座漂亮的高达90英尺的钟楼，从那里可以欣赏周边美好的乡村风光。大楼主入口朝北，人们一进门就被富有品位的室内所吸引。进入大厅前，左右两侧是衣帽间，主要是西式娱乐项目举行时使用，也有可能用作商店。"1893年4月21日的《北华捷报》报道。

报道还提到，业主希望在大陆咖啡馆（Continental Cafe）附近建造一家精美的茶馆。建筑主体是一个80英尺长、40英尺宽的会堂，由柱廊装点。柱廊上方是一个类似的可以俯瞰大厅的走廊。

"这座建筑的主要目的是作为茶馆使用。茶馆建成后，由于其高贵的气质、雅致的装饰、通透而明亮的氛围，将成为一个经典。不过，它也可以用作其他目的。希望举办舞会或其他类似娱乐活动的外国人将可以租用整座建筑，而且如果仅仅只是实现最初的想法，这个地方也将在上海侨民中广受欢迎。"报道写到。

"从现存的安凯第照片看，该建筑具有英国安妮女王复兴风格，清水红砖、塔楼高耸，体量虽大但无不当、且细节丰富，设计和施工的专业水平很高，体现了一种精致手工艺制作和童话般欢乐气氛的结合。这形象成了张园的标志，而这一点恰巧是张园后来招徕游客的名片。"钱宗灏教授评价。

安凯第开张营业后，张园迎来自己的"黄金时代"，这段人气颇旺的时期一直持续到1909年左右。人们到张园来赏花、登安凯第塔楼远眺风景、打弹子、喝茶、看烟火、体验当时很新潮的照相术，甚至乘坐热气球。张园举行过不计其数的各类活动，从生日派对、婚礼、悼念仪式、各类庆典和集会，应有尽有。

著名上海历史学家熊月之在20世纪90年代撰写的一篇论文中，评价张园是"晚清上海第一个公共空间"。

这个花园在晚清时成为政治集会和演讲的举办地。许多革命者，包括孙中山、章太炎和蔡元培都在安凯第举行过演讲。武术家霍

元甲在此秀过武技，画家刘海粟则在此举办过画展。

张园见证了很多"第一"——第一场西式婚礼、第一场妇女演讲、革命者第一次当众剪辫、第一家户外照相馆……

"张园这一公共空间的形成，与上海特殊的政治环境密切相关。租界既是中国领土又不受中国政府直接管辖的特点，使得中国大一统的政治局面出现一道缝隙。由于上海特殊的社会结构，由于租界的缝隙效应，由于东西文化的差异，地处租界的张园，便逐渐演变成上海华人能够自由发表意见的公

共场所，"熊月之写道。

20世纪初，随着半淞园、大世界等新式公园相继开幕后抢走了人气，张园的"黄金时代"走到了尽头。1919年，张叔和去世，此后张园土地陆续被重新分割成28块，被不同的开发商建成石库门住宅，渐渐生长为一片繁华闹市中的里弄街区。

"张园位于南京西路历史风貌区的核心位置。多年前曾有计划将位于张园附近的地铁2号线、12号线和13号线南京西路站连通，受限于当时的建筑保护技术，没有实行。"负责张园城市更新项目的上海静安置业集团有限公司副总工程师李振东说。

"这次的更新项目中，将更多地保护这些富有价值的历史建筑，并充分利用地下空间。"他介绍，从2016年起，静安置业就开始调研张园历史建筑，建立

"一房一册"档案。他们采访了1100多户家庭，调研了170多幢历史建筑。在做建筑记录和档案时还使用GRS和无人机摄影等现代技术。

2020年10月30日世界城市日，在上海社科院主办的石库门城市更新论坛上，静安置业董事长时筠仑透露，张园将设立文化演绎中心和文化展示中心，成为国际文化体验和交流的新地标。

而钱教授认为，张园的建筑形态非常丰富。

"张园的里弄建筑建于20世纪20到30年代，新式里弄、旧式里弄、坊、村、里都有。因为这些里弄建筑由不同的开发商建造，所以形态十分多样，有别于静安别墅等风格单一的里弄，有着一步一景的效果，这就是张园的价值所在。"钱教授评价。

昨天：张园　**今天：**张园　**地址：**威海路590号
建筑师：金斯密（T. W. Kingmill）和艾特金森（Brenan Atkinson）

Red lanterns illuminated grey lane houses and dark wood gates in the Zhangyuan Garden area last month. After celebrating the last Spring Festival residents are packing up their belongings and moving away from a neighborhood full of history sandwiched between Wujiang and Weihai roads.

"I plan to move to a new home not far from here, also in the Jing'an District. I will miss Zhangyuan forever because it's where I grew up," says Xing Jianmin, a middle-aged man, whose family has lived for decades in a room on the second floor of a shikumen (stone-gate) house that boasted a larger interior public space than ordinary shikumen houses.

"I played badminton in the spacious corridor and enjoyed sliding down the handrail of the big staircase when I was a boy," he recalls.

In January, the local government announced Zhangyuan Garden will go through a new round of refurbishment to turn the plot into a mixed-use center of leisure, commerce, fashion and culture. Meanwhile the project will further enable Metro lines 2, 12 and 13 to connect in one underground station. Local residents like Xing received financial compensation for relocating so several of the historical buildings in the area get preserved.

"Zhangyuan Garden, which evolved out of an Englishman's

farm and later a renowned Chinese garden, had been a living museum of shikumen architecture. It had great values for research and preservation," says Tongji University professor Qian Zonghao, who is co-authoring a book on Zhangyuan Garden's architectural history.

Zhangyuan Garden dates back to the 1860s when a British merchant, Groom Francis, purchased a farm. Francis owned a firm named Glover & Co. on Nanjing Road. He had lived in an apartment building on Yuanmingyuan Road but later moved to a farm along the Bubbling Well Road, today's Nanjing Road W.

Chang Su-ho, or Zhang Shuhe, was a Wuxi native who worked for the Shanghai Steam Navigation Co. He bought the farm from Groom and built Weichunyuan Garden for his mother to live in. It had ponds, rockeries, rare flowers, willows and bamboo groves.

After Chang's mother passed away in 1885, he opened the garden to the public at the advice of a friend.

It was at a time when the then Shanghai Municipal Council excluded locals from public gardens. So, many private gardens in the city started charging admission fees, including the Chang's plot.

In 1893 Chang invited two famous architects, T. W. Kingsmill and B. Atkinson, to build the garden's signature building—Arcadia Hall. To make it more attractive,

he not only added new entertainment facilities but also expanded the garden five times, from the original 20 mu (13,340 square meters) to up to 70 mu.

In a 1923 year guide, titled *Shanghai: A Handbook for Travelers and Residents to the Chief Objects of Interest in and Around the Foreign Settlements and Native City*, Zhangyuan Garden, which was then called the Chang Su-ho Garden, was listed as one of the city's renowned gardens.

"The hall is one of the handsomest buildings in Shanghai, and the gardens are good. Displays of fireworks are given in the summer. There are some altogether original effects, quite unlike those Western fireworks. Refreshments may be obtained. The gardens are about 12 years old. Under the present management, many new attractions have been added, such as a water chute and cycle track," as was introduced by the book.

While building operations were going on in the garden in 1893, *the North-China Herald* reported the Arcadia Hall building was "something in the nature of a 'new departure' for a Chinese pleasure garden".

"The general effect of the structure when viewed from the outside is very pleasing," the paper reported on April 21, 1893.

"The style is the Italian Renaissance, and the material a familiar red brick. Over the N.E. corner will be a pretty campanile tower 90ft high, which will give a very fine view over the surrounding country. The principle entrance is at the N., and on entering the visitor will be attracted by its very tasteful appearance. To the right and left, just before entering the hall, are rooms which will be used as cloak rooms when foreign entertainment is being given, but probably at other times they will be utilized as shops."

The report says the idea was to construct a finely built teahouse very closely to the Continental Café. The main part of the building consisted of a fine hall 80 feet long by 40 feet wide, which was adorned by a colonnade that supported a similar promenade looking down into the hall.

"The primary object of the hall is to serve as a teahouse, and when it is finished, on account of its loftiness, tasteful decoration and general airiness and brightness it will be a model one," the report said. "But it will be available for other purposes as well. Foreigners who desire to give a ball or other entertainment of a similar nature will be able to hire the entire building and if the ideal which has been set up is only realized the place will no doubt be very popular with Shanghailanders."

Professor Qian Zonghao discovered from historical postcard photos that the grand Arcadia Hall had red bricks and a steep tower.

"It was so large but was properly designed and built with abundant details, which expressed a combination of refined handicrafts and a merry fairy tale atmosphere. The building became the landmark of Zhangyuan Garden and a name card to attract visitors. It's a pity that this building, which was formerly located between today's 264 and 250 Maoming Road N. had been demolished long time ago," Qian says.

After the opening of the new

Arcadia Hall, Zhangyuan Garden embraced its golden era which lasted until 1909. It became a garden where you could admire flowers, climb to the tower of Arcadia Hall to cast a bird's-eye view of Shanghai, play billiards, drink tea, take photos, which were still rather novel at that time, watch fireworks or even ride hot-air balloons. The garden hosted numerous birthday parties, wedding ceremonies, memorial services, celebrations and big gatherings.

Famous Shanghai historian Xiong Yuezhi, who did one of the first academic researches on Zhangyuan Garden in the 1990s, named it "the first public space in modern China".

In late 1900s, the garden served as a venue for political gatherings and speeches. Revolutionaries such as Dr Sun Yat-sen, Zhang Taiyan and Cai Yuanpei gave speeches at the Arcadia Hall. Chinese martial arts master Huo Yuanjia showcased his skills in front of a big crowd. Renowned Chinese painter Liu Haisu exhibited his first nudes here.

There were many "firsts" in this garden — the first Western-style wedding, the first women's speech, the first time revolutionary figures cut their pigtails (Chinese men wearing single long braid is regarded as a symbol of feudalism) in the public and the first outdoor photography studio.

"The rise for Chang's garden to become such a public space was closely related to the special political environment of Shanghai at that time. The garden, located in the International Concession, was not under the direct jurisdiction of the Chinese government. There was a lot of options for innovations and ideas," Xiong writes in "Zhangyuan Garden: Research of a Shanghai public space in the late Qing Dynasty".

After its peak time in the 1900s, the garden saw a decline at the openings of newer entertainment parks like the Great World Amusement Center in 1918. After Chang Su-ho died in 1919, the compound was gradually divided into up to 28 pieces for selling and reconstructed into a shikumen residential block by different developers.

Today, it is a cluster of shikumen houses surrounded by modern high-rises.

"Zhangyuan Garden sits as a centerpiece of Nanjing Road W. historical area. There was a plan to connect Metro lines 2, 12 and 13 in one stop years ago but technology was not mature for preserving so many old houses," says Li Zhendong, vice chief architect of the state-owned Shanghai Jing'an Real Estate (Group) Co. Ltd., a major developer of this project.

"Now the upcoming regeneration project will be able to preserve these valuable historical buildings and make full use of underground space."

He says an archival book for each building in Zhangyuan Garden was done as part of the research work starting in 2016.

"So far archival, architectural and restorative experts have researched more than 170 buildings and interviewed some 1,100 local families. Modern technologies, such as GRS, drone photographing have been used in making this architectural records," Li says.

Professor Qian notes that Zhangyuan Garden features abundant architectural forms.

"Built from 1920s to 1930s, the compound had a variety of new-style lanes, old–style lanes and the more spacious shikumen mansions. The variety resulted from dozens of early developers and made it differ from other shikumen residential block like Jing'an villa where buildings looked almost identical. Therefore, Zhangyuan Garden has a unique value for conservation," Qian says.

Yesterday: Chang Su-ho Garden　**Today:** Zhangyuan Garden　**Address:** 590 Weihai Rd. **Architects:** T. W. Kingmill and B. Atkinson

激动人心的热气球降落伞表演
Parachute Balloon Spectacular Greeted by Excited "Hi-yahs"

周六下午，对于蜂拥来到张园的几千名华人来说，跳伞是另一项西方野蛮人的发明，让中国人感到震惊。当地人对于热气球还了解一二，但是看到一个妇女从空中飞过，在很明显只有一把伞的帮助下，从一英里的高度降落，当然引起一片"哈呀"的惊疑之声。

在这种情况下，在中国的外国人肯定感到不懂当地语言的弊端。毫无疑问，这些本地人评论被翻译成我们的语言肯定非常有趣。这些人很可能不会像另一些无知的所谓爱国本地人那样，认为中国早在数千年前就已经做过相同的事了。

无论如何，让西人感到满意的是，发现在中国产生一种西方体验时，它应该按照原样那么做。从气球充气到塔谢尔小姐（Van Tassell）最后在奥利弗平房附近的棉田最后下降，一切都顺利进行。确实，出于经济原因，活动开始的时间被推迟了，气球充气膨胀的过程枯燥乏味，但是上升和下降过程与期望的一样好。

六点时刚刚日落，塔谢尔小姐来到气球的后部，表演了一些让人感到惊恐的技艺后，她释放了气球，升到大约4000英尺（1219米）的高度。然后很快降落伞就打开了，她稳稳地落下来，没有任何意外地着陆了。在了不起的一天之内欣赏两次落日之后，这位勇敢的表演者被裹上一件斗篷送回家。热气球在三英里远的地方落下，虽然被及时发现，但村民已经恶意地割掉几乎整个顶部。

当晚接受采访时，塔谢尔谈到因为风的缘故，她降落得非常快。她一直感到在风中降落的速度比没有风时要快。她的第一次跳伞是一次愉快的体验，但此后她意识到这项运动还是有一定危险性的。

Judging from the thousands of wondering Chinese who flocked to Chang Su-ho's garden, Shanghai, on Saturday afternoon, parachuting is another of the inventions of the Western barbarian which come as a shock to celestial notions. Of balloons the natives know something; but the spectacle of a woman flying through the air and descending for nearly a mile, apparently with only the aid of an umbrella, was certainly enough to excite "hi-yahs" without number.

It is on such occasions that foreigners in China must feel the disadvantages of not understanding the language. The comments, translated into our speech, would without doubt be very amusing; and it is highly probable that they were not wanting patriotic natives who felt sure the same kind of thing had been done in the Middle Kingdom thousands of years before.

Anyhow it is some satisfaction to the Westerner to find that when a Western sensation is produced in China it is done as it should be. Everything passed off without a hitch, from the commencement of the inflation to the final descent of Miss Van Tassell in a cotton-field near Oliver's Bungalow. It is true that, for financial reasons, the start was delayed, and that the process of inflation proved rather tedious, but the ascent and descent were all that could be desired.

At six o'clock, just after sunset, Miss Van Tassell went up at the tail of the balloon, and in five minutes' time, after performing some blood-curdling feats on her horizontal bar, she let go, at a height of about 4,000 feet. Very quickly the parachute opened, and she came steadily down, landing without accident, though the shock on coming to the earth was sufficient to throw her on her face. Then, after having had the remarkable experience of seeing the sun set twice in one day, the daring performer was wrapped up in a cloak and taken home. The balloon fell about three miles off. It was rescued in the shortest possible time, but not before the villagers had wantonly cut off nearly the whole of the top sections.

Miss Van Tassell, on being interviewed in the evening, said she fell very rapidly, this being due to the wind. She had always found, she said, that she fell more quickly in wind than in calm. Her first parachute jump

was a delightful sensation, but afterwards she began to realize that there was a certain amount of danger about it. The Van Tassells leave shortly for Manila.

摘自 1890 年 10 月 17 日《北华捷报》

Excerpt from *The North-China Herald*, on October 17, 1890

高大简洁的泰兴大楼曾被上海建筑史学家罗小未称为"a luxury apartment house"(一座奢华公寓楼)。

1934年初建时,这座名为麦特赫斯脱公寓(Medhurst Apartments)的建筑确实是高档住宅楼。

"大楼沿街转角处建造,平面略呈一字形,主立面朝东偏南。公寓中央部分为12层,两翼各10层。底层沿街为商店,上部为住宅。楼内装修精细,建筑形式具现代建筑风格。"罗小未在《上海建筑指南》中写道。

麦特赫斯脱公寓位于静安寺路(今南京西路)和麦特赫斯脱路(今泰兴路)转角的一块基地,建筑面积达8000多平方米,由英商恒业地产公司(Metropolitan Land Co.)投资。

根据同济大学钱宗灏教授的研究,上海租界早期的住宅多为石库门——一种为小刀会起义后涌入租界的移民建造的联排建筑。根据中国人的习惯,石库门设有天井和厢房。20世纪20年代上海出现成套的里弄公寓,钢窗蜡地板与煤卫齐全,现代舒适。

"此后上海的地价不断上涨,开发商开始兴建6-9层的高层公寓。虽然高层公寓中每套平均房

的面积更小，但因为更现代的设计和设施，居住品质反而提升了。上海近代高层公寓主要为装饰艺术风格和现代风格。泰兴大楼是一件晚期装饰艺术风格作品，与现代主义风格趋同。"钱教授说。

他还提到，这座大楼以泰兴路旧名"麦特赫斯脱路"命名，而这条路又以英国领事麦华陀（Walter Henry Medhurst）命名。麦华陀和其父英国传教士麦都斯都对上海城市发展有影响。父亲麦都斯在山东路一带建立了"麦家圈"，在此创立了中国第一个近代印刷所——墨海书馆（The London Missionary Society Press），参与创办上海第一家西医医院——仁济医院。其子麦华陀担任英国领事期间建议用中国省市名来为上海租界道路命名，其中包括南京路。

1934年麦特赫斯脱大楼投入使用前夕，英文《大陆报》刊登报道，称这是一座"上海新的百万美金大楼"。大楼由新瑞和洋行（Davies & Brooke）设计。这家老牌英资建筑事务所还设计过兰心剧院、礼查饭店、外滩7号大北电

报公司和西藏中路东方饭店等标志性建筑。

"现代理念主导了建筑的外观设计，而室内设计则细致考虑到上海居民现代城市生活的需求。"《大陆报》报道评论道。

报道还透露，大楼设计有两种不同类型的公寓——自助式公寓和装修好的服务公寓。这座公寓楼提供餐厅酒吧等设施与各类服务，堪比一家大型现代酒店，又有家居生活的超然宁静。9楼是餐厅，有鸡尾酒吧和独立的休息室。餐厅用现代感的线条装饰，给人温暖愉悦的感觉，而主休息室的现代设计和色彩方案还带有中式元素。

报道特别提到大楼里设有两套阁楼套房，每套都有7个房间，面向一个美丽的、宽敞的屋顶露台。阁楼套房的住客还可以使用露天平台和位于9楼的休息室及餐厅。套房包含客厅、书房、阳光房、3间卧室、3间浴室和带冰箱的厨房。

如此富有现代设计感的公寓对于高层次住客很有吸引力。1938年2月9日《北华捷报》刊登的一则讣告描绘了一位麦特赫斯脱

大楼住客的肖像。

这位住客名叫罗申菲尔德（Julian Rosenfield），是经纪公司A.B. Rosenfeld & Sons的合伙人。2月7日，久病的他突然在麦特赫斯脱大楼家中去世。

罗申菲尔德出生于上海，曾在上海和威海卫（今山东省威海市）上学，回到上海前在美国加州大学和Mount Tamalpals军事学院完成学业。

5年前，他创办了这家经纪公司。罗氏是一位共济会员，也是美国花旗总会、哥伦比亚乡村俱乐部和上海跑马总会的会员。在商业世界里，他是上海股票交易所、美国商会、芝加哥交易所、纽约交易所和加拿大交易所的会员。

根据静安置业副总工程师李振东的研究，投资大楼的恒业地产公司成立于1930年。这个时间与沪上老牌的外商地产公司，如1872年成立的沙逊洋行和1888年成立的业广地产相比，要迟很多。

在军阀混战时期，官僚、地主搜刮的银两大量流入上海租界，而这些官僚地主又十分迷信外商。几位旅沪英国商人发现这一点后，便以少量资金成立房地产公司并发行股票和债券集资，购得建房基地后向银行押款，享受外商银行对其本国商民优惠的利率。他们集资组建英商恒业地产公司后购得静安寺路麦特赫斯脱路口这块面积2.15亩的基地，建造一座公寓带店面房的大楼，借以扩大影响和业务。麦特赫斯脱大楼的建成让恒业公司的信誉蒸蒸日上。由于位置优越，楼上公寓还被一些知名的医师租作诊所，如中华医药会上海分会会长、我国著名的泌尿科医师陈邦典即租用了一套五开间的一组公寓房，为大楼增添了知名度和信誉。

一份恒业地产在外滩17号开股东大会的报告印证了他的研究。根据1938年12月21日《北华捷报》的报道，公司主席史密斯（F. R. Smith）说，有能力的管理和优质餐食让麦特赫斯脱大楼一直保持满住状态，这也证明是公司的一项成功投资。

"公共租界、西区和法租界的租金收益比过去几年都要高，我们公司在这些区域的项目一直带来令人满意的回报。"斯密斯在股东大会上说道。

1955年，恒业地产公司向中国政府提出转让经营，1956年移交房管部门接管。

1971年，上海电信在佘山微波中继站和泰兴大楼分别安装了微波收发信机和抛物面天线，从此上海市民可以收看中央电视台的节目。后来，泰兴大楼又开设了上海长途电话局国际电话室，从这里通过通讯卫星的无线电波，联结着世界各地。在刚刚改革开放的日子里，远隔重洋的亲友在这里接通了电话。

如今，泰兴大楼保持着昔日简洁现代的外表，底层是中国移动公司营业厅，楼上仍为公寓。

昨天：麦特赫斯脱大楼 Medhurst Apartments　**今天：**泰兴大楼
地址：南京西路 934 号
建筑师：新瑞和洋行 Davies and Brooke, Civil Engineers and Architects
参观指南：可以安静地走进公寓大楼，从现状看，很难想象昔日是一家奢华公寓楼。

The gigantic, simple-cut Taixing Apartments on Nanjing Road was once called "a luxury apartment house" by renowned Shanghai architectural historian Luo Xiaowei.

It was formerly an upscale residential building, known as the Medhurst Apartments, when it was built in 1934.

"The simple modern building is found with vertical lines over the entrance, while the wings are marked with strong horizontal lines," Luo writes in her 1990s book *A Guide to Shanghai Architecture*.

"The 8,837-square-meter building was a complex of apartments and shops invested in by Metropolitan Land Co.. The company purchased a 2.15-mu land (1,434 square meters) at the prominent location of the Bubbling Well Road (now Nanjing Road W.) and Medhurst Road (now Taixing Road) to expand business and boast influence," says Li Zhendong, vice chief architect of the Shanghai Jing'an Real Estate (Group) Co. Ltd., who scooped archives for Jing'an District's old houses.

According to the research of Tongji University professor Qian Zonghao, the city's residential architecture developed from early shikumen (stone-gated) houses to three-story apartments emerging in the 1920s.

As Shanghai's land price continued to soar in the 1920s, taller apartment buildings, between six and nine floors began to spring up. Although every flat in the taller buildings was smaller than before, the living quality of flat dwellers improved significantly due to modern design and facilities.

"Tall apartment buildings were in either Art Deco or modern style. The Medhurst Apartments were designed in a late Art Deco style which resembled modern style," Qian says.

The Medhurst Apartments was called "Shanghai's new million-dollar building house" by *the China Press* before its opening. It was designed by Davies & Brooke, a veteran British architectural firm in old Shanghai whose signature works range from Lyceum Theater, Astor House, Great Northern Telegraph Building at No. 7 on the Bund to the Grand Hotel on Xizang Road M., a 5-minute walk from the Nanjing Road pedestrian shopping street.

"Modern conceptions dominate the outward appearance while the interior was arranged after detailed study to fulfill the peculiar needs of the Shanghai resident and the demands of modern

city life," *the China Press* reported on March 1, 1934.

According to the report, the building uniquely housed two types of apartments—self-contained and furnished serviced apartments. The dining room, lounges and cocktail bar, together with other service features, "furnished residents with all the facilities of a big, modern hotel plus the quietness and detachment of life at home."

The ninth floor had been given over to the dining room, which had been furnished with warmth and gaiety along modern lines, with a cocktail bar and secluded lounges. In addition, the modern design and color scheme of the main lounge contained an atmosphere of Chinese motifs.

The report noted that special features of the building were two penthouses, which had seven rooms each and faced out to an attractive, spacious roof garden.

Terraces were available for the penthouse residents, as well as from the ninth floor lounge and dining room. A drawing room, study, sun porch, three bedrooms, three bathrooms and kitchens with Frigidaire were among the facilities of the penthouse apartments.

Apartments with this modern design and facilities were attractive to the city's upper-class dwellers. An obituary in *the North-China Herald* on February 9, 1938 painted a picture of a typical Medhurst apartment resident — Mr. Julian Rosenfield, partner in the brokerage firm of A.B. Rosenfeld & Sons, who unfortunately died suddenly early on February 7 in his home in the Medhurst Apartments after a long illness.

Shanghai-born Rosenfeld was educated in Shanghai and Weihaiwei (in today's Weihai, Shandong Province) and later completed his education at the University of California and the Mount Tamalpals Military Academy before returning to Shanghai.

At the time of his death, he was a partner in the brokerage firm of Rosenfeld & Sons, which he founded about five years earlier. He was Mason and a member of the American Club, the Columbia Country Club and the Shanghai Race Club. In the business world, he was a member of the Shanghai Stock Exchange, the American Chamber of Commerce, the New York Cotton Exchange, the Chicago Board of Trade, the Commodity Exchange Inc., of New York, and the Canadian Commodity Exchange Inc. .

According to Li Zhendong's research, the Metropolitan company was founded in 1930, which was much later than some veteran foreign developers, like the Sassoon & Co. or Shanghai Land Investment Company.

"The Metropolitan company's early founders saw a business opportunity of flooding a large amount of silver into Shanghai settlements brought by Chinese officials and landlords during the Warlord era. So they founded the real estate company without much money and issued stocks and bonds to raise funds. The Medhurst Apartments was a successful investment which boasted the company's reputation," Li says.

"Owing to the great location, some renowned doctors opened clinics in the Medhurst Apartments, such as famous urologist Chen Bangdian, who rented a five-room apartment for his clinicrst. These clinics added fame and faith of this building."

A meeting report of Metropolitan Land Co's shareholders at the No. 17 on the Bund proved his words.

According to the report on *the North-China Herald*, December 21, 1938, Chairman F. R. Smith said capable management, plus the excellent food served in "Medhurst" continued to fill the building to capacity, fully justifying the investment made in this enterprise.

"Rent collections in the International Settlement, the Western District and the French Concession were higher than for the past several years, our properties in these areas continuing to give a satisfactory return," Smith said during the meeting.

In 1955, the building was taken over by the Chinese government and embraced a historical role afterwards. In 1971, Shanghai Telephone Company installed microwave transceivers and parabolic antennas on Sheshan Mountain and in the Medhurst Apartments (now Taixing Apartments) respectively, which enabled people in Shanghai to watch programs sent by Beijing-based CCTV.

Eight years later, it also served as an international call room for the Shanghai Long-Distance Telephone Bureau. With the help of a communication satellite, many Shanghainese managed to talk to their overseas relatives and friends whom they lost contact with for decades.

Today the building houses a China Mobile branch on the ground floor and residential flats upstairs, which has retained its historical role, from a luxury apartment house to an important communication house.

Yesterday: Medhurst Apartments   **Today:** Taixing Apartments
Address: 934 Nanjing Road W.
Architect: Davies and Brooke, Civil Engineers and Architects
Tips: You may enter the building in a quiet way. It's hard to imagine its past as a luxury apartments building from its current condition.

麦特赫斯脱公寓的新型冰箱
New Type of Frigidaire in the Medhurst

　　上海新的豪华公寓楼麦特赫斯脱大楼今天竣工，标志着美国工程公司（American Engineering Corporation）将1934年款的豪华冰箱引入这座城市。

　　住在麦特赫斯脱的上海侨民会在他们的公寓中发现新的豪华冰箱，既美观、方便、品质高，也很经济。这款新的超级63型冰箱具有更大的食品存储容量，带有三个托盘，可一次冷冻七八个冰块。

　　冰箱外部饰面涂有著名的瓷钢材料，而内部则在一个整体的无缝食物隔室中饰以不锈钢瓷。

　　这种新型公寓设备的其他特殊功能包括改进的冷控自动除霜内部照明和自动通风装置。夏日即将到来，将这种冰箱引入上海恰逢其时，毫无疑问会在中外居民中广为流行。

The completion today of Shanghai's new and luxurious apartment hotel, the Medhurst, marks the introduction of the 1934 model Deluxe Frigidaires into the city by the American Engineering Corporation (China), 989 Bubbling Well Road.

Shanghailanders, who live in the Medhurst, will find a new Deluxe Frigidaire in their apartments, which offer new beauty convenience, quality and economy in the low-priced refrigerator field. This new super 63 Frigidaire has a larger food storage capacity with three trays holding 78 cubes of ice at one freezing.

The exterior finish is coated with the famous lifetime porcelain-on-steel while the interior is completed with stainless porcelain in a one-piece seamless food compartment.

Further special features of the new apartment Frigidaire are the improved cold control automatic defrosting interior lighting and the automatic trav releasing. The introduction of the new refrigidaire into Shanghai is timely for the coming summer season and will no doubt prove popular among both foreign and Chinese residents in this city.

摘自 1934 年 3 月 1 日《大陆报》
Excerpt from *The China Press*, on March 1, 1934

1941年10月15日，美琪大戏院开业，被称为新时代远东建筑的一件杰作。这是上海"孤岛时期"建成的最后一家剧院，由中国建筑师范文照设计。

摩登现代的剧院座落于江宁路、奉贤路转角处，是一座两层高的钢筋混凝土框架结构建筑。剧院的英文名"Majestic Theatre"取自毗邻的"Majestic Road"(今南汇路)，其设计满足舞蹈、歌剧和音乐剧等多种演出的需要，也用于放映电影。

剧院附近曾是著名的大华饭店（Majestic Hotel），由西班牙建筑师乐福德（Abelardo Lafuente 1871-1931）设计，1927年蒋介石和宋美龄在此举行婚礼。酒店后来失火烧毁后，所在地块出售重新开发。

在正式开业前数月，剧院发起公开竞赛征集一个动听的中文名。征集活动收到2000多封信件，其中有7个方案都建议取名为"美琪"。这个名字既有"美玉"的美好寓意，发音也近似剧院的英文名"Majestic"。从此，这家剧院就叫做"美琪大戏院"，开业时首映美国福克斯影片公司摄制的《美月琪花》。

美琪大戏院是何挺然创办的联怡电影公司（Shanghai Amusement Co. Ltd.,）投资兴建的第三家戏院。在20世纪30年代，这家公司还建造了北京大戏院和南京大戏院。

其中，位于南京西路两端的南京大戏院和美琪大戏院均由著名中国建筑师范文照设计。这两座剧院生动展示了近代中国第一代建筑师设计风格的重要转变。

建于1930年的南京大戏院由范文照和赵深设计，是上海现存不多的由中国建筑师设计的西方古典主义建筑。建筑设计为改良的文艺复兴风格，外立面的拱廊由彩色灰泥和人造石建造而成。北厅设计有古罗马柱式和大理石楼梯，剧场内有巨大的穹顶和雕刻精美的护墙。

有趣的是，两位中国建筑师在完成这件古典之作以后，设计风格都发生了显著变化。他们先创作了一些将中国元素融入现代建筑的中国古典复兴建筑，如带中式屋顶的八仙桥基督教青年会大楼。

"但他们都抛弃了这种风

格。赵深后来加入的华盖事务所曾发起'摒弃大屋顶运动'。而范文照转向现代风格后，呼吁纠正为建筑添加传统大屋顶的错误。范文照的风格转变是受到两位新同事——美籍瑞典裔建筑师林朋（Carl Lindbom）和中国建筑师伍子昂的影响。1935年范文照曾代表中国参加在英国伦敦举办的第14届国际住房与城镇规划大会和在意大利罗马举办的第13届国际建筑大会，回国后更坚定地拥抱了'功能决定形式'的国际式风

格。范文照1941年设计的美琪大戏院就非常现代。"钱锋说。

除了美琪大戏院，范文照1935年后设计的建筑，如五原路协发公寓（Yafa Apartments）和衡山路集雅公寓（Georgia Apartments）都是现代风格。

美琪大戏院的主入口位于两条街道的转角处，建筑中央是一座圆形巨塔，沿街两个侧厅，减少了建筑与街道之间的冲突。剧院的立面简洁自然，外墙涂成淡黄色奶油色，装饰有一些相同颜色的雕刻

条，营造一份优雅的效果。

剧院入口设有五个长窗，构成了立面的视觉焦点，在入口大厅还悬挂着华丽的水晶吊灯。内部空间则巧妙布置得连续、流动和充满动感。建筑师使用了奶油色水磨石和波浪形线脚来装饰地板和墙壁。

同济大学钱宗灏教授认为，美琪大戏院的弧线形楼梯与邬达克设计的大光明电影院楼梯有异曲同工之妙。这两个大楼梯都演示了装饰艺术风格由早期折线形设计向曲线形的转变。

在《范文照》一书中，建筑师黄元培提到，范文照因为之前与何挺然在南京大戏院项目的良好合作关系，受邀设计美琪大戏院。

"在设计时，范文照仍极度饱和化，布局理性，明确地将休息厅、门厅、售票厅、楼厅、楼梯、穿堂等各功能空间分立，妥善运用，并富于变化，自然流畅，室内还加有艺术雕塑，营造气氛，富丽庄重，楼梯与地坪采磨石子材料，共1597个座位。"

"在外立面部分，范文照在

几何圆形巨塔上做直线条长窗户，供给室内光源外，也形成竖向的垂直语言，巨塔下为一弧形的大雨棚，与巨塔搭配产生一种速度的美感，两侧墙面有数个方窗与横向窗带，在线条、比例与体量之间层次分明。开幕之际，曾被海内外人士誉为'亚洲第一'。"他在书中写到。

美琪大戏院后来成为专映西片的首轮影院，包括京剧大师梅兰芳和芭蕾舞蹈家乌拉诺娃（Galina Sergeevna Ulanova）在内的很多艺术明星都曾在此演出。 1954年，第一届上海人民代表大会也在剧院举行。1989年，它被列入上海市第一批优秀历史建筑，成为上海市市级文物保护单位。

此后，剧院进行了数次翻新整修，其中2010年上海世博会之前的一次大修恢复了历史旧貌，同时改善了剧院的空调和音响系统等设施。如今，美琪大戏院名为"美琪剧场"，虽然体量不大，却是地理位置优越的一个重要文化场所，每年举办多达200场演出。

昨天： 美琪大戏院　**今天：** 上海美琪剧场　**地址：** 江宁路 66 号

建筑师： 范文照（Robert Fan）　**建筑风格：** 装饰艺术风格

参观指南： 剧场仅向观众开放，建议在演出前参观建筑，欣赏处处流动的富有韵律的线条。

The Majestic Theatre was the last theatre built during Shanghai's "lonely island" period when the international settlement was surrounded by Japanese-occupied territory from 1937 to the end of 1941. When it threw open its doors on October 15, 1941, it was regarded as a masterpiece of "a new epoch in Far Eastern architecture".

"The Majestic is a signature work of Chinese architect Fan Wenzhao, or Robert Fan, in a late Art Deco style, more close to modern style," says Tongji University professor Qian Zonghao.

At the corner of Jiangning and Fengxian roads, the 1,597-seat theatre was named after nearby Majestic Road, today's Nanhui Road. Designed to stage dance performances, opera and concerts, the Majestic was also used as a cinema.

Next-door to the theatre stood the Majestic Hotel, where Chiang Kai-shek and Song Mei-ling held their grand wedding ceremony in 1927. The hotel was destroyed in a fire and the land sold for redevelopment.

In search of a Chinese name for the venue, the theater's managers organized a public competition in the months before the official opening. Over 2,000 letters flooded in, with seven of them bearing the same suggestion 美琪 (meiqi), which not only meant "perfect as beautiful jade", but has a pronunciation very similar to "majestic". And so the theater duly became "美琪" to the Chinese audience.

The Majestic was the third cinema owned by Shanghai Amusement Co. Ltd., which built the Beijing and Nanking theaters in the 1930s.

Perched along Nanjing Road, the Nanking Theatre, YMCA building and Majestic stood witness to the transition of architectural styles by Fan and the first-generation of modern Chinese architects.

Built in 1930, Nanking Theatre, today's Shanghai Concert Hall, is a rare surviving example of a Western classical-style building designed by Chinese architects. Fan and fellow University of Pennsylvania graduate Zhao Shen (S. Chao) designed the building in a modified renaissance style with arcades, pillars, a huge dome inside the theater and parapets with delicate carvings.

Later Zhao, Fan and others designed some "Chinese-renaissance" buildings which incorporated both Chinese and Western elements, such as the YMCA building with its upturned eaves and large plate-glass windows — today's Jinjiang Metropolo Hotel Classiq in People's Square.

"They gave up that style and embraced more modern styles — a simplicity of form, space, materials, detail and color. Zhao's firm began to abandon big Chinese roofs while Fan was even more radical. He called for correction of the 'big roof mistakes', especially after European architect Carl Lindbom and Chinese architect Wu Zi'ang joined his firm in 1933," says Qian Feng, another Tongji University professor.

"After his 1935 tour of Europe and representing China at the 14th International Housing and Town Planning Congress in London and the 13th International Architectural Congress in Rome, Fan fully embraced that 'international style' that valued 'form follows function.' His 1941 work, the Majestic Theatre, was a very modern piece," she adds.

In addition to the Majestic, Fan's other works after 1935, such as the Yafa Apartments on Wuyuan Road and Georgia Apartments on Hengshan Road, were all in a modern style.

Facing streets on two sides, the Majestic with a rounded vestibule in the center and two side halls on the street-side flanks reduced the conflict between architecture and

the streets while eliminating as much noise as possible.

The facade is simple, even a bit raw. The whole building is painted yellowish cream and embellished with some sculptured strips in the same color, creating an elegant effect.

The entrance features five long windows that form the focus of the facade. In the entrance hall hang splendid crystal chandeliers. The inner space is smartly arranged to look continuous, free-flowing and dynamic. The architect has used cream-hued terrazzo and wave-shaped architraves to decorate the floors and walls.

"The staircase is smartly de-signed with curves, which resembles the staircase of the Grand Theatre in the People's Square, another modern cinema, designed by Slovakian-Hungarian architect Laszlo Hudec. The two staircases represent late Art Deco style when the hard lines zigzags of the early style had evolved to curves," says professor Qian Zonghao.

In his 2015 book *Robert Fan*, Huang Yuanzhao notes that Fan was awarded the Majestic project because he had a good relationship with the owner of the Nanking Theatre for more than 10 years.

"The layout is rational with clearly separated functional spaces—the waiting and entrance

halls, ticket office, staircase and corridors. These spaces are properly arranged in a natural flowing way. Sculptures embellished the solemn ambience.

"On the facade, Fan's use of long straight windows on the round tower not only provides interior lighting, but also forms vertical language. Even the curved canopy below the huge tower creates a speedy aesthetic together with the tower. The theatre was called 'Asia's first' upon its opening," Huang says in his book.

The Majestic Theatre became one of the first cinemas to show Western movies. A galaxy of stars, including Peking Opera master Mei Lanfang and ballet dancer Galina Sergeevna Ulanova, have performed there. In 1954, the first Shanghai People's Congress was held here.

In 1989 it was listed in the city's first group of excellent historical buildings and became a municipal cultural relic for preservation.

Since then, the theatre has undergone several renovations, most recently before the 2010 Shanghai Expo to revive its original look and improve facilities — from air-conditioning to a new sound system imported from the United States.

"The theatre is not big but it is an important cultural venue in a great location. We host up to 200 performances, including dance, plays and concerts, every year," said manager Ouyang Yejing. "We are updating the main hall in time for the new season later this year."

Yesterday: Majestic Theatre   **Today:** Shanghai Majestic Theatre
Address: 66 Jiangning Road
Architects: Robert Fan (Fan Wenzhao)   **Architectural style:** Art Deco style
Tips: The concert hall is only open to its audiences. I'd suggest visit the building a bit earlier ahead of a performance to admire it.

中国建筑师学会年会
The Society of Chinese Architects

　　一周前，去年由在本地执业的中国建筑师成立的中国建筑师学会，在华安大楼餐厅以晚餐会的形式举行了第一次年会。会议选举范文照先生为会长，吕彦直先生担任副会长，李锦沛先生任财务兼秘书，庄俊先生当选为委员会成员。

　　协会的目标是团结中国建筑师，并共同努力，以维护其尊严和地位、提高职业效率，并在社会发展和进步中为政府当局提供支持。

　　鉴于中国地方政府最近在执业建筑师方面的工作，协会为政府负责公共工程的部门提供了专业意见。

　　这些充满激情的建筑师的雄心计划之一就是协会能有自己的会所。他们希望公众对中国建筑的发展产生兴趣，一些热情的客户可以向协会捐赠会所用房作为礼物。

　　鉴于有大量的学生和制图员希望学习建筑，但却无法接受合适的培训，协会建议学徒工作室纳入未来的会所中，以使这些年轻人有机会接受建筑设计方面的教育。

The Society of Chinese Architects, which was organized last year by the local Chinese practicing architects, held its first annual meeting in the form of a dinner at the China United Apartment dining room a week ago. The following officers were elected: President Mr. Robert Fan; Vice-President, Mr Y.C. Lu; Treasurer and Secretary, Mr Poy G. Lee; Mr T. Chuang was elected to serve on the Board of Directors.

The objects of the society are to unite in fellowship the architects of China and to combine their efforts so as to uphold the dignity and standing, and to promote the efficiency of the profession, and to render support to the public authorities in their civic developments and improvements.

In view of the recent steps taken by the local Chinese Government in relation to the registration of practicing architects, the Society has offered its service to the Public Works Offices of the Government on matters concerning the profession.

One of the most ambitious plans of this group of enthusiastic men is to obtain a club house for the society. It is hoped that general public interest will be given to the advancement of architecture in China to such an extent that the club will be donated to the society as a gift by some enthusiastic patrons.

In view of the fact that there are a great number of students and draftsmen who desire to learn architecture but cannot obtain proper training on these lines, the society proposes to incorporate into their future clubhouse an atelier to give these young men the opportunity of educating themselves on the lines of architectural design.

摘自 1927 年 12 月 10 日《北华捷报》
Excerpt from *The North-China Herald*, on December 10, 1927

百看不厌的何东住宅
Sir Robert Ho Tung's Residence

第一次看邬达克设计的何东花园，是透过玻璃墙。当时在陕西北路一家店午餐，坐在全明的玻璃墙边，一个绿色花园映入眼帘，美得惊人。

一个月后飞北京的航班上，又在航空杂志上读到介绍这座花园别墅的文章。原来，带绿色花园的白色别墅曾是香港富商何东（Sir Robert Ho Tung）的住宅。

后来，终于有机会走进何东住宅细细欣赏。这样逐渐地接近一座历史建筑，无形中增添了一份特别的魅力。

近代房地产巨商何东是香港开埠后的首富，也是汇丰银行等多家企业的大股东，因成显赫，曾获多国爵士或勋位。何东的父亲是荷兰裔犹太人何仕文（Charles H.M. Bosman），后入英国籍，母亲为祖籍广东的施氏。已故澳门赌王何鸿燊是何东的侄孙。1931年12月8日《北华捷报》一篇报道何东爵士金婚纪念的文章回顾了他的"精彩人生"。

"爵士先生60年前出生于香港，他有三个弟弟三个姐妹，是这个大家庭的长子。他的父母是穷人，但是小罗伯特在七岁时进入一所中文学校，在那里他表现出学习的天赋。接下来，他在香港中央学校（现为女王大学）学习英语，并通过竞争性考试赢得了广州海关的职位，开始了自己的职业生涯。因为海关的职位无法满足他的雄心，年轻的何东于1880年辞职，成为了怡和洋行买办的初级助理。起初，他每月只领取15美元，外加年度奖金。但他极高的才干、天生的商业能力和干劲是如此显著，以至于他在1900年离开公司前已经升任总买办。从那时起，罗伯特爵士赢得了殖民地最高的金融和商业成就，如今被誉为香港金融实力的重要支柱之一。"报道写道。

这篇文章还列举了何东爵士担任过的众多公司职务，涵盖了航运、能源、土地投资、保险和抵押贷款、缆绳制造、酒店、水泥和工程建设等经济领域。此外，他还为几乎每个香港华人的慈善组织而服务，对香港大学的捐赠基金捐款超过26万美金，在香港殖民地开办九龙英国学校，并设立了很多奖学金。

何东住宅是邬达克的早期作

品之一，当时他初到克利洋行，为旅居上海的外国富商设计了多所带有大花园的古典风格豪宅，如万国储蓄会经理盘滕先生（Mr. Beudin）和马迪耶先生（Mr. Madier）的别墅。何东住宅的原业主为赫希斯特生物公司上海分部（Shanghai Plant of Hoechst Chemicals）的总裁卡茨（Wm Katz），后来别墅转给了何东。

何东住宅也令人想起邬达克的另一件作品——有"爱神花园"美名的巨鹿路675号刘吉生住宅（今上海市作家协会）。两座花园住宅都是为富商设计建造的新古典主义作品，也都是邬达克的早期作品。它们的风格宛若姊妹楼一样，却有着不同的美丽。

《上海邬达克建筑地图》作者、同济大学华霞虹教授介绍，何东住宅的建筑为二层混合结构，平屋顶，采用新古典主义风格，檐口厚重，主立面多以爱奥尼式列柱或壁柱予以强调。如起居室外南立面门廊有四根贯通两层的巨柱，西侧半圆形阳光房的外墙中间嵌有两根，东面主入口上方则是两组双壁柱。东、南两面二层的弧形阳台均有雕饰精美的牛腿。

何东住宅的室内设计精美。最引人注目的是黑白大理石地坪和巨大的螺旋型楼梯。房间铺柚木地板，饰雕花护壁，主要房间均设有形式各异的壁炉，连吊顶的石膏线脚也各不相同。华教授介绍，壁炉与木家具的雕饰都是精工细作，部分陈设由邬达克亲自设计。锅炉房、暖气水汀等配套设施也一应俱全。

根据邬达克的家书，他曾亲自监理卡茨住宅的施工，最后为便于工作还搬进已造好的一个房间居住。不幸的是，这座造价4.5万元的豪宅在竣工之际遭遇火灾，公司不得不从头开始建造。根据1920年9月11日《北华捷报》对该火灾的报道，台球室遭到严重破坏，房屋的其余部分也受到强烈的高温与烟熏的损坏。

在设计白色别墅的日子里，初到上海不久的邬达克几乎每天都给家人写信，随信附上很小的照片（6×4厘米），精心黏贴在明信片大小的纸板上，纸板背面画满铅笔素描，还写上解释和评论。在家信里，邬达克主要是不断地向父亲介绍自己的生活和工作。他遗憾自己作为一名建筑师，在上海无法得到提高。因为其他人的水平都不如他，所以邬达克认为他们的称赞或者批评都没有意义。

邬达克还抱怨除了工程设备的介绍，这里专业期刊的质量仅相当于故乡15年前的水准，而在上海又看不到那些高质量的期刊。他很想阅读欧洲的专业期刊，特别是维也纳和德国，所以下定决心每在上海工作三年就回家六个月，以便阅读期刊，了解其他研究成果。

他请父亲寄来《建筑师》（*Der Architekt*）、《柏林建筑世界》和《匈牙利建筑》（*Magyar Epitomuveszet*），还有自己的关于建筑和艺术的书籍。在信中他提到正在施工的卡茨住宅，并流露出对于传统新古典主义设计的厌倦。这让他失去了灵感，感觉自己好像一个初学者。

何东住宅的入口位于陕西北路，参观者映入眼帘的先是建筑的东立面，却已十分精美。东门装饰有带三角形装饰的门楣，两根爱奥尼克柱支撑着一个迷你阳台。南立面呈现近似的风格，但规模更加宏伟，通高两层的爱奥尼克柱组成了美好的门廊。在阳台上可以欣赏中式风格的花园，小桥流水、曲径山石，点缀着参天古树。

虽然邬达克家书充满了抱怨和厌倦之情，何东住宅还是成为一座经典耐看的建筑。在白色别墅竣

工后的二十年间，年轻的邬达克就像曾担任买办助理的何东一样展露才华、抓住机遇，在南京路沿线一次次尝试更摩登现代的建筑风格，达到职业生涯的巅峰。

1949年后，何东家族迁回香港。1958年，中华书局《辞海》编辑所（今上海辞书出版社）迁入。该楼曾被改造为40套小型办公室出租，如今由上海辞书出版社使用。

昨天： 何东住宅（初建时为卡茨住宅） **今天：** 上海辞书出版社 **地址：** 陕西北路 457 号
建造年代： 1920 **建筑师：** 邬达克 **建筑风格：** 古典主义风格
参观指南： 不对外开放。

My first contact with the Ho Tung's Residence was behind a piece of glass. During a lunch at an organic hotpot restaurant on Shaanxi Road, a breathtakingly beautiful garden stunned me through a full glass wall.

A month later on a plane from Shanghai to Beijing I read an article on airline magazine about the secret garden and the building it attached to. The villa was once home of Hong Kong tycoon Ho Tung.

I finally had a close look at the residence with a small group of old house fans recently. The step-by-step contact with the house has added special charisma. It's like a casual glance at someone from afar, hear some of his stories later and finally got a chance to meet him.

The villa was initially designed for Wm Katz, director of the Shanghai Plant of Hoechst Chemicals, who later sold it to Ho Tung.

Sir Robert Ho Tung was born in 1862 in Hong Kong where he became the wealthiest man of his time and a major stockholder in many enterprises including the HSBC Bank.

Keen on public affairs and charity, he was knighted by the British Crown for his donation

during World War I. And during the long war he also increased his investment in Shanghai and acquired quite a lot of properties in the north Bund area. Macao billionaire Stanley Ho Hung Sun, nicknamed "The King of Gambling", is his grandnephew.

An article on *the North-China Herald* on December 8, 1931 introduces his unusual life to the detail.

"Born in Hongkong 69 years ago, Sir Robert was the eldest son of a large family of four brothers and three sisters. His parents were poor people, but at the age of seven, young Robert was sent to a Chinese school, where he showed a natural gift for learning. He next attended the Hongkong Central School (now Queen's College) learning English and began his career by winning by competitive examination a post in the Maritime Customs at Canton.

At the post in the Customs did not offer sufficient scope for his

ambitions, young Ho Tung resigned in 1880 and became a junior assistant to the Compradore of Messrs. Jardine, Matheson & Col. Ltd. At first he only received $ 15 per month, plus an annual bonus but his high intelligence, natural business ability, and energy was so marked that before he left the firm in 1900, he had risen to be chief Compradore. Since that time, Sir Robert has won his way to the highest pinnacles of financial and business success in the Colony, and today he is described as one of the great pillars of Hongkong's financial strength," the 1931 report says.

The report also listed the many business activities he served on the Board of Directors of the Hongkong Whampoa Dock Co., Hongkong Electric Co., Hongkong Land Investment & Agency Co. Ltd, Hongkong, Canton & Macao Steamboat Co., Hongkong Fire Insurance, Hongkong & Shanghai Hotels Ltd. In addition, Sir Robert also served as an official of almost every philanthropic organization for the Chinese of Hongkong that he served.

The residence of Ho Tung mirrored another Hudec work-tycoon Liu Jisheng's residence on Julu Road (now the Shanghai Writer's Association). Both villas are his early works and are essentially neoclassical in style.

The east gate is the first thing that impresses any visitor, which is graced by a huge lintel with triangular decoration and two Ionic columns that support a mini-balcony.

The front—the south facade—is in the same style but on a much grander scale. Four huge Ionic columns mushroom up to the second floor, which makes a nice porch and so elegantly half hides a shallow balcony on the second floor.

White French windows in interestingly different shapes and sizes, a flat roof surrounded with parapets and railings—everything you could imagine for a dream house, this has it all.

Inside, the building retains a strikingly beautiful black-and-white marble floor and the original grand spiral staircase with its patterned iron railings. The fireplaces and wood furniture were embellished with exquisite carvings.

According to Hudec's family letter, he was supervising the construction on the site. Unfortunately the villa which cost up to US$47,000 to build was destroyed in a big fire when it was near completion. They had to start the project all over again.

The Ho's family returned to Hong Kong after 1949 and the state-owned Shanghai Lexicographical Publishing House used the villa after 1958. It was once renovated and then leased to a company providing service offices mainly for foreign companies. Now it's used by the publishing house.

The main facade of this foreign villa faces a big Chinese garden that once stunned me in the restaurant. The garden is filled with camphor trees, old vines and labyrinths.

Yesterday: Ho Tung's Residence   **Today:** Shanghai Lexicographical Publishing House
Address: 457 Shaanxi Rd. N.   **Date of Construction:** 1920
Architect: L. E. Hudec   **Architectural style:** Western Classical Style

火灾新闻
Fire in Sinza

　　星期四凌晨2点47分,消防队接到报警称在爱文义路(Avenue Road, 今北京西路)和西摩路(Seymour Road, 今陕西北路)转角处发生火灾。消防队的新闻分部发现卡茨先生(Mr. W. Katz)位于西摩路36号住所一楼的台球室在熊熊燃烧。几台消防喷雾器开始工作后,大火迅速得到控制并被扑灭。这所房子刚刚完工,起火点位于台球室下面的加热室内的某个地方,或者在房间里存放的家具之间,烧着了地板。火势迅速蔓延开来,幸亏消防队迅疾的工作,否则整个房子可能都被损毁了。幸运的是,房屋里几乎没有家具,实际的火灾损坏仅限于台球室,这里遭到严重破坏。房屋的其余部分也受到强烈的高温与烟熏的损坏。

　　消防队长官在执行任务期间死里逃生。他从地板一块烧焦的部分跌落到下面正在燃烧的加热室。幸运的是,他随身带着一台消防喷雾器,他被队友们救出,瑟瑟发抖,瘀伤严重,逃离了火场。

At 2:47 a.m. on Thursday the Fire Brigade received a telephone call to a fire at the corner of Avenue and Seymour Roads. The Sinza Division found the billiard room on the ground floor of No. 36 Seymour Road, the residence of Mr. W. Katz, well alight. Several jets were got to work and the fire was quickly held and extinguished. The house had just been finished and the fire started somewhere in the heating chamber below the billiard room, or amongst the furniture stored in the room, and had got a hold on the floor. It was spreading quickly and but for the prompt work of the Brigade, the whole house might have been destroyed. Fortunately the premises were practically unfurnished, and the actual fire damaged was confined to the billiard room, which was badly damaged, the remainder of the house being damaged by heat and smoke, both of which were intense.

The Chief Officer during the operations had a very narrow escape, falling through a burnt portion of the floor to the heating chamber below, which was in flames. Fortunately he had a jet with him, and was got out by members of the Brigade, escaping with a severe shaking and bruises.

摘自 1920 年 9 月 11 日《北华捷报》
Excerpt from *The North-China Herald,* on Sep. 11, 1920

鸿达的摩登学校

A Modern School Designed by C. H. Gonda

1930年11月，英文期刊*The China Builder*刊登了建筑师鸿达（C. H. Gonda）绘制的上海犹太学校设计图。这张草图令人印象深刻：浓郁树荫烘托着摩登校舍，男女学生在校园中漫步，朝气蓬勃。新校舍位于今天陕西北路500号西摩会堂的院内。

根据这篇题为"新上海犹太学校大楼"的报道，学校由已故的佩里先生（Mr. Perry）慷慨捐建。旅居香港的佩里留下遗嘱，捐赠15万两银用于建造犹太学校新楼，条件是上海犹太社区需募集同等数目的款项。

项目很快启动，犹太社区成立了委员会负责建造事宜。他们购置了一块位于西摩路（今陕西北路）、新闸路转角邻近西摩会堂的地皮，委托鸿达设计校舍。西摩会堂是一座犹太会堂，又名拉结会堂（Ohel Rachel Synagogue），系犹太富商亚可布·沙逊（Jacob Sassoon）为悼念亡妻拉结（Rachel）而捐资建造。

"工程已经开工，从方案和草图可以看出，该建筑将按照荷兰和美国最现代的学校建筑形式来建造。在设计时，建筑师特别注意让所有教室都有最多的日照和空气流通。宽大通风的走廊和充足的楼梯令教室之间的交通很方便。所有多余的、毫无意义的装饰都被去除了。该建筑只用最好的材料建成，以便为在校儿童提供最好的服务和最卫生的环境。宽敞的礼堂位于底楼，可用于所有的社交和节日活动，也可作为不同组织的集会中心。"1930年的期刊报道。

文章特别提到，鸿达先生多年来倡导采用一种新的建筑风格，而草图显示他为这座校园建筑也选择了这种新风格——建筑的表现形式严格符合建筑结构，将简约与现代实用性结合在一起。

鸿达和他的老乡、国际饭店设计师邬达克一样，都是20世纪

二三十年代活跃在上海的外国建筑师。他比邬达克大4岁，两位建筑师算是同龄人。同为第一次世界大战后到魔都打拼的东欧老乡，鸿达的人生经历和职业发展，都与邬达克有惊人的相似之处。

1889年6月22日，鸿达出生于匈牙利珍珠市的一个犹太家庭，父亲是商人。鸿达在维也纳技术学院学习过建筑，也曾到巴黎和伦敦学习工作。一战爆发后，就像很多奥匈帝国的士兵一样，鸿达和邬达克应征入伍、获得勋章、不幸被俘后被送往西伯利亚战俘营。

他在战俘营的际遇与邬达克有所不同。在那里，鸿达遇到后来的妻子——俄国著名建筑师弗谢沃洛多维奇（Vsevolodovich）的女儿埃夫多基娅（Evdokia）。后者是一位有两个儿子的离婚单亲妈妈，她聘请会讲多国语言的鸿达担任孩子们的家庭教师。没想到后来两人坠入爱河，于1919年结婚，1920年9月15日双双来到上海展开新的人生旅程。

邬达克是1918年从西伯利亚战俘营辗转逃到上海，先到美商克利洋行打工，1924年自己创业，公司后来开在自己设计的真光大楼（位于今外滩源）。和邬达克一样，初来乍到的鸿达也是先在英商公平洋行任职，1928年创办鸿达洋行，公司也开在自己的建筑作品里——同样位于外滩源的光陆大楼。

当时的上海约有20国公民享受治外法权的保护，即外国人在华犯罪却可免于中国法律的审判。可是邬达克和鸿达因为来自解体的奥匈帝国而无法享受这个待遇，所以工作起来必须格外小心，避免犯错。一旦和中国客户发生纠纷打起官司，两人在中国法庭是要吃亏的。每个硬币都有两面。也正因如此，华人精英更青睐这样"中立的"建筑师，他们由此打开了华人市场并取得成功。邬达克的国际饭店、大光明电影院和吴同文住

宅，鸿达的外滩14号交通银行、新新百货等力作都是与中国业主合作的结晶。

与邬达克相比，鸿达现存作品的数量虽然不算很多，但风格现代前卫，个性更加鲜明，令人过目难忘。其中，外滩—南京路沿线的作品有外滩14号总工会大楼、光陆大楼、东亚银行大楼、新新公司（今第一食品商店）和犹太学校。

在南京路上，鸿达还操刀过1930年惠罗公司的改造工程，他将这座19世纪古典主义风格的老牌百货公司改造成一间简洁现代的商店。此外，淮海路上的国泰电影

院（1932）也是鸿达的代表作，影院的垂直线条和具有表现主义风格的塔楼引人注目。

2019年，匈牙利驻上海总领事馆与匈牙利建筑师协会合作，在匈牙利国家档案馆和奥地利国家档案馆的帮助下，由匈牙利艺术史学家埃斯泰尔·巴尔达瓦里（Eszter Baldavári）执笔，编写了画册《鸿达：匈牙利超现代建筑师》。

这本书也提到西摩路犹太学校这个建筑，认为鸿达开拓人脉的速度惊人，可能与其子的同学关系有关。"鸿达的儿子乔治·W. 费多罗夫（George W. Fedoroff）在回忆录里提及，家中男孩就读上海西童男书院，同学中不乏商界名门之后，如哈同和沙逊家族。由此

不难推测，可能正是借助这些关系他才赢得上海犹太学校的设计项目。"

这本书还写到，历史照片显示鸿达原本想建一座平顶建筑，与美国著名建筑师弗兰克·劳埃德·赖特（Frank Lloyd Wright）的作品异曲同工。砖砌的校舍具有朴实的高大窗户和石材框架，外观简朴，而正门上方的悬挑上却带有装饰。入口处铺有四边红色的灰色马赛克地砖，地砖延伸到建筑内部，而室内设有内置木制储物柜。

根据1930年期刊 *The China Builder* 的报道，这所学校可容纳约250名学生，因为部分学生在校用餐，所以设计了充裕的就餐空间。最先进的供暖系统、现代化的电灯装置以及所有能确保儿童安全的最新消防器材，使这座建筑的机械装备更加完善，也应用了最先进的结构方法。建筑造价约为20万两白银。

在这所摩登校舍草图发表的一年前，英文报纸《上海星期天报》(*The Shanghai Sunday Times*)刊登了一篇犀利幽默的现

代主义建筑宣言。

"我们生活在一个机器时代。我们有飞行机器、飞机、交通机器、烹饪机器、电器，所以我们还需要一个生活机器——住宅。虽然没有人会向他的汽车经销商要一辆意大利文艺复兴式的汽车，但在住宅里，这样的风格要求比比皆是……房子的女主人，烫着卷发，男孩一样的身材，穿着短裙，在她路易十四式的客厅里，为一位下着灯笼短裤、上穿花纹套头衫、外披粗花呢夹克、晒得黝黑的运动型男士调制鸡尾酒。"

这篇文章令人想起现代主义建筑主要倡导者、法国建筑师勒·柯布西耶在《走向新建筑》（1925）中的观点。文章的神秘作者署名为"ADNOG"，如果将这几个字母倒序，就能发现他真正的大名——"Gonda"（鸿达）。

昨天：上海犹太学校　**今天：**上海市教育系统妇女工作委员会
地址：陕西北路 500 号院内　**建造年代：**1930 年　**建筑师：**鸿达（C. H. Gonda）
建筑风格：现代风格
参观指南：建筑不对外开放，建议参观外滩—南京路沿线的鸿达作品：外滩 14 号总工会大楼、南京东路 100 号惠罗百货、南京东路 720 号新新公司。

In November 1930, The *China Builder* published a drawing of the Shanghai Jewish School designed by architect C. H. Gonda. The drawing is impressive: a modern school building set off by lush trees, with boys and girls happily wandering in the campus. The school was built on the grounds of the former Ohel Rachel Synagogue on Seymour Road, at 500 Shaanxi Road N. today.

According to the 1930 report entitled "New Shanghai Jewish School Building", the school was donated by the late Mr. Perry, a resident of Hong Kong. He left a will and donated 150,000 taels of silver for the construction of the new building of the Jewish school, on the condition that the Shanghai Jewish community should raise the same amount of money.

The project was launched soon and the Jewish community established a committee responsible for the construction. They purchased a piece of land near the Ohel Rachel Synagogue at the corner of Seymour and Sinza Roads and commissioned Gonda to design the school. The synagogue was built by Jewish tycoon Jacob Sassoon to memorize his late wife Rachel.

"Construction work has already started and from the plans and sketches it can be seen that the building is going to be constructed along the most modern lines of School building adapted for this purpose in Holland and America. Special care has been taken in designing this building to give a maximum of daylight and access of air to all class rooms. Wide and airy corridors with ample staircases provide easy way of communication between the classrooms. All superfluous and meaningless ornaments have been dispensed with; the building is constructed of only the very best material so as to give a maximum of service and the most possible hygienic surroundings for the School children. A spacious Auditorium is located on the Ground Floor, which will serve for all social and festive functions and also as a center of assembly for different organizations," the 1930 journal reported.

According to the article, it could be seen from the perspective sketch that Mr. Gonda, who had for many years already advocated through his architectural work the adaption of a new style in architecture, had also chosen for this building an architectural expression which was strictly in conformity with the structural qualities of the building and which combined simplicity with the modern line of utility. Renowned for his pursuit of an ultramodern style, Gonda left a galaxy of signature works in Shanghai, including several buildings sprinkled along the Nanjing Road.

Gonda, like his fellow and Park Hotel designer Laszlo Hudec, was also well-known foreign architect active in Shanghai through the 1920s and 1930s. Gonda was 4 years older than Hudec and they both went to Shanghai after World War I. Their life experienc es and professional developments were strikingly similar to each other.

Gonda was born to a Jewish family in Gyongyos on June 22, 1889, whose father was a merchant. After his father died, Gonda moved to Vienna with his family and studied at the Technical College of Vienna's school of architecture. He made his way to Paris, where he likely received a diploma from the renowned Ecole des Beaux-Arts, and later worked in London.

When World War I broke out, Gonda was drafted, awarded a silver medal for valor, captured and sent to a Siberian prisoner of war camp, just like Hudec and so many soldiers in the Austro-Hungarian army.

During this time, he met Evdokia Nikolayevna Dmitrieff, daughter of a renowned Russian architect. The divorced mother hired Gonda, a prisoner who could speak Hungarian, German, English, French and Russian, to teach her two sons.

Gonda and Evdokia soon fell in love and got married in 1919. On September 15, 1920, the couple arrived in Shanghai for a new

chapter of life.

Both Gonda and Hudec came to the right city at the right time as Shanghai was embracing a "golden era" between the two world wars. Hudec worked as a draftsman in an American architectural firm. He became a partner after only two years before opening his own firm in 1925. Likewise, Gonda first worked at a British architectural firm, was quickly promoted and then went on to open his architectural firm in 1928. The family moved into a magnificent house with a lush garden, tennis court and several servants on today's Xikang Road in Jing'an District, not far from the Jewish school.

Specializing in commercial buildings, Gonda's office was located in one of his signature works, the Capitol Building on to-day's Huqiu Road, an eight-story Art Deco building, housing a modern, comfortable theatre, offices and apartments.

In 2019, the Consulate General of Hungary in Shanghai and the Association of Hungarian Architects cooperated to make a book entitled *Gonda, Shanghai's Ultramodern Hungarian Architect.*

According to the book, it is believed that Gonda made connections in Shanghai through his sons. Gonda's adopted son George W. Fedoroff mentioned in his memoirs that the boys attended the Shanghai Public School where fellow classmates were the scions of Shanghai's most renowned merchant families, including the Hardoons and the Sassoons. "One can speculate that it might have been this connection that won him the Shanghai Jewish School commission."

Today, the building is used by the Workers' Union of Shanghai Educational Committee. The facade and interior are mostly intact.

According to the book, archival images show that Gonda's original concept was a flat-roofed building reminiscent of the works of celebrated American architect Frank Lloyd Wright. The tall win-

dows and stone frames of this brick-clad school are simple, but traces of ornamentation appear on the cantilevered overhang of the main entrance.

The entryway is paved with gray mosaic tiles with a red border, which extends into the building's interior, which features built-in wooden lockers.

According to the report on the 1930 journal, this school could accommodate about 250 students. Because some students ate at the school, ample dining space was designed. A most up-to-date heating system, modern electric light installation and all those up-to-date firefighting appliances which guaranteed the utmost safety to the children completed the me-chanical outfit of this building, which was in strict keeping with the rest of the most modern structural methods to be applied in this building. The construction cost was about 200,000 taels of silver.

One year before this impressive drawing of modern school building was released, another English newspaper *The Shanghai Sunday Times* published a modern architectural manifesto in a humorous, sarcastic tone.

"No one ever asked his motor car dealer for a motor car in Italian Renaissance style, the request for residences in that style are frequent... And people of our modern age do not think how utterly ridiculous it is to see the lady of the house in her drawing room

Louis XIV, with shingled hair, boyish figure and short skirt, shaking a cocktail for a sun-burned, athletic gentleman in plus-fours and a tweed jacket over a checkered pullover."

The statement mirrored opinions of French modern architecture pioneer Le Corbsier in his book *Towards a New Architecture* published in 1925. The author of the article mysteriously signed as "ADNOG". If reverse these letters, his real name will show up—"Gonda".

Yesterday: Shanghai Jewish School
Today: The Workers' Union of Shanghai Educational Committee
Address: 500 Shaanxi Road N.   **Architect:** C. H. Gonda
Architectural style: modern style   **Built in** 1930
Tips: The building is not open to the public. It is recommended to visit the works of Gonda from the Bund through Nanjing Road: No. 14 on the Bund, Huiluo Department Store at 100 Nanjing Road E. and Sun Sun Co. at 720 Nanjing Road E..

精美舒适的西班牙公寓
A Spanish-style Apartments Building

华业公寓位于南京西路一个院落的深处。高耸的大楼像一座西班牙式城堡，与周边低矮的里弄形成对比。

"华业公寓是一座钢筋混凝土结构的复古主义建筑，设计为西班牙风格与拜占庭式样的混合风格。拜占庭式样建筑在土耳其和俄罗斯较多，上海很少，一般有5个顶，华业公寓也是：中间一个，边上四个。"同济大学钱宗灏教授说。

1934年，当这座"宫殿般雄伟的"公寓楼落成时，英文《大陆报》撰文形容这座新大楼"好像一个巨人展开他的双臂——4层楼高的双翼"。

"西班牙建筑一直被认为是低矮的但富有艺术感。华业公寓也很艺术，但却一点也不低矮。如果它建在西班牙，可能被称为是一座'摩天楼'。但是它特别有艺术气息，屋顶和檐口很有效果，阳台令人印象深刻，而拱窗给整体氛围带来一丝真正的南部的气息。"报道写到。

这座公寓大楼由华商公司（Cosmopolitan Trust Company）投资，位于静安寺路（今南京西路）靠近西摩路（今陕西北路），建成时周边环境"安静、干净而便利"。由于位于一

个院落内，大楼与马路上的噪音灰尘保持了一段距离，但又能方便地抵达购物市场、跑马总会、剧院和商业区。

根据《大陆报》报道，华业公寓有三个单元，分别位于南侧、中部和北侧。每个单元的设计都尽最大程度地追求居住者的舒适与便利，使用最好的建筑材料建成。

大楼呈一个巨大的"H"型，两翼由封闭式走道相连，大厅位于中央单元。

华业大楼提供了形式多样的公寓房型，从一房、两房、三房到四房公寓都有，还有包含6个房间的复式公寓和8个房间的阁楼套房。

其中，每套公寓均设有配餐室、厨房、浴室、衣柜、佣人房、佣人洗手间和工作阳台。每套公寓都带有一个大阳台，是休息、休闲和娱乐的理想之地。所有公寓和大部分的主要房间、卧室都为南向布局。

大楼的底楼设计有宽敞的入口大厅、三个大行李间、一个理发店、儿童游戏室、大楼经理办公室和18个车库。整个项目占地7亩，在室外留有足够的空间建造了一个美好而迷人的花园。如今，花园已经缩小很多，但仍然种着历史悠久的樟树。

杨嘉佑在《上海老房子的故事》一书中提到，上海很多开发商发现建造里弄或花园洋房盈利十分有限。当公寓建筑在海外兴起后，他们转为在上海建造高档公寓租赁获利，华业公寓就是这样一个投资项目。

华业公寓还是美国出生的中国建筑师李锦沛（Poy Gum Lee）的代表作之一。

同济大学副校长伍江在《上海百年建筑史1840-1949》中写到，李锦沛是近代上海一位多产建筑师，作品风格比较混杂。早期多为简化的西方复古式样，且喜爱将中国传统建筑式样融于西式建筑之中，后来设计风格也受到新建筑的影响。

李锦沛还与两位曾在美国学习的中国建筑师——毕业于宾夕法尼亚大学的范文照和赵深共同设计南京大戏院（今上海音乐厅）和中国基督教青年会大楼（今锦江都城青年会酒店）。

不过，李锦沛的人生轨迹与他们不同。李锦沛于1900年出生于纽约，曾在麻省理工学院和哥伦比亚大学学习，后来获得纽约州立

大学学位。他毕业后曾在美国建筑师茂飞（Henry Murphy）的事务所工作，而茂飞后来在中国设计了大量中国传统复兴建筑，包括南京灵谷寺阵亡将士纪念塔和燕京大学（今北京大学）。

1923年，李锦沛来到上海担任基督教青年会建筑处的副建筑师。这位美国土生土长的建筑师在上海设计了不少中国风浓郁的作品，如中国基督教青年会大楼和圆明园路基督教女子青年会大楼，两座建筑都有藻井雅致的大堂。

研究近代中国建筑师的同济

大学钱锋教授提到，李锦沛在中国设计了一系列基督教青年会建筑。1929中山陵设计师吕彦直因病去世后，李锦沛接过重任将未竟的设计任务完成。而李锦沛、吕彦直、范文照和赵深都曾经在纽约茂飞事务所工作。传统中国建筑行业只有工匠和手工艺人的概念，李锦沛这一批华人建筑师被称为近代中国第一代建筑师。他们中的很多人20世纪初曾赴欧美留学，回国后将所学技艺用于建设正在向现代化转型的中国。

不过，李锦沛、范文照、赵深和其他很多同时代的中国建筑师，后来都转向更为现代的风格。

华业大楼就是一座简洁现代的西班牙式公寓。

2015年，美国华侨博物馆举办了介绍李锦沛的特别展览。这位来自纽约唐人街的设计师在1945年因战乱离开上海回到纽约。他曾经把在美国学到的西方建筑技术引入中国，22年后又把中国古典复兴风格从中国带到纽约唐人街，用在很多作品上。"李锦沛是第一个为唐人街的美国华人做设计的美国华裔建筑师。"纽约特展如此评价他。

这个展览题为"中国风格，再发现李锦沛建筑1923-1968"，既展示了这位年轻的建筑师与同事在中山陵前的合影，也有他为纽约唐人街项目设计的草图。其中很多项目都有着中式大屋顶和彩绘装饰，与李锦沛的几个上海项目非常神似。

如今，华业大楼的大厅停放着两行自行车。与上海很多老房子一样，华业大楼的居民比昔日数量增加很多。乘坐青草色的电梯可以来到顶楼，眺望一排排红砖里弄，风景无敌。

从楼梯走下来，可以发现每一层的公共空间都堆着杂物：花盆、旧鞋、蒙尘的自行车、湿拖把和大大小小的纸盒子。空中悬挂着很多竹竿，挂着滴水的衣服。空气中弥漫着洗衣粉和香醋混合的气味，这是普通上海人家生活的味道。

不过，西班牙公寓的精美，点点滴滴还在。大厅屋顶装饰有大幅雕花玻璃，楼梯两侧是白色西班牙式螺旋柱。地面铺着暗红色调的马赛克地砖，虽然磨损不少，却如1934年时一样耐看。

昨天：华业公寓（Cosmopolitan Apartments）　　**今天：**华业公寓

地址：南京西路 1213 号

参观指南：欣赏西班牙式建筑细节和迷人小花园。

Tucked away in a residential compound on Nanjing Road W., the Hua Ye Apartments (Cosmopolitan Apartments) is shaped like a Spanish castle, towering above the alleyway houses.

"The steel and concrete structure is designed in a mix of Spanish and Byzantine styles. The Byzantine-style buildings, widely seen in Turkey and Russia, often have five tops. The Cosmopolitan Apartments also have five tops, a very rare example in Shanghai," says Tongji University professor Qian Zonghao.

When the "palatial and imposing" apartments building was completed in 1934, *The China Press* on August 16 described the newest and most up-to-date residential building in Shanghai as "a tall gi-

ant with outstretched arms which form the two 4-story wings".

"Spanish houses are commonly known to be low and artistic. The Cosmopolitan Apartments is artistic but far from being low. If it were built in Spain, it would probably be called a 'skyscraper'. But it is distinctly artistic; the roof and eaves are effective; the balconies impressive while the arch-windows give a real southern touch to the whole atmosphere," the report says.

The residential apartment building was the property of the Cosmopolitan Trust Company.

Located on the southern end of Seymour Road (now Shaanxi Road), just half a block off Bubbling Well Road (now Nanjing Road W.), the apartments building stands still in quiet, clean and convenient surroundings.

Set back away from the hustle and bustle of the thoroughfare, it was within easy reach of a market, the race course, theatre and business districts when it was built.

According to *The China Press*, the Cosmopolitan Apartments contained three units — south, center and north, each arranged to give maximum comfort and convenience and constructed with the best building materials.

Shaped like a big "H" the two wings of the building are linked by enclosed hallways leading into the main lobby in the central unit.

The apartments in the building are varied. There are single rooms and two, three and four-roomed apartments, duplex apartments with six rooms and penthouses with eight rooms.

Attached to each apartment was a pantry, kitchen, bathrooms, closets, servants' quarters, servants' washroom and rear service verandah. A large verandah was attached to each apartment making it an ideal place for rest, leisure and recreation. All the apartments and most of the main rooms and bedrooms faced south.

The building was also designed with a large entrance lobby on the ground floor, three large baggage rooms, a barber shop, children's playroom, a building manager's office and 18 garages. The land occupied was 7 mow (4,669 square meters) thus leaving sufficient space outdoors for a nice, attractive garden. Now the garden, facing the building, has shrunk. It is small and planted with period camphor trees.

According to Yang Jiayou's book *The story of Shanghai Classic Houses*, local real estate developers found there was little money or profit to be made building alleyway houses and garden villas. So, as apartment buildings started to be in vogue overseas, they switched to build luxurious apartments for lease in Shanghai, such as the Cosmopolitan Apartments.

The Cosmopolitan Apartments was a signature work of American-born Chinese architect Poy Gum Lee (Li Jinpei).

According to Wu Jiang's book *A history of Shanghai Architecture*

1840-1949, Lee came to China from the United States in 1923 and took over the work of constructing Dr Sun Yat-sen's Mausoleum in Nanjing after architect Lu Yanzhi suddenly died of disease in 1929. Wu described Lee as a "prolific architect in modern Shanghai designing in a variety of architectural styles".

Lee and two other US-trained Chinese architects, Fan Wenzhao and Zhao Shen, co-designed Nanking Theatre, today's Shanghai Concert Hall and Chinese YMCA building.

"Unlike most architects of his time, born in China but trained overseas, Lee was born in New York in 1900 and studied architecture in Price College, MIT, Columbia University and won a

diplomat from New York State University," says another Tongji University professor Qian Feng who has researched modern China's first-generation architects.

"Before coming to Shanghai as a YMCA architect in 1923, Lee had worked in the New York office of American architect Henry Murphy, a foremost architectural proponent of the incorporation of Chinese architectural elements into modern construction. Familiar with Murphy's manners and treatments, Lee later used the new style extensively in his China projects including the Chinese YMCA building," Qian says.

Lee's architectural education in several renowned American universities coincided with the emergence of this modern Chinese style. A year after the East-meets-West Chinese YMCA building was completed, he adapted Chinese architectural elements and motifs on the eight-story bureau for National Committee of the Young Women's Christian Association of China which still perches on Yuanmingyuan Road near the Bund.

"Like Fan, Zhao and other Chinese architects, Lee later turned to a more modern style and a noteworthy work of his was the Cosmopolitan Apartments, a simple-cut Spanish-style building with Art Deco details," Qian adds.

However Lee's successful career in China was cut short by the Japanese occupation, and in 1945 he repatriated to design projects in the Chinatown of New York where he was born and grew up.

This time he brought architectural modernism from China to Chinatown and became "the first Chinese American architect to design for Chinese American clients in Chinatown".

As a tribute to the architect that bridged two cultures, the Museum of Chinese in America hosted an exhibition titled "Chinese Style, Rediscovering the Architecture of Poy Gum Lee 1923-1968" in 2015.

Today, two lines of bicycles juxtapose the lobby of the Cosmopolitan Apartments. The building is like many of the city's old houses and shared by more residents than ever before. A grass-hued elevator takes people to the top floor. It offers a breathtaking view of a congregation of red-brick alleyway houses down under.

Walking downstairs the passageway, you may find each floor crowded with flower basins, worn shoes, dusty bicycles, wet mops and boxes of all sizes. The space overhead is sometimes crisscrossed by bamboo poles hanging with air-drying clothes. The air is scented in a mingling of washing powder and Chinese vinegar — a smell of local daily lives.

But traces of the Spanish building's past are everywhere. The lobby ceiling is adorned by a huge patterned glass. Two white spiral-shaped columns grace the entrance of the staircase. The floors are paved with mosaic bricks in a dark red hue, partially worn but still stylish. You only need to close your eyes, though, and you're back in 1934.

Yesterday: Cosmopolitan Apartments   **Today:** Hua Ye Apartments
Address: 1213 Nanjing Rd W.
Tips: Enter from the lane's entrance on Nanjing Road and walk ahead for about two minutes. The building faces a small garden with stone table and stools.

新公寓楼使用国产砖
China-made Bricks Used on New Apartment

　　在面砖和屋面瓦的制造中，中国已经占据了举足轻重的地位，其结果是，国内几乎所有建筑物都使用了国内产品。由于本地制造的瓷砖和砖头的损耗与进口产品不相上下，因此在建筑项目里使用国产材料有很大的经济因素的考量。

　　在高档面砖中，琉璃和西班牙屋面瓦等均由来自宜兴的中国琉璃瓦公司（China Glazing Color Tile Company）生产，位于九江路的Cathay Quarry Tile Company是其唯一的经销商。

　　华业公寓所用的红色屋面瓦就是这个本地经销商提供的。

China has come very much to the fore in the making of face bricks and roofing tiles with the result that the domestic product is used in practically all of the buildings in the country. Since locally-made tile and brick stands the wear and tear on a par with the imported article, the patronizing home industry is a tremendous economic factor in construction work.

Among the high grade face bricks Liu Li, Spanish and Chun roofing tiles are those coming from the China Glazing Color Tile Company of I-Hsing, for which the Cathay Quarry Tile Company on Kuikiang Road is the sole distributor.

The red roofing tile which has been used on the Cosmopolitan Apartments was supplied by the local distributor.

摘自 1934 年 8 月 16 日《大陆报》
Excerpt from *The China Press*, on August 16, 1934

传奇不断的花园

An Eventful Hub and a Centerpiece of Nanjing Road W.

上海展览中心是南京西路的中心，也是一块传奇不断的土地。

1954年，上海展览中心的前身——中苏友好大厦在已荒芜的爱俪园原址建成。爱俪园由犹太富商哈同修建，他曾经拥有近半条南京路的地产。

"爱俪园是哈同给爱妻的一个礼物，占地300亩，小桥流水、奇山怪石，景致之佳居上海私人花园之冠，被誉为'海上大观园'。"研究上海犹太人历史的上海社科院王健教授说。

哈同的人生好像一面镜子，映射出近代上海冒险家乐园的真实景象。1868年，出身贫苦的哈同从巴格达来到上海闯荡。他身无分文，在老沙逊洋行从最底层的"司阍"（看门人）干起，因为勤勉又有头脑，很快掌握了上海地产投资的诀窍。1886年，哈同加入新沙逊洋行主管房地产部，1901年在南京路成立哈同洋行从事贸易和房地产投资，后来成为上海滩著名的地产大王。

《走在历史的记忆里——南京路1840s-1950s》一书记载，哈同发迹后建造私家花园爱俪园，

又称哈同花园，是沪上一大胜景。院内曾兴办圣明智大学，延请王国维、罗振玉等名家来授课，并刊印佛经，出版一批学术著作。著名画家徐悲鸿早年到上海，曾被介绍到此画仓颉像，并在此与蒋碧薇相识，后由哈同资助出国留学。

爱俪园毗邻的街道也被命名为哈同路（Hardoon Road），就是今天的铜仁路。

王健教授介绍，哈同在原公共租界工部局和法租界公董局都担任过董事，这是不多见的。

"这也是因为哈同对于城市发展独到的眼光。他出任新沙逊洋行主管房地产的大班协理后，仔细研究分析了上海房地产未来的发展走向，决定将投资的重点放在南京路。当时西藏路一带还是郊外，是他建议公共租界应该向西发展，直到今天静安寺一带的位置。而当时其他人也有向北和向南发展的建议。"王健说。

独具慧眼的哈同认为"南京路居虹口、南市之中，西接静安寺，东达黄浦，揽其形胜，实为全市枢纽，其繁盛必为沪滨冠。"因此，他凭借其自己过人的眼光与

投机策略，不断低价购入南京路的地产。后来也正如他所料，南京路果然成为上海最繁华的商业街，哈同的财富也随着南京路的快速发展不断地增值。

王健教授统计，哈同1931年6月19日病逝时已拥有土地449.098亩，市房812幢，住房544幢，办公大楼24幢，旅馆饭店4幢，仓库3座。其中包括16块南京路黄金地段的地产，面积达111.578亩，占南京路地产总面积的44.23%。

哈同去世后，他的夫人罗迦陵继承了丈夫的财产，成为亚洲最富有的女人。英文《字林西报》刊文写道，"这对夫妇在一起快乐地生活了45年，互相奉献。哈同对罗迦陵敬意有加，总是称她为'我的妻子'。"

上海社科院研究员张生发现，哈同在静安区内的地产以"爱俪园"为轴心，向东西两侧展开，东起西摩路（今陕西北路），西至哈同路（今铜仁路）西侧。

他认为哈同之所以选择静安区块作为公司业务的核心地段，除

了该区块本身蕴涵的巨大商业价值外，与他深爱的妻子罗迦陵(Liza Hardoon1864-1941年)有关。罗迦陵，又名俪穟（或俪蕤），中法混血儿，出身贫苦，身世复杂，传说颇多。其中比较可信的说法是，罗迦陵1864年出生在涌泉浜旁的罗家村。1901年，哈同按照夫人的愿望，在罗迦陵的出生地购得一片土地，花费9年时间打造了一座花园，作为两人的居所。1910年竣工，夫妻俩各用名字中的一个字，即，用"欧司·爱·哈同"中的"爱"字和"罗俪蕤"中的"俪"字，组合为"爱俪园"，即通常所说的"哈同花园"。

1895年哈同迎娶罗迦陵后，在上海安家立业，妻子对他的影响很大。罗迦陵劝说哈同信奉佛教，爱上中国文化，赞助佛教书籍出版，并创办教育机构。没有子嗣的哈同夫妇领养了十多个中外孤儿。

根据陈喆华、周向频的论文《民国上海私家园林爱俪园研究》，爱俪园全园由僧人黄宗仰主持设计，始建于1903年冬，至1909年落成。黄宗仰不仅取法古典园林，以生平游历会心之景物点

缀园林，且在造园期间远赴东瀛借鉴日本的园林艺术，融汇成建筑形制各异、中日乃至西式元素相配的园林景致。

童寯先生在《论园》中提及爱俪园"为现存园之最大者，近代建构，中西夹杂。其他如'徐园''半淞园''九果园'均不值一顾"。他将爱俪园与豫园、也是园等几座名园并置而论，足可见爱俪园在上海近代园林史中的地位。

爱俪园中有大片草坪和林地，点缀着茅亭和石亭，有花圃、长廊、假山石洞、湖水、木曲桥、石舫、草庐、荷花池、学堂和家庵等，整体结构呈现封闭内敛的传统宅院特征。值得一提的时，爱俪园的水系源自涌泉浜活水，由"涌泉小筑"引入，贯通于整个园林的东半部，而园林丰富的景致皆围绕水系展开。南京西路和静安寺的旧英文名，"Bubbling Well Road"和"Bubbling Well Temple"都因涌泉浜而得名，而来自静安涌泉的活水为南京西路中心位置的这座园林带来了灵动的气息。

因为没有子嗣，哈同夫妇收养了近20个中国和外籍孤儿。王健教授曾见过其中一位外籍养女。"她能说一口流利的普通话，告诉我哈同夫妇喜欢看京剧，在家中用筷子吃饭。"王健说。

爱俪园在鼎盛时期有近80个景点，居住着800余人，其中包括保镖、管家、仆人、僧人、老师和学生等。不过，传奇花园的盛景没有持续很久。1941年罗迦陵也去世后，她的养子女们争夺遗产，爱俪园也因无人打理而渐渐荒芜，到1949年前已是一个废园。

虽然存在时间不久，同济大学钱宗灏教授认为，爱俪园仍堪称上海近代史上一座很有影响力的名园。他提到，曾经生活在这座花园里的人，如哈同、罗迦陵、黄宗仰、姬觉弥，都是近代上海的传奇人物。此外，孙中山、慈禧太后、徐志摩等名人也曾到爱俪园参加与园主有关的活动，很多佛经和学术著作在爱俪园印刷出版。著名画家徐悲鸿也曾在爱俪园居住，并在此遇到后来的夫人蒋碧薇，他们都在哈同的资助下赴欧留学。

虽然花园已逝，但这些关于

爱俪园的城市记忆留存至今。

1953年，这座传奇花园迎来新的命运。当时，中国和苏联计划在北京、上海和武汉建造三座中苏友好大厦。在上海的选址包括四平路汽车修理厂、广中路农场和南京西路爱俪园。最终，昔日哈同的花园因为其位于市中心的便利位置和合适的面积而被选中。

1954年中苏友好大厦建设项目开工时，《新民晚报》于5月4日刊登的报道称这是"上海的一座规模巨大的社会主义建筑"。

报道提到，中苏友好大厦建造在延安中路以北、南京西路以南、铜仁路以东、西康路以西的大块空地上。这座雄伟的建筑物包括了中央大厅、工业馆、文化馆、农业馆、电影馆等建筑物。整个建筑占用土地面积九万五千多平方公尺。建筑物本身面积约一万七千多平方公尺，体积约二十七万多立方公尺。中央大厅上有一尖塔形的建筑，塔尖装置一颗巨大红星，完工后入夜将发放光芒。塔顶红星距地面有一百多公尺，将是全市最高的建筑物。从延安中路大门进去，前面有一个喷水池，进去便是中央大厅，再进去，是工业馆。工业馆后面有一个可容纳一千人的电影院。中央大厅的两翼是文化馆和农业馆。所有这些都是按照苏联民族形式设计。

中苏友好大厦是由苏联著名建筑师、斯大林奖金获得者安德烈耶夫，工程师、斯大林奖金获得者郭赫曼和建筑师吉斯诺娃设计的。中国的工程师、技术员七十多人在苏联专家帮助下，完成了初步设计和技术设计。整个建筑工程也将在苏联专家的帮助下，全部由中国工人用中国的材料来完成。

"这座建筑物的建造象征中

苏两国人民的伟大友谊，也表现出苏联建筑方面的辉煌成就。"《新民晚报》报道。

"中苏友好大厦是一座典型的俄罗斯建筑，给上海建筑增加了一份色彩。因为俄罗斯是永久冻土，而上海是软土地基。当时俄罗斯建筑师的方案经过中国建筑师陈植的改良，现在仍沉降但没有倾斜，应该是陈植的功劳。"同济大学钱宗灏教授说。

如今，中苏友好大厦已改名为上海展览中心。建筑保持着20世纪50年代初建时的风貌，蜜色巨柱和雕塑雄伟华丽，也有宁静的花园点缀其间。上海展览中心也是上海举办重要活动的地点之一，每年的两会和上海书展都在此召开。这里还经常举行如蓬皮杜艺术中心大展之类的重要艺术展览，仿佛还是一个传奇不断的"海上大观园"。

昨天：爱俪园（哈同花园） **今天：**上海展览中心 **地址：**南京西路 1333 号
建筑风格：俄罗斯民族风格
参观指南：展览中心建于 1954 年，原为中苏友谊大厦，现已向公众开放，该展览中心几乎全年都举办各种展览。

The Shanghai Exhibition Center, or the former Sino-Soviet Friendship Building, is an eventful hub and a centerpiece of Nanjing Road W. .

In 1954, this landmark was constructed on the site of a decayed garden belonging to Jewish tycoon Silas Aaron Hardoon, who owned half of the properties along Nanjing Road in the early 20th century of Shanghai.

"Mr and Mrs Hardoon's former home, the beautiful 'Aili Garden' built on the current site of Shanghai Exhibition Center, was a gift from Hardoon to his beloved wife. Covering an area of some 300 mu, or 200,100 square meters, the garden's picturesque scenery topped the city's private gardens and was nicknamed 'The Grand-View Garden of Shanghai', " says professor Wang Jian from Shanghai Academy of Social Sciences, author of the book *Shanghai Jewish Cultural Map*.

According to the book *Nanjing Road, 1840s to 1950s*, Hardoon constructed the private garden named Aili Garden, also known as the Hardoon's Garden, after making his fortune from investing in the city's real estate market. The garden had become a prosperous scenic spot in Shanghai, where a college was initiated and many famous Chinese scholars and artists, including Wang Guowei and Luo Zhenyu, were invited to teach lessons.

The garden's neighboring street was named Hardoon Road, which is today's Tongren Road. Hardoon's own legendary life had become a mirror of old Shanghai, the paradise of adventurers.

Born into a poor Jewish family in Baghdad, he came to Shanghai penniless to work for the David Sassoon, Sons & Company as a gatekeeper in 1868. But the hard-working foreigner quickly became a genius in the acquisition of commercial property, chiefly retail property along Shanghai's main thoroughfare.

"Hardoon was the only man in the history of Shanghai that had served as member of the board for both Shanghai Municipal Council (that ruled the International Settlement) and French Municipal Council (that governed the French Concession) owing to his vision on the city's development," says professor Wang.

At that time Xizang Road was still a suburban area and it was Hardoon that suggested the International Settlement should expand toward the west to today's

Jing'an Temple. And there used to be other opinions like extending to the north or the south.

Hardoon also profited from his vision. Afterward he founded his own company on Nanjing Road and made a huge profit from investing in the city's booming real estate.

After marriage to Shanghai-born woman Luo Jialing in 1895, the former lonely expatriate finally had a warm home in the city. A decade later he built the fancy garden as a token of love for his wife.

According to Chen Zhehua and Zhou Xiangpin's co-authored academic paper "The Research of Aili Garden in Shanghai", the garden was designed by a famous Buddhist monk Huang Zongyang, who started building it in 1903 and completed it in 1909.

The East-meets-West garden was like a fantasy land of old Shanghai, featuring large lawns, lush trees, water ponds, rockeries, wooden bridges and a rainbow of pavilions in different shapes and made of diverse materials.

Water in the garden was directed from the Bubbling Well on Nanjing Road W. , which used to be called Bubbling Well Road after the well in front of the Bubbling Well Temple, today's Jing'an Temple.

Having studied in Japan for years, Huang combined Chinese classic garden art with the Japanese and Western garden design and decoration.

Hardoon's wife Luo Jialing, or Liza Hardoon, had great influence on her husband.

"She persuaded Hardoon to believe in Buddha, sponsor the publishing of Buddhist books, found a university of wealth and wisdom, and to love Chinese culture. Having no children of their own, they adopted nearly 20 Western and Chinese orphans. One of Hardoon's Western adopted daughters, who spoke fluent mandarin and Shanghai dialect, told me the Hardoons appreciated Peking Opera and used chopsticks at home," Wang recalled.

When Hardoon died in 1931, Luo fell heir to the bulk of her husband's estate and became Asia's wealthiest woman. *The North-China Daily News* reported that "the couple lived together very happily for 45 years and were devoted to each other".

According to the book *Shanghai-style Gardens*, Aili Garden, at its prime time, had 80 scenic spots

and housed up to 800 people, including bodyguards, butlers, servants, monks, teachers and students.

However, this wonderland did not last long. After Luo passed away in 1941, many of their adopted children fought for legacies and the garden lacked proper maintaining. It was occupied by the Japanese army after 1941 and was completely left to ruin until 1949.

Though gone with the winds too soon, Tongji University professor Qian Zonghao noted, it remained an influential garden in modern Shanghai history.

"People who had lived in this garden, including Hardoon, Luo Jialing, monk Huang Zongyang and butler Ji Juemi were part of the legend in the modern history of Shanghai. In addition, a gal-

axy of nobilities, revolutionaries and literary figures from Empress Cixi, Dr. Sun Yat-sen to poet Xu Zhimo were all associated with the garden's owners or joined events here.

"Besides, a large number of Buddhist scripts and academic works were published in the garden, too. When famous artist Xu Beihong came to Shanghai, he lived in the garden where he met his future wife Jiang Biwei. Both later studied in Europe with Hardoon's financial support," Qian says.

So despite the fact the garden is gone, the memory of it still lives on.

The ruins of the Aili Garden confronted a new fate in 1953 when the Chinese and Soviet Union governments decided to build three Sino-Soviet Friendship Buildings in Beijing, Shanghai and Wuhan. In Shanghai, the officials chose among three possible sites — an automobile repair plant on Siping Road, a farm on Guangzhong Road and Aili Garden on Nanjing Road W.. Hardoon's garden was finally chosen for its central and convenient location and proper size.

When the project of Sino-Soviet Friendship Building kicked off in Shanghai in 1954, *Xinmin Evening News* called it a "gigantic socialism architecture" of the city in a news report on May 4.

The report said this grand architecture covering an area of more than 95,000 square meters would include a central hall, industrial hall, cultural hall, agricultural hall and a cinema with a capacity of 1,000 people.

"The central hall has a steep tower. A huge red star, which glistens at night, will be installed on the top. With the tower-top red star at a height of more than 100 meters, it will be the tallest building in the city," the report said.

"The exhibition center is typical Russian-style architecture, adding a special color to Shanghai's architectural landscape," Qian says.

The construction was designed by several award-winning architects from the Soviet Union in cooperation with Chen Zhi, one of the first-generation Chinese modern architects. The project was built with Chinese materials by Chinese workers.

Professor Qian notes that due to Shanghai's soft soil, which is different from Russia's solid frozen soil, the exhibition center has sunk a little bit over the years, but not tilted thanks to Chen Zhi's adaptation on Russian architects' plan.

Graced by many huge, honey-hued columns and sculptures, it has hosted several of the city's most important events, including the municipal congress meeting, the annual Shanghai Book Fair and the exhibition showcasing "Masterpieces from the Centre Pompidou 1906-1977" in 2016.

Standing in the prominent downtown location, the exhibition center still serves as a grand-view garden that houses important figures and new stories in Shanghai.

Yesterday: Aili Garden (Hardoon's Garden)   **Today:** Shanghai Exhibition Center
Address: Nanjing Road W.   **Architectural Style:** National style of Soviet Union
Tips: Built in 1954 as the former Sino-Soviet Friendship Building, the Exhibition Center now opens to the public, which hosts a variety of exhibitions almost throughout the year.

哈同夫人的 70 周岁诞辰
Mrs Hardoon's 70th Birthday Celebration

8月27日，已故犹太富翁哈同（S. Aaron Hardoon）的遗孀在静安寺路1375号哈同花园举行盛大活动，庆祝自己的70周年生日诞辰。在花园正门外竖起了一个红色的大拱门，不计其数的灯笼和电灯照亮了从正门通往园内楼宇的道路。

这一天里，包括许多中外精英在内的居住在上海的人纷纷赶来参观花园，并向这位以慈善而闻名的哈同夫人致敬。

由于哈同夫人是一位热心的佛教徒，数十名佛教法师参加了庆祝活动，仪式也是按照佛教仪式举行的。为了娱乐来宾，有特邀的演员在其中一座楼里特别搭建的舞台上进行戏剧表演。为了祈福长寿，仪式还燃放了成千上万的鞭炮。

然后，来宾们被邀请到一幢楼中的一个宽敞的大厅。大厅墙壁上挂着许多用丝绸制成的红色卷轴，上面书写着哈同夫人的事迹。现场有几百个花篮，这些花篮来自哈同夫人和她先夫的朋友。

已故的哈同先生职业生涯起步于仓库管理员，后来他创造了一笔据称是上海最多的财富。他去世后，遗产由他的遗孀管理。哈同太太曾被她的已故丈夫的一些亲戚告到中国的英国法庭，这些亲戚要求分享哈同的巨额财产。

The spacious Hardoon garden at 1375 Bubbling Well Road was the scene of great festivities on August 27, the occasion of the 70th birthday of Mrs S. Aaron Hardoon, widow of the late Jewish multi-millionaire. Outside the main gate of the garden a large archway of red was erected while innumerable lanterns and electric lights formed an illuminated entrance over the path leading from the main gate to the residential buildings of the garden.

Throughout the day, streams of local residents, including many leading Chinese and foreigners, visited the garden and paid their respects to Mrs Hardoon, known for her philanthropic acts.

Scores of Buddhist priests participated in the celebrations, as Mrs Hardoon is an ardent Buddhist, and the ceremony was performed in accordance with Buddhist rites. For the entertainment of the guests, actors were invited to give theatrical performances on a specially-erected stage in one of the residential buildings. Thousands of firecrackers were let off as a good omen for long life.

The guests were then invited to a spacious hall in one of the residential buildings where numerous red scrolls made of silk were hung on the wall, bearing characters eulogizing Mrs Hardoon's deeds. Hundreds of baskets of flowers were in evidence, these being from the friends of both Mrs Hardoon and her deceased husband.

The late Mr. Hardoon, who started his career as a godown watchman, eventually built a fortune reputed to be the largest in Shanghai. After his death, the estate had been administered by his widow who was once named as the defendant, in the British Court in China by some of her deceased husband's relatives who claimed a share of the Hardoon millions.

摘自 1933 年 8 月 30 日《北华捷报》
Excerpt from *The North-China Herald*, on August 30, 1933

郭氏兄弟的双子楼
The Kwok brothers' Twin Villas

    郭氏兄弟的双子楼是一对白色优雅的百年别墅，深藏在一个南京西路的花园里，却映射了南京路这条"上海第五大道"的发展史。

    白色别墅建造于20世纪20年代，是郭乐（Kwok Lok）和郭泉（Kwok Chuen）的宅邸。郭氏兄弟都是澳洲回国的华侨，在南京路创办了著名的永安公司。

    别墅的建筑面积分别都在1200平米左右，高达三层，设计为法国古典主义风格。并列的两座小楼建筑风格近似，视觉效果和谐，却并非一模一样。

兄长郭乐的别墅在东侧，立面较为平坦，而西侧郭泉别墅的立面则设计了弧形的阳台，有起伏变化的效果。

两座别墅共享的花园设计有绿树、假山和带小石桥的水法，精致灵动。室内的宽大木质扶梯让人印象深刻，通往一间间装饰有柚木护墙板的卧室。

双子别墅位于静安寺路和哈同路（今铜仁路）转角的位置，地段显赫。这块地皮属于拥有近半条南京路地产的犹太富商哈同（Silas Aaron Hardoon）。哈同的宅邸"爱俪园"就位于双子别墅的斜对面，如今是上海展览中心。哈同和郭氏兄弟都选择在南京东路营业，但居住于位于南京西路的花园。

对于郭氏兄弟来说，这并非第一次租用哈同的地皮。20世纪10年代，他们曾高价向哈同租下南京路东侧的一块土地以建造永安公司，不过后来证明是相当成功的投资。

永安公司是南京路"四大公司"开业的第二家。与第一家先施公司相比，永安百货不仅生意更好，后来还建成当时南京路的第一高楼——永安新厦（今七重天宾馆）。

上海档案馆研究员张姚俊翻开馆藏的"四大公司"档案，发现它们的发家史有相似之处。永安公司创办者郭氏兄弟和其他三家创办人——先施公司老板马应彪、新新公司创始人李敏周和大新公司控股人蔡昌，都来自地处珠江出海口的香山县（今广东中山）。他们早年在澳洲经营果栏（即水果批发店）或杂货店起家，然后带着实业救国的理想回国二次创业。

"尽管永安、先施和大新公司均在香港和广州取得斐然业绩，但他们不约而同地把目光瞄准'殷商巨贾咸集'的上海，选择在当时申城地价最高的南京路落地生根，这不能不说是'英雄所见略同'。"张姚俊说。

用向空袋里扔黄豆的方法计算南京路两侧的行人数量后，郭氏兄弟发现南京路南侧的人流更多，决定将永安公司开在这里。他们向哈同租用土地时，这位犹太富商提出了高昂租金和苛刻合同，要

求30年后地皮和建筑所有权必须归还哈同。哈同喜欢把土地租给大型百货公司以获得最高租金。和郭氏兄弟签约后,哈同又把永安斜对面的地皮租给四大百货的第三家——新新公司,后来又把南京路九江路口的一块土地租给大陆银行以建造大陆商场。在昔日哈同土地上建造的这些百货公司今日犹存,都作为购物中心使用。

郭氏兄弟在深思熟虑后接受了哈同的要求。虽然后来永安公司的建造因为资金问题有所拖延,时间证明他们的决定是正确的。

郭氏兄弟为公司取名"永安",期望可以在激烈的商业竞争中取得稳定的发展。永安公司后来的成功源于他们的营销智慧。1918年8月20日开始,郭氏兄弟便在《申报》上连续刊登广告。9月5日开业后,公司原本准备销售两个月的货品在20天内售罄,当时的盛况由此可见一斑。

"四大公司都绞尽脑汁用各种促销手段吸引顾客,而永安百货将女营业员用到了极致。他们招聘年轻貌美、端庄秀丽又略懂英文的上海小姐推销美国康克令金笔,销售非常'火爆'。1936年,著名新闻人徐铸成到沪后专程去永安买

笔。他细细打量了女售货员，对举止优雅的'康克令小姐'发出了'果然明眸皓齿，不负众望'的赞叹。"他说。

此外，永安百货每年四季和周年庆都举办大促销活动，并提供类似信用卡的"记账消费"服务，让高端客人可以先购买后付款。永安百货还是上海最早设置橱窗展示商品的商店。此外，室内时装秀、送货上门、发送礼券等服务也让商店增色不少。"永安"的好口彩让礼券成为深受欢迎的礼品。

为了在南京路激烈的竞争中胜出，永安公司聘请大名鼎鼎的公和洋行设计了巴洛克风格的百货公司大楼，1932年又请美国建筑师哈沙德（Elliot Hazzard）在老楼边的三角形基地盖起一座19层高的摩天楼，与老楼以天桥相连，是当时南京路最高的建筑。如今，这座简洁的钢构巨厦仍屹立在永安老楼旁边。

同济大学郑时龄院士在《上海近代建筑风格》新版中提到，郭氏兄弟位于南京西路1418号的双子别墅由英商毕士莱洋行（Percy M. Beesley, Architect）设计。英国建筑师毕士莱（Percy

Montagu Beesley）于1906年前到上海，1907年在离南京西路不远的新闸路建立毕士莱洋行，承接土木工程和建筑设计事务，直到1920年代尚见于记载。书中还提到，位于外滩南苏州路79号的教会公寓（Union Church Apts）也是毕士莱洋行的作品。

如今，双子别墅由上海市政府外事办公室和上海市对外友好协会办公使用，经常接待来自海外的代表团和国际友人。白色小楼前的草坪上矗立着一座形似和平鸽的铜雕，大理石底座上用多国语言刻着"友谊"，仿佛和昔日主人"永安"的期冀不谋而合。

昨天： 郭氏兄弟住宅　**今天：** 上海市政府外事办公室　**地址：** 南京西路 1418 号
建造年代： 1924 年　**建筑师：** 毕士莱洋行　**建筑风格：** 西方古典风格
参观指南： 别墅不对公众开放，但从南京路和铜仁路可以欣赏到其外观。

Tucked away behind a stylish garden on Nanjing Road W. , a pair of century-old white villas remain elegant, the homes of Chinese merchant brothers surnamed Kwok (usually referred to as Guo in pinyin).

The twin villas also mirrored the development of Nanjing Road, often called Shanghai's Fifth Avenue. The former landlord, the Kwok brothers and architects of the villas were connected with each other and interwoven in the history of this legendary road that symbolized old Shanghai.

According to Lou Chenghao and Xue Shunsheng's 2008 book *Shanghai Old Houses*, the twin villas were built in the 1920s for Kwok Lok and Kwok Chuen, who returned from Australia and opened the Wing On Department Store on Nanjing Road.

The twin villas, each at around 1,200 square meters, feature three floors in a French classic style. The juxtaposing houses look harmonious with each other but they are not identical.

The eastern villa for the elderly brother Kwok Lok is designed with a comparatively flat facade while the western one, for younger brother Kwok Chuen, is graced by curved verandas in the front.

The garden shared by the villas is also well-designed with lush

trees, rockeries and a tiny stone bridge that links with a stylish fountain. Inside, a big, beautiful wooden staircase leads to bedrooms which are all spacious and decorated with teak-wood dado.

Perched on the prominent location of the Bubbling Well Road (today's Nanjing Road W.) and Hardoon Road (today's Tongren Road), the site of the villas belonged to Jewish tycoon Silas Aaron Hardoon, who owned half of the properties along Nanjing Road in the early 20th century. Hardoon's own home, the renowned Aili Garden, was on the other side of Nanjing Road W. , which is today's Shanghai Exhibition Center.

It's not the first time that the Kwok brothers made a deal with Hardoon. In the 1910s, they rented a piece of land at a hefty price from the tycoon on the eastern side of Nanjing Road for building Wing On Department Store which turned out to be a successful investment.

The Wing On Department Store was the second of the four big Chinese department stores on Nanjing Road — the other three being Sincere Co., Sun Sun and The Sun.

"Wing On not only enjoyed better business than the first one, Sincere Co., but also built the tallest building on the popular shop-

ping street," says Zhang Yaojun, a researcher at the Shanghai Archives Bureau who had studied archives left by the four big stores. According to his research, the Kwok brothers, quite like owners of the other three big stores, were born in China's Guangdong Province and left home at an early age for Australia where they earned first bucket of gold from fruit wholesale business. With an idea to save China through commerce, they returned to start up business for the second time. Though these big stores had achieved successes previously in Hong Kong and Guangzhou, their founders all cast eyes on Shanghai, particularly the city's most expensive shopping street — Nanjing Road.

After calculating the amount of pedestrians on both sides of Nanjing Road by throwing beans into two empty bags, the Kwok brothers decided to rent the site on the southern side of Nanjing Road which appeared to attract more people to walk by. The land was owned by Hardoon who asked for a big price and a strict contract — ownership of both the building and the site would both return to Hardoon after 30 years.

According to Shanghai historian Shen Ji's research, Har-

doon preferred to retain his best sites for big department stores and big companies, for the best rental price. After signing contract with the Kwok brothers, he rent another site opposite Wing On to the third big department store, Sun Sun Co. Later on he made the same contract with Chinese-owned Continental Bank by renting a land on the crossroad of Nanjing and Jiujiang roads for constructing the Continental Emporium. All these buildings built on Hardoon's land on Nanjing Road remain today and still function as big stores.

"The Kwok brothers agreed to the deal after careful considerations. Though the construction of the store was delayed due to funding problems, time proved their visions correct," says Zhang.

After choosing the site for their new store, the Kwok brothers decided to name the new store Wing On, literally meaning "perpetual peace". The name originated from their fruit store in Australia showed their expectation to make safe and stable business in the fierce commercial competition. And they made it with wits and strategies.

In 1932, Wing On constructed a new 19-floor building on the tri-

angle-shaped site adjacent to the 1918 premise which was the tallest building on Nanjing Road of its times.

The store's success was described as "a notable example of shop building in Shanghai on an architectural scale" by *The Shanghai Times* in 1918. The department store had roof gardens and offered a variety of entertainment options besides shopping.

In addition to varied smart promotions like employing young, beautiful "Miss Conklin" to sell American Conklin fountain pens, Wing On also introduced shop window display, organized indoor fashion shows, offered delivery service and issued gift coupons to attract customers.

According to Professor Zheng Shiling's book *The Evolution of Shanghai Architecture in Modern Times*, the Kwok brothers' white villas were designed by British firm Percy M. Beesley, British architect Percy Montagu Beesley arrived in Shanghai before 1906. In 1907, he established Beesley firm on Xinzha Road, not far from the Bubbling Well Road, to undertake civil engineering and architectural design services. His architectural practices were seen in records until in the 1920s. The Union Church Apts at 79 South Suzhou Road on the Bund is also a work of Bessley.

Today the twin villas serve

as the administration offices for Shanghai Foreign Affairs Office and Shanghai People's Association for Friendship with Foreign Countries (SPAFFC) to receive friends and official delegations from abroad. On the lawn fronting the white villas stands a copper sculpture with two embracing hands visualizing either a magnolia flower — the city flower, or a pigeon — the symbol of peace, the marble base of which inscribed with the word "friendship" in different languages, to symbolize the city's sincere wish for more friends from afar.

Yesterday: Kwok Brothers Residence   **Built in** 1924
Today: Shanghai Foreign Affairs Office   **Address:** 1418 Nanjing Road W.
Architect: Percy M. Beesley, Architect   **Architectural style:** Western classic style
Tips: The villas are not open to the public but their facades can be admired from Nanjing and Tongren roads.

永安百货：诞生自澳洲的上海偶像

The Store of Perpetual Peace: a Shanghai Icon Born in Australia

永安百货是上海最著名的地标之一。

它那面向两条街的立面在夜晚霓虹灯的照耀下熠熠生辉，针状尖顶好像一把闪烁的利剑，刺穿黑暗的天空——这就是上海的永安百货。

这是永安的意思——永远平安。这家伟大的百货商店总是从地下室到屋顶都挤满了购物者，它有着悠久而富有变化的发展历史，已经成长为远东地区最大、最著名的商店之一。

永安百货堪称是一个荣耀版的"上海伍尔沃思"（Woolworth为美国著名百货商店），兼顾低廉售价和高品质商品。从安全别针到加热器/火炉，从吊袜带到地毯，从盐到袜子，应有尽有。商店位于南京路和浙江路交界处的"小岛"上，是这座城市最繁忙的十字路口之一。夜幕降临时，这里成为一片璀璨的仙境。

早在1800年左右，几位精明的旅居悉尼的中国广东商人成立了一家小公司，在澳大利亚首都悉尼开了一家小店。这些海外华商给他们的小店取名"永安"。

这家商店为这些在海外闯荡的商人们带来了丰厚回报。随着它的发展，商人们最终回到中国。

1916年，J. B. Lock、郭标和其他几位商人在香港开设了另一家永安百货。事实证明那家店也十分成功，以至于两年后，他们决定成立一家新公司，并在繁华的大都市上海开设一家新店。

目前，永安百货的资本为250万元港币（32万元美金）。商店没有迁移过地址，但原来并非像现在有那么大的规模。14年来永安百货一直位于南京路——店铺面向浙江路的大部分都是五年后、即1923年添加的。

这家商店的发展突飞猛进，如今已成为一个蓬勃发展的有实力的企业，拥有约1000名员工。

它的许多业务还包括在上海的三家棉纺织厂。这三家纺织厂与永安商店相关，也结合了许多其他外部利益。1931年，永安公司的资本约为1000万美元，其业务总额约为1500万美元。

The store of perpetual peace is one of the best-known and most famous landmarks in Shanghai.

Its two-street front brilliant at night with neon light, its needle-like spire piercing the dark sky-like a flashing sword — that is Wing On, a Shanghai institution.

For that is what Wing On means — perpetual peace. This great department store, always crammed with shoppers from basement to roof, has had a long and varied history and has grown to be one of the largest and most famous stores in the Far East.

Wing On is a glorified Shanghai Woolworth's, combining low prices and high quality goods. Everything from safety pins to baseburner heater/stoves, from garters to rugs, from salt to socks, can be found in the teeming isles of the big store at the corner of Nanking and Chekiang Roads — one of the busiest crossroads in this city, and a fairyland of blazing light after nightfall.

Back in 1800, or the thereabouts, several astute Chinese merchants, living far from their Canton homes in Sydney, formed a small company and opened a small store in that Australian capital. These overseas merchants called their modest little shop Wing On.

The store brought rich returns to these self-exiled merchants. As it grew the merchants eventually returned to China.

In 1916, J. B. Lock, Kwok Bew, and others opened another Wing On store in Hong Kong. It proved so successful that two years later, in 1918, it was decided to form a new company and open a new store in the thriving metropolis of Shanghai.

The present Wing On store was capitalized at HK$2,500,000 (US$320,000). It has never moved, but it is not always as large as it is today. For 14 years, Wing On occupied a position along Nanking Road only — the large part of the store which fronts on Chekiang Road was added five years later, in 1923.

The store has grown by leaps and bounds, and today it is a thriving, wealthy concern, employing about 1,000 people.

Its many ramifications include three cotton textile mills in Shanghai which are associated with the store and combines many other outside interests. Its capital today is approximately US$10 million in 1931, and its business amounted to about US$15 million.

摘自 1932 年 12 月 5 日《大陆报》

Excerpt from *the China Press*, on December 5, 1932

2019年5月16日，设计巴黎卢浮宫玻璃金字塔的华裔建筑大师贝聿铭（Ieoh Ming Pei）在纽约去世，享年102岁。

贝氏家族在上海市静安区南阳路170号曾有一座花园别墅。中西合璧的小楼今日犹存，映射了贝家自明朝以来绵延发展15代的传奇历史。

"贝宅由中都工程司设计，手法是装饰艺术风格，细部是中国风格的。"同济大学郑时龄院士在一次主题为"上海20世纪30年代建筑"的讲座中专门讲到这座别墅。

"别墅布局像中国老式厅堂，中间是客厅，两边是厢房。花园里有个亭子也相当精彩，又是现代的，但又带有一种中国的传统的味道。花园墙壁雕刻着100个'寿'字。"他介绍。

南阳路贝宅长期以来一直被误认为贝聿铭父亲、中国银行副总裁贝祖诒的宅邸，其实它是贝氏另一脉颜料大王贝润生的产业。

1917年，贝润生买下早已荒废的苏州名园狮子林，而贝聿铭童年时曾在这座明代园林里度过很多难忘的时光。狮子林的园林艺术曾启发了很多艺术家和诗人，也影响了贝聿铭一生的审美与建筑设计。

撰写贝聿铭传记（*I.M. Pei,*

Mandarin of Modernism）的美国学者康奈尔（Michael Cannell）发现，贝氏家族的历史可追溯至明朝。这个庞大的家族文化底蕴深厚，培养了很多诗人、画家、书法家和银行家，贝聿铭为第15代子孙。

贝氏祖先于明代来到苏州行医售药，其子孙刻苦节俭、行善积德，将祖传的药铺生意不断做大，发展成为江浙地区最著名的药材行。到18世纪时，贝氏家族已在当地拥有大量土地。

贝聿铭的祖父贝理泰参与创建上海商业储蓄银行，他的许多儿孙都投身金融界，为中国现代金融业的发展做出了贡献，其中最著名的就是贝聿铭的父亲贝祖诒。

而贝润生则来自贝氏家族人丁寥落、家业衰败的一脉，他从小就是被贝氏义庄的月米抚养长大的，16岁时去上海一家颜料行做学徒，后来发展为老上海的"颜料大王"和"地产大王"。

康奈尔说，拥有狮子林花园给这位大亨带来"一种出身高贵的感觉"。他在书中写道，"拥有一个花园体现了对美和学识的正确欣赏，这大致相当于一个来历不高的人从贫穷的贵族手中收购了一个城堡……园林的新主人们可以放弃围墙外的世俗职责，像高级官员一样在此种植竹子、练习书法和在水边凉亭里接待客人"。

贝润生还买下周围的民房宅基并打通狮子林进行整修，不过这座恢复壮丽景象的园林并非他的私家园林。由于贝润生少年穷困时曾得到族人的帮助，他将承训义庄、家族祠堂和家族学校设在这里，资助家族里的穷学生。后来苏州人将"狮子林"作为贝氏家族之代称者，即源于此。

虽然规模小了很多，南阳路的贝宅也富有"狮子林"的神韵。别墅离繁华的南京西路很近，却有一个宁静的花园，精巧地布置着凉亭、假山、灌木和鹅卵石小径。

根据静安置业副总工程师李振东的研究，房屋的建筑面积1311平方米，园地面积2011平方米，业主贝润生曾任德商德孚洋行买办。一战时期因为北洋政府决定参加以英、法、美、日等国组联的"协约国"阵线对德宣战，德孚洋行在回国前将大量储备颜料让与贝润生。随着战事延长，远东颜料市场货源奇缺，贝润生以数倍、甚至数十倍的高价销售颜料获得暴利，战后恢复生产后他又以与德商的关系获得垄断经营地位，继续获取厚利，成为巨富。后来，贝润生又把大量资金投入房地产。由于上海社会情况复杂，他担心子女遭绑票，不敢让子女外出接受教育。他的儿子贝焕章就是由专职家庭教师在家授课的。

上海档案馆资料显示，20世纪二三十年代，由于经营房地产利润丰厚、风险小，吸引不少贝润生这样的江浙富商把钱投入了这个领域。如浙江生丝商人刘姓一家，就

在福州路广西路一带拥有会乐里、会香里、洪德里、昭德里等十多条弄堂。有颜料大王之称的洞庭东山人贝润生，1918年以后开始向房地产投资，短短十几年，他就拥有各类房屋近千幢，面积16万平方米以上。到1949年，华商房地产商人大约有3000多家，拥有近6万幢房屋，总面积在1000万平方米以上。其中，占有1万平方米以上的有160多户，占有3万平方米以上的也有30多户，其中就包括贝润生。

根据建筑学家曹伟所著的《上海住宅》一书，贝宅采用西方的钢结构和混凝土结构，并采用了安全性和舒适性最先进的现代设备，例如钢制玻璃窗、空调和电梯。同时，中国风格的影响又很明显，窗户都装饰有汉字"寿"的彩色图案。旋转的楼梯形状像一条

巨大的龙。别墅内部也装饰着很多中国传统建筑的细节，二楼有一个供奉佛龛的房间。

郑时龄院士提到，设计这座中西合璧别墅的中都工程司由顾鹏程于1935年创办，而顾鹏程毕业于同济大学土木工程系。别墅设计采用的装饰艺术风格源于1925年巴黎召开的装饰艺术博览会，后来传遍了世界。这种风格带有现代的意味，是现代建筑，又带有装饰，同时受到俄国芭蕾舞和古埃及考古的影响。

"上海就像纽约和巴黎一样，是一座装饰艺术风格建筑的城市。"他说。

2015年，世界装饰艺术大会（World Congress on Art Deco）曾在上海举办，主办方选择在这座贝氏花园举行开幕酒会。当晚，中西合璧的建筑立面被灯光染成红色和紫色，花园里聚集了专程从世界各地来参会的Art Deco资深爱好者。

贝润生有两个儿子、七个女儿，他把最小的女儿贝娟琳嫁给了年轻的颜料商人——吴同文，将铜仁路一块地皮作为女儿的嫁妆赠送给新婚夫妇。吴同文聘请斯裔匈籍建筑师邬达克在这块基地设计了一座豪宅，就是著名的"绿房子"，离"贝宅"仅有几分钟步行之遥。

"绿房子"和"贝宅"都装有电梯，这在当时是非常罕见的设计。贝氏花园落成一年后的1935年，年轻的贝聿铭离开上海赴美学习建筑。1949年后，这里由上海机电设计研究院使用，昔日舞厅被改为食堂，楼上则是年轻员工的宿舍。

如今，别墅已改造为一家精品酒店和餐厅。贝家花园的新客人们喜欢在苏式园林风格的花园里徜徉，欣赏这座现代别墅里层出不穷的中国元素，特别是墙上的100个"寿"字，仿佛在透露一个家族绵延兴盛的秘密。

昨天： 贝宅　**今天：** 贝轩大酒店　**地址：** 南阳路 170 号

建造年代： 1934 年　**建筑师：** 中都工程司　**建筑风格：** 带中国元素的装饰艺术风格

参观指南： 建筑对住宿或就餐客人开放。

World-renowned Suzhou-born architect Ieoh Ming Pei — better known as I.M. Pei — who designed the Louvre's glass pyramid and Qatar's iconic Museum of Islamic Art, died aged 102 in New York on May 16, 2019.

An East-meets-West garden villa at 170 Nanyang Road in Jing'an District showcases the history of the legendary Pei family which has prospered for 15 generations since the Ming Dynasty (1368-1644).

"The villa is designed in Art Deco style with many traditional Chinese details," says Tongji University professor Zheng Shiling during a lecture about the city's architectural scene in the 1930s.

"It has an old Chinese layout with a sitting hall in the middle and bedrooms on both sides. The garden courtyard is graced by a well-designed pavilion which is modern-style but features traditional Chinese ambience."

He adds that there's a wall in the garden inscribed with 100 Chinese characters shou, or longevity.

The garden house, often known as the Pei Villa, has long been mistaken for a home of I.M. Pei's father, Tsuyee Pei, a banker who headed the Bank of China.

But it was in fact a property of Pei Runsheng, a dye tycoon from another branch of the Pei family.

It was Pei Runsheng who also purchased the renowned garden — Lion Grove Garden (Shizilin) in Suzhou in 1917.

During his childhood, I.M. Pei spent many hours in this 14th-century garden built by the abbot of an adjacent Buddhist monastery, playing hide-and-seek with his cousins and studying the Chinese classics.

The sanctuary that inspired monks, artists and poets for centuries impacted his aesthetic attitude and architectural design.

American scholar Michael Cannell traced history of the Pei family to the Ming Dynasty in his book *I.M. Pei, Mandarin of Modernism*.

According to Cannell, I.M. Pei belonged to the 15th generation of this large, prosperous lineage of poets, painters, calligraphers and bankers based in Suzhou, a bastion of ornamental gardens and old Chinese crafts such as silk, embroidery and scroll painting.

The first Pei arrived in Suzhou during the middle of the Ming Dynasty (1368-1644) to practice medicine and sell curative herbs from a stall in the marketplace

of the Xuanmiao Taoist Temple
(Temple of Mystery).

His descendants developed the business into a shop purveying a variety of Chinese medicines using fungi, crushed leaves and ginseng.

By the 18th century, the Peis had become a great land-owning family in the area.

I.M.'s grandfather, Litai Pei, was a powerful and learned man ranking in the top of the ruling gentry. Pei Litai groomed his sons for banking careers, such as his third son, Tsuyee.

Tycoon Runsheng came from a poor branch of the Pei clan. It is said he parlayed two silver dollars his grandfather gave him into a fortune and thus became a tycoon.

Cannell said the tycoon's ownership of the Lion Grove Garden "lent him a sense of gentility".

"To own a garden demonstrated a proper appreciation of aesthetic and scholarly matters," Cannel wrote in the book. "It was the rough equivalent of a parvenu (person of lowly origin) acquiring a chateau from an impoverished aristocrat.

"Its new inhabitants could renounce the worldly duties outside its walls and devote themselves, as mandarins should, to cultivating bamboo, practicing calligraphy and receiving guests in waterside pavilions."

As Pei Runsheng had received support from relatives when he was young and poor, he later set up the Pei Ancestral Hall in the Lion Grove Garden and would make generous donations to help other members within the big family, as well as people living in disaster-stricken areas, and poor students.

Although on a much smaller scale, the Pei Villa on Nanyang Road mirrors the tycoon's Suzhou Garden in some ways.

Just behind downtown Nanjing Road W., formerly known as Bubbling Well Road, the garden house provided a tranquil place with lawns, a pavilion, rockeries, pebble paths and shrubs.

According to Li Zhendong, vice chief architect of the Shanghai Jing'an Real Estate (Group) Co. Ltd., where many of Jing'an District's housing archives were preserved, the villa covers up to 2,011 square meters of land on this prominent location.

"Pei Runsheng made his first bucket of gold from dealing dye with German firms before and after World War I," Li said.

"He then invested most of his capital in real estate in Shanghai and owned nearly 1,000 buildings, including some tall buildings at the crossroads of Jinling and Sichuan roads near the Bund.

"He was so wealthy that his son, Pei Huanzhang, was asked to attend home school to prevent from been kidnapped."

According to the Shanghai Archives Bureau, modern Shanghai's high-profit, low-risk real estate market in the 1920s-1930s attracted many wealthy merchants such as Pei from neighboring Zhejiang and Jiangsu provinces.

For instance, a silk tycoon surnamed Liu owned dozens of lanes on Fuzhou and Guangxi roads.

Almost one year after the purchase of Lion Grove Garden in Suzhou, Pei Runsheng started investing in Shanghai's real estate and his property gradually added up to 160,000 square meters.

By 1949, according to archive records, there were more than 3,000 Chinese merchants who owned up to 60,000 buildings and houses that covered more than 10 million square meters. Among the top 30, each had more than 30,000 square meters, including Pei Runsheng.

As architectural scholar Cao Wei wrote in his book, *Shanghai Housing After its Opening to Foreigners*, the villa features a Western

steel and concrete structure and the newest modern equipment of its times for safety and comfort, such as steel-framed glass windows, air conditioning and an elevator.

At the same time, the Chinese influence is strong. The windows are decorated with the colored pattern of the Chinese character shou.

The swirling staircase is shaped like a huge dragon. The interior of the villa is lavishly embellished with traditional Chinese architectural details. There's a room for a Buddhist shrine on the second floor.

The East-meets-West Art Deco villa was designed by Chinese architect Gu Pengcheng who grad-

uated from Tongji University and opened an architectural firm in 1935.

Art Deco took its name, short for Arts Décoratifs, from the Exposition Internationale des Arts Décoratifs et Industriels Modernes in Paris in 1925.

The style had been inspired by Russian ballet and the archaeological discoveries of ancient Egypt.

The Art Deco vogue coincided with Shanghai's real estate boom from the 1920s to the 1930s and had a great impact on the city's architectural scene.

"Just like New York and Paris, Shanghai was then a center of many Art Deco buildings," Zheng says.

In 2015, when the World Art

Deco Congress was hosted in Shanghai, the organizer chose to kick off the congress in the Pei Villa.

Fronting the facade which turned red and purple by a light show, the garden welcomed Art Deco aficionados from around the world.

Pei Runsheng had two sons and seven daughters. His youngest daughter, Pei Juanlin, married a younger dye tycoon named Wu Tongwen.

Pei gave land on Tongren Road to his daughter as a dowry.

Wu commissioned renowned Hungarian-Slovak architect Laszlo Hudec to design the famous Green House, which was only a few minutes' walk from the Pei Villa.

Both the Green House and the Pei Villa were equipped with an elevator — a novelty in private residences at that time.

The young I.M. Pei left Shanghai to study architecture in the United States in 1935, one year after the completion of this garden villa.

In the 1950s, the villa was used by the Shanghai Institute of Mechanical and Electrical Engineering.

The dancing hall was converted to a dining hall and the bedrooms on the upper floors became a dormitory for young employees.

Today, the villa with refractory brick walls has been turned into a boutique hotel and restaurant. Diners love to wander in the Suzhou-style garden and admire Chinese elements here and there, especially the wall of 100 characters of longevity inscribed by a family of long, successful history.

Yesterday: The Pei Villa   **Today:** PEI Mansion Hotel   **Address:** 170 Nanyang Road
Date of construction: 1934   **Architect:** Gu Pengcheng
Architectural Style: Art Deco with Chinese elements
Tips: The garden villa is open to customers of the restaurant/boutique hotel.

　　1934年的一个冬日，哈同路257号别墅传出悲怆的琴声。弹奏古琴的是"报业大王"史量才的妻子沈秋水。是年11月13日，史量才在沪杭高速被国民党特务暗杀。

　　"他是中国新闻史上的重要人物。史量才为人正直，坚持将真相告知公众。"上海档案馆研究员张姚俊评价道。

　　史量才曾任《申报》总经理。在他去世前，《申报》是上海发行量最大的中文报纸。

　　他生于1880年，20岁参加科举考中秀才，此后经历丰富：1901年考入杭州蚕学馆学习，在泗泾办养正小学堂，后来又创办上海第一家女子蚕桑学校。1910到1915年间，他在松江盐务局和沪关清理处等担任公职。

"这段时期的工作让史量才对政界的尔虞我诈深感厌恶。他转向新闻业，希望通过舆论力量促进社会正义。"张姚俊说。

1912年，史量才接办《申报》，担任总经理。《申报》由美国人美查创办于1872年，是近代中国历史最悠久的报纸之一，但史量才接办时发行量仅有几千份。

时间证明他是一位眼光超前、能力出众的出版人。史量才为这份报纸改进经营、聘请贤能、重视广告、削减开销，同时争取江浙一带金融财团的支持。后来，《申报》的抗战评论又大大增加了报纸的影响力和发行量。

1930年4月5日，美商《密勒氏评论报》（*The China Weekly Review*）介绍，《申报》日发行量达15万份之多，是全国最有影响力的报纸之一。史量才本人也成为"上海教育、社会和慈善事业中最杰出的人物之一，是许多大学、医院和慈善社团的负责

人"。与此同时，史量才在商业领域也做得风生水起，投资了数家银行、药店、棉纺厂和书店等。

史量才位于哈同路（今铜仁路）的住宅是一座砖木结构的法国乡村风格别墅，米黄色外墙，顶部覆盖红瓦。

根据静安区房管局资料，别墅占地面积1222平方米，高三层，兴建于1922年。主立面构图对称、比例和谐，有坡屋顶和老虎窗，二层有敞廊。敞廊栏板和一层平台栏板图案精美，具有中国传统特征。住宅既有西方建筑的柱式、壁炉和装饰等，又有中国式样的门

窗，门前布置了一对石狮，中西合璧。别墅由丰盛投资建筑开发公司设计并建造，一层为客厅、画室、阳光室、餐厅、书房等，二层为客厅和卧室，三层主要是卧室。

2005年—2006年，上海章明建筑设计事务所对小楼进行了修缮，发现当年住宅由史量才、原配夫人庞明德、二夫人沈秋水以及原配夫人之子史咏赓四人居住。1934年史量才遇害后，夫人沈秋水将其改作仁济育婴堂，1949年后先后用作上海静安区党史办公室、地址办公室、市水务局办公室等，如今由上海市人民对外友好协会办公使用。

这座花园小楼保持了历史旧貌，室内装饰有华丽的天花，地上铺设着图案精美的马赛克地坪，壁炉和大楼梯都用米色花纹的大理石制成。

小巧精致的花园草坪茂盛，绿树荫浓。院落里还有一座带有中国传统装饰的红色建筑，据说曾是史家的经堂和存放祖先牌位的地方。

1932年1月，史量才在此寓所约请沪上工商文化界二十余人，组成商讨时事的"壬申俱乐部"，期望以报纸作为宣传武器来鼓舞士气，共抗外敌。随着史量才的影响力越来越大，他坚持抗战和新闻自由的态度为日后的悲剧埋下伏笔。

"1933年蒋介石谋杀国民党左翼领导人邓演达后，宋庆龄写了一封英文抗议信，这封信的中译版在史量才的帮助下出版，激怒了蒋介石，而《申报》对国民党政府不抵抗政策的揭露也损害了蒋介石政权的形象，促使他下决心要除掉史量才。"张姚俊说。

根据档案记载，1934年11月13日，时年55岁的史量才与沈秋水、儿子、侄女和一名儿子的邓姓同学一起乘私家车返回上海。他们在沈秋水位于杭州的住所短暂休假后，驶入沪杭高速公路。

汽车行驶到杭州与海宁间时被一辆别克敞篷车拦住。车上有7个人，他们刺穿了史量才的汽车轮胎，开枪打死了司机和邓姓同学，又追杀史量才到一个公路边的小屋，并当场杀死了他。他的尸体被扔进一个干燥的水箱。1934年11月14日，英文《大陆报》专门配照片报道了这起案件。

史量才的遇刺震惊上海，人们纷纷表示哀悼，认为是国家的巨大损失。1934年12月23日，有1300多人参加了在中国商会举行的追悼会，许多著名人物出席追悼会或致挽联。

主持追悼会的上海特别市市长吴铁成赞扬史量才毕生的事业。他回忆道，史量才一生致力于四项社会公益工作，他是中国新闻业的先驱之一，值得纪念，他也促进了教育和文化事业的发展。总的来说，他对有利于国家和人民福祉的任何事物都有兴趣。在这段中日敌对时期，他为了维护上海的和平与秩序付出时间和热心，这一点应该特别被铭记下来。

根据1934年12月24日《大陆报》报道，吴市长又指出，上海本地的团体机构应该继续开展史量才尚未完成的促进社会福祉的任务，这些工作都是这位已故报人长期奉献付出的。

复旦大学博士研究员叶冲在题为《报人办报——史良才的报人主体意识》的论文中，评价史量才看到了大众化报纸生存发展的另一条道路，即把报纸读者定位于人民，这在中国是前所未有的。在他之前，无论是外国传教士、商人、

中国官员或知识分子，各派力量办报都是为了彰显本党力量或赚钱，而报纸作为大众传播工具的作用被淡化了。

"从这个角度讲，史量才与《申报》开创了一个新的时代。"他写到。

在当年有关史量才去世和追悼活动的报道中，《大众画报》刊登的一张照片最打动人。

这张黑白照片展示了史量才哈同路住所设立的灵堂和穿白衣的沈秋水。图片说明写到，沈女士在先生的遗体旁抚七弦古琴致哀，琴声凄咽，吊唁者为之泣下。

据说，史量才与沈秋水都痴爱古琴，高山流水，互为知音。史量才安葬后，失去知音挚爱的沈秋水焚烧了古琴，到史量才为她而建的杭州秋水山庄隐居，度过余生。

昨天：史量才故居　**今天：**上海市人民对外友好协会　**地址：**铜仁路 257 号
建造年代：1922 年
参观指南：该建筑物不对公众开放，但可以从铜仁路欣赏到。

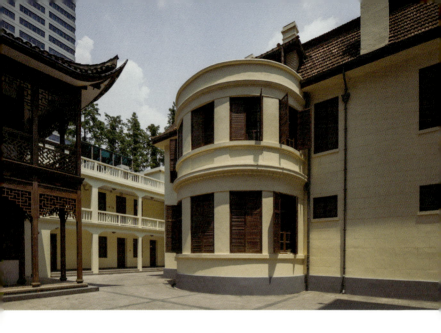

At the quiet stylish garden villa at 257 Tongren Road, a mourning tune from a guqin (traditional string instrument) can be heard coming from the chic abode one wintertime day in 1934. The sorrowful lament is being played by the wife of Shi Liangcai (Shih Liang-ts'ai), a journalist, publisher and long regarded as China's answer to "Joseph Pulitzer".

Shi had been assassinated, on November 13, on his way back via the Hu-Hang Highway (between Shanghai and Hangzhou) by a Kuomintang secret agent.

"A significant person in Chinese journalistic history, Shi was a newspaperman with an upright heart who always tried to tell the truth to the public," said Zhang Yaojun, a researcher of modern Shanghai history from the Shanghai Archives.

Shi grew up in Songjiang, now part of Shanghai. He was proprietor of the Shun Pao (Shanghai News), the most widely circulated Chinese newspaper in Shanghai before he passed away in 1934.

Shi had a versatile working experience after he passed the Xiucai Examinations of the Imperial Court (for civil service recruitment) during the Qing Dynasty (1644-1911) — the equivalent to a bachelor's degree, at the age of 20.

Five years later, he turned to

studying silk farming at Zhejiang Sericulture College and started the first Women's Sericulture School in Shanghai.

In addition, he held several political positions between 1910-1915, including the posts of director of the Salt Administration Bureau of Suzhou and director of Customs Revenue Administration of the Shanghai Circuit during both the Qing and Republic of China years.

"While serving these posts, Shi was deeply disappointed with Chinese political circles, which were full of deceit and blackmail," Zhang said. "He then switched to the newspaper business, hoping to arouse ethic consciousness and social justice through journalism in China."

Shi became the publisher of the Shun Pao in 1912 when the paper was still in a precarious stage with a daily circulation of only a few thousand copies. A competent publisher, he employed talent, improved management, focused on advertising, reduced costs and successfully won support from financiers in the neighboring Jiangsu and Zhejiang provinces.

After 1931, Shun Pao's opinion of the war against Japanese invaders enhanced the paper's influence and circulation.

According to "Who's who in China," a column in The China Weekly Review dated April 5, 1930, the paper grew to be one of the most influential newspapers in the country with a daily circulation of more than 150,000 copies. Shi himself also became "one of the most prominent persons among the local gentry of Shanghai in educational, social and philanthropic endeavors, being the director of a number of universities, hospitals and philanthropic societies".

He was also one of the most successful business promoters in Shanghai being financially interested in several banks, drug stores, cotton yarn factories and bookstores. The column also stated his residence address on Hardoon Road, which is today's Tongren Road.

Shi's residence on Tongren Road is a yellow-hued brick-and-wood structure topped by red tiles.

According to archives of Jing'an District Housing and Land Management Bureau, it is a French country-style villa built by Shi in 1922. Covering an area of 1,222 square meters, the facade of the three-story villa is graced by

open-air verandas on the second and third floors, and classical orders in varied sizes and styles.

Now used as the office of Shanghai People's Association for Friendship with Foreign Countries, the building is well preserved inside and out. The interior is richly decorated by plaster cornices on the ceiling and patterned mosaic floors. Both fireplaces and a grand staircase are fashioned from marble with grey-creamy patterns.

The small, stylish garden is planted with lush lawns and trees. Also in the yard, a red building with traditional Chinese decorations is said to have been used as Shi family's ancestral hall.

In 1932, Shi founded a club named "Ren Shen (after the Chinese name of the Year of the Monkey)" at this residence to unite patriotic Chinese capitalists and intellectuals. They often gathered to discuss strategies to fight the Japanese invaders. Shi's later tragedy resulted from his growing social influence, Anti-Japanese attitudes and free journalism opinion.

"After Chiang Kai-shek murdered Deng Yanda, a left-wing leader of Kuomintang party, in 1933, Soong Ching Ling, widow of Dr. Sun Yat-sen, wrote an English letter of protest. With Shi's help and resources, a Chinese translation of the letter was published by local news agencies which irritated Chiang," Zhang says.

Shun Pao's expose of Kuomintang government's non-resistance policy during the war impaired the image and interest of Chiang's regime, aroused his hatred and finally made him decide to "shut Shi up for good".

According to archive files, on November 13, 1934, the 55-year-old was returning home, in company with his wife Shen Qiushui, son Shi Yonggeng, niece Shen Lijuan, and the son's schoolmate Deng Zuxun in his private motorcar, to Shanghai via the Hu-Hang Highway following a brief vacation at his wife's residence in the lakeside city of Hangzhou.

Their car was halted by the henchmen's car, a Buick convertible, at Wenjiabu, midway between Hangzhou and Haining. Seven men piled from the obstructing vehicle, punctured the tires of Shi's car, shot the chauffeur and Deng dead and pursued Shi into a roadside hut where they killed him on the spot. His body was dropped into a dry cistern.

"Deng, 23, was a schoolmate at the Hangchow (today Hangzhou) Christian College of Shi Yonggeng, son of the publisher, who managed to run to safety together with Shi's wife and niece, except for a bullet in the arm of Shen Qiushui that was later removed in Hangchow," *The China Press* reported on November 14, 1934, with a photo of Shi's car, a Studebaker.

Shi's assassination was a great shock in Shanghai, widely mourned as a serious loss to the country. More than 1,300 people attended a memorial service held at the Chinese Chamber of Commerce on December 23, 1934. Many noted figures of the times attended the service or presented mourning scrolls.

Mayor Wu Te-chen of the Municipality of Greater Shanghai, who presided over the ceremonies, eulogized the life endeavors of the murdered publisher.

Mayor Wu recalled that Shi devoted his lifetime to four lines of social welfare work. He should be commemorated as one of the pioneers of journalism in China. His name was also associated with enterprises for the promotion of education and culture.

Generally, Shi took interest in anything that proved to be for the well-being of the nation and the people at large. He should be particularly remembered for the time and enthusiasm given to the preservation of peace and order in Shanghai during the Sino-Japanese hostilities.

Wu further pointed out that local participating groups should carry on the unfinished task of promoting social welfare in Shanghai, to which the late newspaper publisher had dedicated himself, *The China Press* reported on December 24, 1934.

In a paper titled "Analysis about Shi Liangcai's Subject Consciousness of Journalist," Fudan University PhD researcher Ye Chong finds that Shi created a "golden era" of Shun Pao under his management.

"Shi found a way of publishing a newspaper for the general public which was unprecedented in China. Before Shi, Chinese or foreign newspapermen published newspapers either for the purpose of missionary, earning money, enhancing their own political powers or gaining political positions. Unlike them, Shi and his Shun Pao initiated a new epoch of free journalism," Ye said.

Among the Chinese and En-

glish newspaper reports of Shi's death and memorial service, a small photo in a bilingual picture magazine named "Dazhong Huabao" was most touching.

The magazine published a photo showing the mourning hall of Shi's Hardoon Road residence where his wife Shen Qiushui was seen in white attire playing guqin. It says "Mrs Shi is playing a mourning tune on a seven-string guqin before the body of Mr Shi. The tune sounded like sobbing and visiting mourners cried on hearing the tune".

It is said Shi got to know Shen through her skills on guqin performance. Shen later burnt the guqin after the burial of Shi and lived a quiet, reclusive life in Qiushui Shanzhuang, a villa bestowed by Shi to her in Hangzhou.

Yesterday: Shi Liangcai Residence
Today: Shanghai People's Association for Friendship with Foreign Countries (SPAFFC)
Address: 257 Tongren Road   **Built in** 1922
Tips: The building is not open to the public, but it can be admired from Tongren Road.

为期三天的史量才悼念仪式
3-Day Ceremony Begun for Late Shi Liangcai

今天是为期三天的悼念仪式的第二天，很多亲朋好友到《申报》出版商史量才位于哈同路的家中瞻仰遗体。今天史先生的遗体将运到杭州安葬。

仪式于昨天开始，在《申报》主编的带领下，史家亲属和《申报》员工向这位已故的出版人表示敬意。

周六下午，仪式将以一个令人印象深刻的游行活动结束。届时，载有史先生遗体的棺材将从哈同路住宅一路游行至北站，以运往杭州。

Many friends and relatives will visit Shi's home at Hardoon Road to pay homage to the late Mr Shi Liangcai, publisher of the Shun Pao and part owner of the Sin Wan Pao, today, the second day of a three-day ceremony on the occasion of the removal of Mr Shi's body to Hangchow for burial.

The ceremony began yesterday when members of the Shi family and employees of the Shun Pao headed by Mr Chang Wen-ho, chief editor of that newspaper who officiated at the service, paid their respects to the late newspaper publisher.

The ceremony will be wound up with an impressive procession on Saturday afternoon when the casket containing the remains of Mr Shi will be paraded from the Hardoon Road residence to North Station for entrainment to Hangchow.

摘自 1935 年 5 月 17 日《大陆报》

Excerpt from *The China Press,* on May 17, 1935

永不过时的绿房子

The Green House

　　如果时光倒流，你是一位年轻有为的商人，有两房太太和多名子女，会想要一个什么样的新家呢？1936年，斯裔匈籍建筑师邬达克为颜料商人吴同文设计了一座完美的"梦之屋"，位于今铜仁路和北京西路转角处。这座现代风格的别墅被称为"绿房子"，是当年的"远东第一豪宅"。

　　对邬达克来说，"绿房子"是继国际饭店和大光明电影院之后的最后一件代表作，同时也是一根"救命稻草"。这个项目让

他的事务所度过了20世纪30年代末一段艰难的时光。

　　"绿房子"得名于建筑外立面和围墙上所用的绿色釉面砖。做军绿色颜料起家的吴同文视绿色为自己的幸运色，因此要求住宅通体设计为绿色。邬达克在向工部局申请的文件上，就把这个项目称为"绿房子"。

　　打造"远东第一豪宅"不仅靠优秀的建筑师，也需要兼具品位和财力的业主，而吴同文正是这样的业主。

　　1927年，吴同文娶了来自苏

州的颜料大亨——贝润生的小女儿贝娟琳为妻，嫁妆是一块3.33亩的土地。贝润生送了一份真正的厚礼，这块土地不仅位于黄金地段，周边两条相交的马路——哈同路（今铜仁路）和爱文义路（今北京西路）还暗含了女婿的名字——"同文"，门牌号码是"哈同路333号"。

到1935年时，30岁还不到的吴同文过着优裕的生活。他又娶了姨太太，两房太太都育有子女，想建造一个新家。

对于邬达克来说，这个项目难度不小。3.33亩的基地对于别墅不算大，又贴着道路。吴同文的要求也很高，希望两房太太互不干扰，一大家人在此舒适生活。而吴家人的生活方式中西合璧，老母亲需要一个中式佛堂，吴同文则喜欢打弹子、喝咖啡和跳舞，经常在家中举办西式派对。

1934年12月1日"远东第一高楼"国际饭店开业时，设计饭店的邬达克刚刚迎来职业生涯的巅峰，接到一个个摩天大楼的项目。但很快1935年"银元危机"就爆发了，白银流向海外，上海经济下滑，建造活动几乎停滞。邬达克的事务所很快从门庭若市变得门可罗雀。

不过幸运的是，"绿房子"这个项目让邬达克继续经营缩小规模的事务所。因此，他投入了全部心力。设计图纸显示，邬达克反复做了几轮修改，不断精益求精地优化设计，打磨出"绿房子"这件经典之作。

《上海邬达克建筑地图》作者、同济大学华霞虹教授认为，邬达克当时的情况很像美国建筑师赖特（Frank Lloyd Wright）。1934年到1937年间，赖特在美国宾州西南部为富商考夫曼（Edgar Kaufmann）设计了载入建筑史册的名宅流水别墅（Falling Water House）——一座悬挑于瀑布上的现代主义建筑。

这两座单体别墅建造时间接近，都为富商而设计，两位建筑师当时都陷入了困境——邬达克很久没有像样的委托项目，而赖特也遭遇职业瓶颈，官司缠身，年纪也大了，他的能力遭到怀

疑。

"两位建筑师在困境时拼搏一下，让世界对他们刮目相看，是很有意思的事情。大多数人喜欢传统风格的住宅，要把住宅设计得非常摩登，不是那么容易实现的。业主要有很前卫的观念，还要有机缘巧合。"华教授说。

经过一年反复修改，"绿房子"于1935年11月开工，1938年竣工。

邬达克为吴同文设计一个极其摩登现代、设施先进的新家。他对吴同文说这个房子50年或100年都不会过时。

住宅高达四层，这在上海近代花园住宅中十分罕见。建筑不仅精确地嵌入所在基地，邬达克还根据一家人的生活、工作、社交的需要，对空间做了精妙设计，仿佛"量体裁衣"。

他根据功能将建筑分为两部分：将别墅朝马路的北立面设计得封闭高耸，避免马路的尘嚣，主要是中式客厅和仆人房等，面向花园的南立面则明亮而开放，设计有酒吧、台球室和餐厅等西式社交空间。每层都有弧形大露台，在都市里也能亲近自然的气息。三楼和四楼分别是太太和姨太太及其各自子女的卧室，分层居住，互不干扰。

邬达克还设计了一个贯通的圆柱形阳光房，可以在室内享受阳光美景。从街道上眺望"绿房子"，圆柱形阳光房也成为了街区的亮点，是很特别的建筑设计手法。

"绿房子"的设计还体现了现代主义"有机建筑"的理念，有自由的平面和流动的空间，与传统的封闭式的古典主义豪宅有很大差异。

走进"绿房子"就能感到空间十分流畅，可以从一个空间很自然地走到另外一个空间，楼层之间也有弧形阳台巧妙连接，整个空间的动线设计是流动的。

此外，邬达克还把底层车道架空，让车道从一楼中间穿过建筑，这样做有两个好处：保留整块花园不被车道打扰，因为在建筑的一层车道可以挡风遮雨，上下车很舒适。现代主义建筑大师柯布西耶(Le Corbusier)在其名作萨伏伊别墅（The Villa Saboye）就有类似的设计。

别墅的室内装饰精美。"绿房子"虽然不大，走进去却像个精巧的迷宫。这么多的弧线、转门、楼梯和墙面处理，过渡都很流畅，空间使用合理，处处都有精致细节。一楼舞厅配有弹簧地板，有多个浴室和制冷供暖系统，还有一台荷叶状的电梯，这是上海首个在私宅中安装的电梯。

1959年，建筑师章明在参与写作《上海近代建筑史稿》时考察过"绿房子"，她记忆犹新，当时吴家仍住在"绿房子"里。

"佛堂、小电梯和楼梯非常精致，弧形窗户美好。墙上的所

267

有意大利洞石都经过精心挑选，具有清晰而不间断的曲线图案，非常漂亮。"这位曾修缮邬达克作品大光明电影院和慕尔堂的建筑师回忆。

1939年4月，匈牙利建筑杂志《空间与形式》（*Teres Forma*）指出："这栋房子显然是远东和欧美生活方式一个奇异的混合体。它包含中国生活方式所需的一切，从祠堂到几个家庭套房，当然，除此之外，它还包含一个酒吧，可以在此开办鸡尾酒会。

1948年，后来成为著名翻译家的钱绍昌17岁，应同学邀请经常参加绿房子周末的跳舞晚会。

钱绍昌回忆："绿房子有一个华丽的圆形舞厅，上面铺着弹跳的地板。聚会大约有10个人，包括吴家人。我不知道如何跳舞，但吴同文的姨太太非常好，她是最好的舞者，总是一步一步地教我，直到我掌握了Waltz、Blues和Rumba。之后，我终于有勇气邀请吴家的女儿们跳舞！"

绿房子落成后，被1940年8月的《国际建筑》等杂志报道，《中国月刊》（*China Monthly*）的一辑将之描述为"远东地区最现代、最奢华的住宅"。

华教授评论说："绿房子的独特之处在于，东西方生活方式高度融合，被完全隐藏在现代外观的背后，成为无与伦比的统一体。邬达克显然对上海的社交生活有深刻的了解，并很好地控制了建筑风格。这个建筑也反映了上海的地域性，寸土寸金的城市，如何用好高密度城市里的这块地，很有意义，经济而有效。"

而1939年的匈牙利杂志《空间与形式》也透彻地对其进行了解释。

"今天的东方人有多么渴望西方的生活方式，但同时也坚持自己古老的生活方式。他们不能要么全旧，要么全新，新旧都有其价值所在。因此，一种独特的中西融合得以形成……那些对今日之中国哪怕有些许了解的人都会认为，这幢了不起的家庭住宅是对这个遥远国度的人们的高度精确的表现。"

2014年，"绿房子"在历时三年的修缮后，焕发昔日光彩。

昨天：吴同文住宅　**今天：**上海市城市规划设计研究院　**建造年代：**1935-1938年
建筑师：邬达克　**建筑风格：**国际式风格
参观指南：从铜仁路和北京路可欣赏到立面。

269

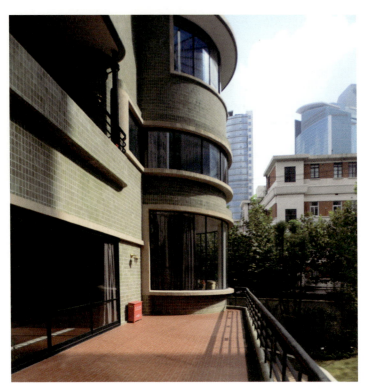

Imagine you are a rich young man who has a wife, a concubine and a plot in downtown Shanghai endowed by your father-in-law. What kind of dream house would you build on it?

In 1936 Laszlo Hudec designed such a dream house for Chinese tycoon D.V. Woo around the corner of Hardoon Road (today's Tongren Road) and Avenue Road (today's Beijing Road W.). It was a modern-style villa widely known as "the Green House", which was regarded as one of the largest and most luxurious residences in the Far East.

"The Green House and the Grand Theatre are my two favorite Hudec buildings," says Tongji University associate professor Hua Xiahong, co-author of *Shanghai Hudec Architecture* and *The Green House*.

"Shanghai is filled with old garden residences, but only a few of them are modern-style architectures with artistic creativeness in design and a high level of completeness in construction. And even fewer of those have kept the feel of Shanghai's east-meet-west modern era till today," she says.

To Hudec, this was another signature work following the huge success of the Park Hotel and the Grand Theatre. Meanwhile, it was a savior for his company to make through the uneasy late 1930s.

The house' nickname comes from the green-colored glazed tiles on the facade and surrounding walls of the residence. It was a choice of the owner Woo who made his first bucket of gold from selling green pigments for military use and thus regarded green as his lucky color.

A well-designed private residence requires not only a smart architect, but also a good owner, a person of good wealth and taste. Mr. Woo was such a good owner.

In 1927 he married the little daughter of Suzhou tycoon Bei Runsheng, who gave the plot to him as a precious dowry. The gift was meaningful because the two roads' Chinese names, Hatong Lu and Aiwenyi Lu, contained Woo's Chinese given name, "Tongwen".

"From then on Woo's fate

was kind of locked to this special plot," says Prof. Hua, adding that the address "No. 333 Hardoon Road" may be purchased and precisely represented the size of the plot –3.33 Mu (around 2,221 square meters).

In 1935 Woo was barely 30 but he enjoyed an affluent life with a wife, a mistress and a bunch of children. But it was a difficult job for Hudec since the new home would house such a big family but the plot irregular and not very large.

Moreover the Chinese family's life style was rather western. Woo had an English name and was keen on a range of western hobbies from billiard balls, dancing parties to drinking coffee. So he would pursuit and embrace this utterly modern home, which was unconventionally designed inside out, technologically advanced as

well. Hudec had to mix up all the intentional space usages together to suit the Woos' east-meet-west life style.

Hudec's career reached a prime after the grand opening of Park Hotel on December 1, 1934. He was widely reported and received commissions of skyscraper one after another.

But soon Shanghai's economy was dragged down by the 1935 international silver crisis and constructions came to a halt almost completely in the city. In family letters, Hudec complained about the empty waiting room of his office, where people used to queue up to talk to him.

Without "the green house,' the only noteworthy commission after 1935, Hudec was not even able to pay the cost of maintaining his office. However more free time allowed the architect to revise the design again and again to make it a perfect house.

Prof. Hua said Hudec's situation mirrored that of famous American architect Frank Lloyd Wright of almost same period when designing the legendary Falling Water House for tycoon Edgar Kaufmann in southwestern Pennsylvania, which hanged over a waterfall.

"Both projects were designed for a rich merchant and both architects fell to a predicament at that time," the professor says. "Hudec had no big projects to do while Wright in his professional bottleneck was aging and soaked in lawsuits. So both of them went all out to make a hit and make the world look at them differently. It's very interesting."

After back-and-forth revises for nearly a year, the project finally kicked off in November of 1935 and completed in 1938. Hudec's solution for housing such a big, influential east-meet-west family was a four-floor modern residence which showcases the essence of organic architecture.

The building has an acute angles and concise layout, which merges perfectly with the base. The main body approaches the road on the north, which connects with the curved surrounding walls on the corner as a unity.

"Woo certainly chose the right man. Hudec was so good at designing within a limited plot. He was like a talented tailor who could make a suit out of an irregular cloth," Hua chuckles.

"He tailor made such a unique building, which could only grow on the site. It was like an urban

living machine anchoring on the plot. Both the functions and the forms were precisely fit for the plot."

The center of the ground floor was designed as passage for cars through which Hudec has made the land for transportation as compact as possible. Probably he had borrowed the idea from Le Corbusier's famous "The Five Points", which suggested elevate the building from the damp earth so as to give the space for a garden beneath it.

In Green House, the connection between the living space and the garden therefore remained uninterrupted. Meanwhile it also prevented people from rain or hot sun when getting on and off their cars beneath the elevated floor.

He also divided the building into two parts according to functions. The western-style social space including a bar, a billiard room, a dining hall and main bedrooms face an open garden. The Chinese-style sitting hall, the ancestral room and servants' room on the northern side are in a more closed style.

The southern facade is stylish. The cylinder-shaped sun parlor is four floors high, which contrasts with the big balcony full of smooth curves that is shrinking layer by layer. The cast iron patterns on the staircase and balcony are in Art Deco style. The sun parlor is made with imported curved glass. Even the glass door

is in a curved shape.

The interior is embellished in a luxurious style. It's not very large, but it's like a delicate labyrinth, with so many curves, rotating doors and smooth architectural details.

The dancing hall is equipped with sprung floors. The villa is installed with gas supply, bathrooms and cooling and heating systems. An elevator in a unique lotus leaf shape was the first to be installed in any private residences in Shanghai.

The 85-year-old Chinese architect Zhang Ming, who had restored Hudec's Grand Theatre and Moore Memorial Hall, still had a clear memory of the house when she visited it nearly half a century ago.

"The curved windows looked so nice. Inside, it was a dressing room of one of Woo's daughters, as far as I remember," she recalls of a survey around 1959 for completing the city's first architectural history book after 1949. The Woo's family was still living in the Green House then.

"The ancestral hall, the small elevator and the staircase were all so refined. All the Italian travertine on the walls had been all carefully selected, with clear and uninterrupted curved patterns, very beautiful."

In 1939 Hungarian architectural magazine Teres Forma (Space and Form) had pointed out, "The building is apparently a peculiar

mix of the Far Eastern and European or American way of life. It contains all that is required by the Chinese lifestyle, from the ancestral hall to several family suites and it has—of course set apart from these—a bar for cocktail parties."

Famous translator Qian Shaochang remembered dancing parties in the Green House. At the age of 17 in 1948, he was often invited to weekend dancing parties there by his classmate Li Qiwen, who was an intimate friend of Woo's younger son.

"The Green House had a sumptuous round-shaped dancing hall with sprung floors," Qian recalls. "The party had around 10 people including Woo's family. I didn't know how to dance but Woo's concubine was very nice and she was the best dancer. She always taught me step by step until I grasped Waltz, Blues and Rumba. After that I finally had the courage to invite Woo's daughters to dance!"

"What is unique for the Green House was a highly mingled space of East-meet-West life styles, which was concealed behind utterly modern appearance and became an unparalleled unity," Prof. Hua comments.

"The most interesting part to decipher the Green House is to sample the complications and contradictions of Chinese elites in a metropolis like Shanghai in the 1930s and 1940s. Hudec obviously had a deep understanding of Shanghai's social life and a good control of architectural expressions to go along with."

Perhaps the 1939 Hungarian magazine has explained it in a more thorough way.

"How much today's oriental people long for the western life style, while also clinging to their own ancient mode of living. They cannot let go either of the old or the new, which both have their own value; thus, a unique merging of East and West comes into being...We believe (the architect) has superbly got right what today's Chinese need and thus satisfied the wish of his client the most perfect...To those with any idea about today's China and today's Chinese this monumental family house will come across as a highly accurate expression of the people of this remote country," the magazine reports.

And these words still sound profound for today's China and Chinese.

Yesterday: D. V. Woo's Residence
Today: Shanghai Urban Planning and Design Institute
Architect: L.E.Hudec   **Built in:** 1935-1938
Tips: The facade can be appreciated from Tongren Road and Beijing Rd. W. .

雷士德的遗产
The Inheritance of Henry Lester

1932年9月，雷士德医药研究院（Henry Lester Institute of Medical Research）即将落成。简洁现代的大楼高达三层，阳光充足，设有演讲厅、医学图书馆、会议室和实验室等。英文《大陆报》称这是"远东地区最大、设备最好的研究型医院，可与国际上任何同类机构媲美"。

研究院是根据英国富商、慈善家雷士德先生（Henry Lester）的遗愿而建造的，位于今日北京西路1320号。

根据1932年9月15日《大陆报》的报道，演讲厅设计有讲台，后面还有准备间（preparation rooms）。与图书馆相连的是一个期刊室。一层还有一些会议室和办公室。

"正门大厅的门廊一侧是门房间和电话室，另一侧面向电梯。长长的走廊向两侧延伸开来，在这些走廊上分布着办公室。上到将用作实验室的二楼，会发现类似的空间布置。每个房间将有专门的特殊用途。三楼除了其他实验室和办公室，还会有一个大型医学研究博物馆。大楼是平屋顶，阳光充足，空间开放而且充足。"报道描述。

上海医药工业研究院原党务部部长胡国樑曾撰文回忆，建筑挑高4米左右，窗户大，采光好，冬暖夏凉。室内地板、门墙都为柚

279

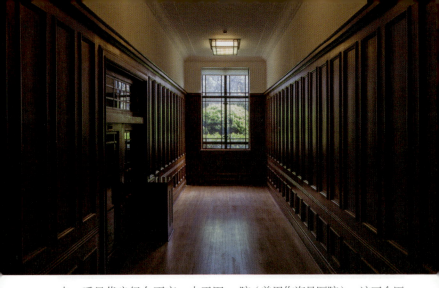

木，质量优良经久不变。由于围墙很高，从外面只能看到建筑顶部和绿树，大楼一直披着神秘的面纱，直到20世纪90年代末，围墙由实墙改为栅栏。1949年后，这里先后挂牌"华东工业部上海工业试验所""轻工业部上海工业试验所""食品工业部上海科学研究所"，直至1957年，这里成为"化工部上海医药工业研究所"，1960年改名为"上海医药工业研究院"，如今由上海现代制药公司办公使用。

医学研究院是根据雷士德的遗嘱而建立的三个主要慈善项目之一，另外两个项目是雷士德医院（今仁济医院西院）和雷士德工学院（曾用作海员医院）。这三个历史建筑今日犹存，都是雷士德留给上海这座城市的遗产。

1840年2月26日，雷士德（Henry Lester）出生于英国南部港口城市南安普敦市。他曾在伦敦接受建筑师和土地勘测师的训练，1863年到上海后受雇于工部局负责公共租界土地测量的工作，后来也为法租界测量土地。这些工作都完成后，雷士德回归建筑师的角色。他先与一名建筑师合作，但很快独立创业，沿着黄浦江岸设计建造了许多著名的洋行、码头和仓库。

1913年，雷士德又与强生（George A. Johnson）和马立斯

（Gordan Morriss）联合创办德和洋行（Lester, Johnson & Morriss），专营建筑设计、土木工程、测绘检验、房地产抵押放款等业务。德和洋行发展成为近代上海实力最强的设计事务所之一，承接的项目包括外滩5号日清大楼、外滩17号字林西报大楼和南京路先施公司大楼等。

1926年5月14日，雷士德在上海公济医院（the General Hospital，今上海第一人民医院）病逝，安葬于静安寺公墓（今静安公园）。《北华捷报》和《大陆报》等英文报纸纷纷撰文回顾雷士德的一生，评价他是一个有远见的人，很早发现了上海的潜力，大量投资不动产。而他在上海的运气特别好，从一开始就很成功，无论做什么都能"点石成金"，做成了上海历史上最大的几笔土地交易。雷士德在去世前已成为上海最大的土地拥有者之一。

报道估算，雷士德拥有价值约300万英镑的财富，也有传闻称他的财产达500万英镑之多。英国学者Peter Hibbard曾在《上海外滩》中评价，雷士德的洋行既做建筑设计与建造项目，又做土地和地产交易，开创了先河，堪称在上海投资最成功的英国建筑师。

不过虽然投资如此成功，雷士德的个人生活却与住华丽别墅的上海富豪们形成强烈反差。终身未婚的他生活非常简朴，穿别人的旧衣，交友不多，喜欢步行和乘公交汽车，被认为是上海英侨社区最吝啬的人。

雷士德在外滩规矩会堂和上海总会居住多年，被认为是总会"最早、最奇怪的会员"。上海总会成立于1861年，又名英国总会，会员全部为男性。今日位于外滩2号的华尔道夫酒店是1911年落成的总会新楼，这里提供英国绅士需要享受的一切，包括远东最长的L型长吧、弹子房、江景绝佳的餐厅和阅览室等。"点石成金"的雷士德却很少去总会酒吧消费，除了为会员提供免费蛋糕和葡萄酒的平安夜。

雷士德每天都在外滩滨江漫步。1926年的《北华捷报》写到，在上海最有趣的事情莫过于在外滩偶遇散步的雷士德，听他讲述过去的变迁，了解这座城市的地价在过去60年间暴涨了多少。

富豪雷士德简朴生活的谜团在他去世后揭开。雷士德去世时除了一名在军中服役的侄子没有亲属，他留下一份惊人的遗嘱，除了少量遗产赠予个人，将几乎所有遗产留在上海用以成立"雷士德基金会"，发展医疗、教育和慈善事业。

他生前指定用遗产资助建造仁济医院新大楼、雷士德医药研究院和雷士德工程研究院和学校。此外，一些慈善组织也得到捐助，如上海聋哑学校、虹口华德路圣路加医院、忆定盘路中国盲人院、董家渡穷苦小姊妹会、虹口黄包车夫会、南市穷苦精神病院等。遗嘱还

设立5万两银子的雷士德奖学金，面向在上海就学的所有国籍、无论宗教信仰的14岁以下的男女学生。从这份遗嘱可以看出，雷士德十分关心城市弱势群体，同时重视医学和教育事业，富有长远发展的眼光。

1927年，雷士德基金会即按照这份遗嘱开展筹建工作，由雷士德创办的德和洋行负责设计。这三大项目在20世纪30年代陆续建成使用。

1931年，仁济医院位于山东路的新大楼首先落成，展开作为现代化医院的新一页。在《仁济医院九十五年1844-1938》（*Ninety-Five Years A Shanghai Hospital 1844-1938*）一书中，医院董事会秘书埃利斯顿（Eric S. Elliston）提到雷士德与这所面向华人的慈善医院有深厚的关系。早在1873年，雷士德曾负责仁济医院男子病房的设计工作，此后长期为医院提供数额不小的捐赠。在1924年12月订立的最后一份遗嘱中，雷士德捐赠100万两款项用于建造仁济医院新楼，此外还赠予医院四块地皮。

雷士德的这笔捐赠附有几项条件，除了提出医院需改名为"雷士德华人医院"（The Lester Chinese Hospital），还要求医院为穷苦病人免费治疗。1927年，医院又收到一张数额达64358.99两的支票，款项是来自雷士德赠予土地的收入。埃利斯顿透露，仁济医院新大楼原计划盖5层，因为后来决定让雷士德医药研究院使用其中一层，大楼加建为6层。

1931年12月15日，英文《北华捷报》介绍了雷士德医院的"新家"，提到雷士德医药研究院的临床部将设在新大楼的五层。

1932年，选址在爱文义路（今北京西路）的雷士德医药研究院落成。有意思的是，雷士德捐建的两家医学机构——仁济医院与雷士德医药研究院，不仅曾在一起办公——研究院一度设在医院新楼五楼，还开展良好的密切合作。研究院接办了医院的化验部，帮助其开展细菌学、血清学、临床化学、病理学、临床造影等方面的研究应用。埃利斯顿评价，研究院的医学专家对医院提供了给力的帮助，而供研究院使用的五楼保留了一些病房，以供专家研究临床疾病。合作有机结合了基础研究与临床治疗，而两家医学机构都为近代中国培养了很多医疗技术人才，也为今天上海的医疗卫生事业奠定了一定的基础。

1934年，根据雷士德遗嘱兴建的第三个项目——雷士德工学院及学校在东熙华德路（今虹口区东长治路）完工。占地达10000平方米的工学院是一座引人瞩目的装饰艺术风格建筑，提供科学技术方面的培训教育。1935年入学的著名规划师、建筑师陈占祥在传记中回忆，这所英式教育的学校为有才华的贫困学生提供奖学金。他的老师、来自英国利物浦的建筑师米勒（H. Miller）教给他"建筑师的责任和终极力量"。

如今距雷士德逝世已近百年，但他留下的遗产仍闪耀着光芒。

2014年，雷士德捐建的仁济医院新楼历经修缮重新投入使用，昔日宽敞的大病房和水磨石楼梯犹存。仁济医院已发展为一所集医疗、教学、科研于一体的综合性三级甲等医院。今年疫情发生后，医院派出172人的医护人员队伍，前往武汉雷神山医院等三所医院驰援。

由于第二次世界大战，雷士德工学院及学校仅持续了不到10年的时间，却培养了数百名杰出的"雷士德男孩"，他们成长为各领域的优秀专业人才。2004年，上海市历史博物馆和雷士德工学院校友会共同举办"雷士德工学院建校70周年纪念特展"。约200件展品涵盖了雷士德本人和雷士德工学院的相关资料，还展示了"雷士德男孩"毕业后的成就。工学院大楼保存至今，由海员医院使用多年。

1957年，雷士德医药研究院这座伟岸的建筑成为化工部上海医药工业研究院，幸运地延续了昔日功能。这里荟萃了一大批来自各大药厂的知名专家和科研人员，如雷兴翰、童村等，声名远播，成为中国医药工业系统中科研实力最强的研发机构之一。

在为《遗产与记忆——雷士德、雷士德工学院和她的学生们》一书撰写的前言里，熊月之写道："在数以万计的近代寓沪外侨中，来自英国的雷士德特立独行，品德高尚，闪射出夺目的光彩……雷士德以其毕生的辛劳，全部的积蓄，书写了一个大写的'善'字，也是一个大写的'爱'字，对弱势群体的善与爱，对儿童的善与爱，对上海的善与爱。"

在上海这座城市，孤身一人的雷士德深居简出，度过了63年漫漫人生岁月。在那份写满

"善"与"爱"的遗嘱中,他还写下一段话:"在将近60年中,我主要和永久的家一直在中国的上海,现在如此,以后也将如此。自从很久以前我选择中国作为定居地以来,这里就是我的家了。"

上海曾经给雷士德带来巨大的机遇和财富,他最终把获得的财富又赠予这座城市最需要帮助的人,仿佛形成了一个爱与能量的完美闭环。"上海人"雷士德的故事如此独特,如此真实动人。

如今,雷士德设立于1926年的"亨利·雷士德"信托基金仍在运作,赴英深造的中国学者如果研究用于造福中国人民,就可以申请雷士德奖学金。基金会的网站是英文的,但首页写着中文"上海"两个字,并附有一段声明。

"亨利·雷士德信托由曾在上海度过大半人生岁月的亨利·雷士德命名,他于1926年去世。他在上海赚到了财富,所以在他身后,将他的财富用于造福上海人民是最正确、最恰当的。这项善举持续到了今日,用于教育奖学金。"

昨天: 雷士德医药研究院 **今天:** 上海现代制药股份有限公司 **地址:** 北京西路 1320 号
建造年代: 1934 年 **建筑师:** 德和洋行(Lester Johnson & Morris)
参观指南: 大楼不对外开放,但可以从北京西路欣赏建筑的立面。雷士德工学院旧址位于东长治路 505 号。

When the building at 1320 Beijing Road was near completion in September 1932, *the China Press* said it would be "the largest and most finely equipped research hospital of its kind in the Far East and is equal to most anywhere in the world".

The establishment of the Henry Lester Institute of Medical Research realized the Last Will and Testament of Henry Lester, a British millionaire landowner and philanthropist whose name is intimately associated with early Shanghai history.

"Among the tens of thousands of expatriates living in modern Shanghai, Henry Lester with his unique character and noble virtue glittered brilliantly," famous Shanghai historian Xiong Yuezhi wrote in the preface for the book *Bequest and Memory* by Fang Yunfang.

The medical research institute had been built entirely for research purposes where a staff of physicians and scientists had some headquarters.

Sitting well back from the street, the institute was surrounded by a brick wall; the entrances were guarded by heavy bronze grills. There was a three-story building and on either end of the ground floor were large rooms, one of which had been used as a lecture room and the other as a medical library.

According to *the China Press* on September 15, 1932, the lecture room contained a stage and preparation rooms behind it. The library had a journal room in connection with it. The remainder of the ground floor was used for conference rooms and offices.

"On entering the main entrance hall, flanked on either side by the porter's office and telephone office, one faces the elevator. Long corridors extend away on either side, on to which open the offices. Ascending to the first floor, which will house laboratories, one finds a similar arrangement of space. Each room will be devoted to a special use. The third floor, beside housing other laboratories and offices, will contain a large museum of medical research. The roof is flat and is open and sunlit, containing much space," *the China Press* said.

The medical research institute was one of the two major philanthropic projects constructed to realize Lester's will.

The other one was a three-story structure in Art Deco style for a combined Lester school — the Henry Lester Institute of Technical Education, which is located on today's Dongchangzhi Road in Hongkou District.

The object of the school was to provide sound fundamental training in the sciences and technology for boys preparing to enter the building and allied trades. In the technical institute more advanced and more theoretical training would be given.

Both the medical research institute and the institute of technical education were designed by the architects of Lester Johnson and Morriss, a firm co-founded by Henry Lester.

Born in 1840 in Southamp-

ton, Lester, who had received his training in London as an architect and land surveyor, came to Shanghai in 1863-1864 to survey the settlement for the Shanghai Municipal Council. He also served in the Public Works Department of the French Council. It is said he followed a doctor's advice and embarked on a journey to Shanghai after an unknown disease took the lives of all three of his brothers.

It seemed he made the right choice and Shanghai became his lucky city. After his service in the municipal council was completed, he started his own business.

His company, Lester Johnson & Morris, became one of the most well-known architectural firms in town. A man of great foresight, he saw the potential of Shanghai and made large investments in property. Prior to his death, he was one of the largest landowners in Shanghai. Most of his property was used for the purpose of Chinese buildings.

With so much money and land in hand, Lester was unlike most tycoons in modern Shanghai who often lived an extravagant life by building gorgeous mansions and hosting parties night after night.

He never married, lived in the dormitory of Shanghai Club on the Bund, had no cars and often took buses. He seldom bought new clothes and most of his clothes were gifts from friends.

Before he died in May 1926, Lester bequeathed most of his assets to philanthropy, including the St. Luke's Hospital, the Institution for the Chinese Blind, the Children's Refugee, The Little Sisters of the Poor, The Shanghai Mission for Ricsha Men and St. Joseph's Asylum for the Poor.

He also left the bulk of his fortune for the re-establishment of the Cathedral School, for the building of the Lester Chinese Hospital and a Henry Lester School and Institute of Technical Education.

In carrying out the latter provisions, the Trustees and their advisors decided to establish two institutes, one for medical research and the other for technical education. The Lester school was to be closely associated with the technical institute.

"I declare that for about 60 years my principal and permanent home has always been and that it still is and will be in Shanghai in China and that long since I chose China as my domicile and such is my domicile now," Lester stated in his will.

Time flies but Lester's legacy still glitters in the city he loved.

The Lester Chinese Hospital turned to be today's Shanghai Renji Hospital on Shandong Road. The Lester school lasted only for less than 10 years due to World War II but nurtured hundreds of outstanding "Lester Boys" who grew up to be Chinese professionals in all aspects of life. Shanghai History Museum hosted a special exhibition dedicated to the Lester school and its students in 2004.

The medical research institute was fortunate to always be tied with medical or scientific research after the Shanghai Institute of Pharmaceutical Industry was founded here in 1957.

"The walls of the building at 1320 Beijing Road W. were tall and people could only see the top of a grand building and lush green trees. They had to admire the grandeur of the building only when the gate opened occasionally. Our institute has always been shrouded with a mysterious veil until the solid surrounding walls were replaced by railings during a renovation in the 1990s. It had congregated a large amount of renowned experts and excellent technicians from large medical factories, such as Lei Xinghan and Tong Cun. It was reputed as the best comprehensive medical and pharmaceutical research institute in China," Hu Guoliang,

the late office director of the institute, wrote in an article about the building.

Today, the China State Institute of Pharmaceutical Industry, which originated from the Shanghai Institute of Pharmaceutical Industry, rent the building to its branch company, the listed Shanghai Shyndec Pharmaceutical Co. Ltd..

After Lester died in 1926, he was buried 10 minutes' walk from this institute built according to his Will. He rested in peace in the now Jing'an Park, which had been Bubbling Well Cemetery for local expatriates since 1898.

"Many American and European expatriates who first came to Shanghai boasted cultural privilege and despised Chinese culture. But with extensive contact with and a deeper understanding of Chinese people, some of them gradually paid more attention to or even loved Chinese culture. They became more friendly to the country. Lester was a typical example of its kind," Xiong said during a recent lecture.

Today, the Lester Trust still supports Chinese students and scholars to study or research in the United Kingdom. In the conditions for applications, "the grant will give a Chinese citizen, whose knowledge and skill obtained, will be for the benefit of the people of China".

The official English website for the Lester Foundation contained two big Chinese characters which are "Shanghai".

Yesterday: Henry Lester Institute of Medical Research
Today: Shanghai Shyndec Pharmaceutical Co. Ltd.   **Address:** 1320 Beijing Road W.
Built in 1934   **Architect:** Lester Johnson & Morris
Tips: The building is not open to the public but you can see the facade on Beijing Road.

研究古代中医药
Ancient Chinese Medicine Studied

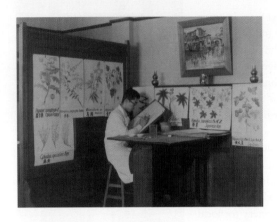

雷士德医药研究院发现古老的疗法有许多治疗作用。

很多人认为，驴皮、羊眼、鹿角、狗脑、奇怪草药等的疗愈用途，在民间传说和妖魔论中交织在一起，实在是空洞的中国迷信。

不过，生理科学部负责人博耐德·雷德博士（Dr. Bernard Read）和雷士德医药研究院的同事们正在进行广泛的调查，这可能会大大减少人们对中医药的怀疑态度。

雷士德医药研究院的态度是，在可以将当今西方世界的医学科学强加给中国人民之前，必须对传统中医实践的基础进行实验性观察。

有理由相信，当某些治疗方法在中国、印度已经持续使用了多个世纪，而且有历史文献表明，尽管没有直接的联系，这些疗法在更古老的文明也有使用，那么基本可以认为这些疗法是有疗效的。

在中国称为"阿胶"的熬煮驴皮被广泛用作血液再生剂和体内止血药，并且是体弱人士、尤其是那些患有肺结核的人们的普遍营养品。这种现象引发对其特性的的化学和生理研究。T. G. Ni博士发现阿胶中含有大量的甘氨酸、胱氨酸、赖氨酸、精氨酸和组氨酸，口服后可提高钙氮的吸收并提高血液中的钙含量，而静脉注射阿胶可有效恢复出血和休克后的循环低下。进一步关于阿胶在肌肉萎缩中的有益作用的研究正在进行中。去年在杭州，仅一家商店就交易了25万元的驴皮。

雷德博士在关于"新型药理和古代医学"的报告中说："值得注意的是，1909年英国药典的现代医学仅包含9种动物来源的物质，而几乎所有这些物质，都是像猪油和蜂蜡一样无害的东西。当现代科学转向肝脏、胃、来自眼睛的维生素A、肾上腺素等时，在古代医学中发现了这么多动物组织的应用是令人惊奇的。"

在上述最新发表的报告中，雷德博士介绍了一张表格，其中列出了传统中医使用的6种家畜的26个部位。这些动物包括牛、马、猪、鸡、绵羊和狗。

梅花鹿等物种的天鹅绒质地的角制成的粉末状药物，受到中国人的高度认可。俄罗斯科学家最近的研究表明鹿角含有雄性荷尔蒙激素。

羊眼的虹膜和晶状体用来治疗视力模糊和结膜炎。鹰、鹦鹉和鲭鱼的眼睛用于治疗夜盲症。最近，瓦尔德（Wald）从绵羊、猪、牛和青蛙的虹膜中分离出维生素A。

在传统中医里，建议猪肝治疗夜盲症、脚气病等，最近人们发现猪肝富含维生素A、B、C、D、E。有很多这样的例子，比如荠菜。因为草药明显缺乏强大的原理，因此被抛在一边，现在已被证明荠菜适度地富含三种维生素，这也很好地证明了中国古人使用荠菜来治疗很多疾病。

在中国，人们保存有30到50个世纪的非常准确的医学经验记录。这些记录并非神圣机构的积累，而是迄今为止的经验发现，只是在20世纪科学的相当粗糙的筛子中才被筛选出来。

Lester Institute of Medical Research Finds Many Healing Properties in Old Remedies.

It may seem to many that the healing use made of donkey skin, sheeps' eyes, deer's horn, dog's brain, odd herbs, etc. . All interwoven as they are in folk-lore and demonology, is just so much empty Chinese superstition, and that it is unfortunate that such great faith is placed in such absurd remedies.

However, an extensive survey now being undertaken by Dr. Bernard Read, head of the Division of Physiological Sciences and his associates at the Henry Lester Institute of Medical Research may greatly diminish popular scepticism.

It is the attitude of the Lester Institute that before today's medical science of the western world can be imposed on the Chinese people, due regard must be given to the empirical observations which form the basis of the old Chinese medical practice.

Reason has suggested that when certain therapeutic practices have been in constant use for a great many centuries not only in China but in India and with no apparent relationship in the still more ancient civilizations, as revealed in old manuscripts, it is at least likely that some real benefit is derived.

The phenomenally widespread use in China of boiled down donkey skin, called "Ah-Chiao", as a blood regenerator, and internal styptic, and a general nutritive for weak people, especially those suffering from tuberculosis, has led to an investigation into its particular character both chemical and physiological. Dr. T. G. Ni finds that it contains a large amount of glycine, cystine, lysine, argenine and hystidine. Administered orally it improves the calcium nitrogen absorption and raises the calcium level of the blood. This Ah-Chiao used intravenously was found to be effective in restoring a depressed circulation after hemmorhage and shock. Further work is proceeding on its beneficial effects in muscular atrophy. In Hangchow last year there was a quarter-million dollars trade of the donkey skin in one store alone.

"It is of interest to note," states Dr. Bernard Read in his report on "The Newer Pharmacology and Ancient Medicine", "that the modern medicine of the 1909 British Pharmacopoeia only included nine substances of animal origin, and those nearly all, quite innocuous things like lard and wax. While modern science is turning to liver, stomach, vitamin A from the eye, adrenalin, etc., it is remarkable to find the use of so many animal tissues in ancient medicine."

In his recently published report mentioned above, Dr. Read presents a table showing twenty-six parts of six domestic animals used in old Chinese medicine. These animals include the cow, horse, pig, chicken, sheep and dog.

The velvet horn of the Skia deer and other species is taken as a drug in powder form and is very highly regarded by the Chinese. Recent studies by Russian scientists show that the male sex hormone is present.

The iris and lens of the sheep's eyes were given for dimness of vision and conjunctivitis. The eyes of the hawk, parrot and mackerel, were administered for night blindness. Recently Wald has isolated vitamin A from the iris of sheep's, pig's, cattle and frogs.

In old Chinese medicine, pig's liver was recommended for night blindness, beri-beri, emancipation etc. And has fairly recently found to be rich in vitamins A, B, C, D and E. A great many instances of this sort are cited. Shephard's purse is given as an excellent example of a medicinal herb cast aside for its apparent lack of potent principles which has been shown to be moderately rich in three of the vitamins and well justifies the old Chinese use of it for a number of maladies.

In China there has been preserved for something between 30 and 50 centuries remarkably accurate records of human experience in the field of medicine. These records are not accumulations of divine institutions but empirical findings which up to the present have only been sifted with the very coarse sieve of last century science.

摘自 1935 年 7 月 24 日《北华捷报》
Excerpt from *the North - China Herald*, on July 24, 1935

超级抢手的公寓

Little-known Apartments Showcase Hudec's Unique Legacy

俗称"绿房子"的吴同文住宅坐落于铜仁路北京西路转角，是建筑师邬达克的代表作之一。"绿房子"对面的红砖公寓楼也是他的作品。这座昔日名为"爱文义公寓"的大楼知名度不高，当年却十分抢手。

爱文义公寓今天叫联华公寓，1931年由联合房地产公司（Union Real Estate Co.）投资兴建，次年落成。大楼设计有56套公寓。

"大楼开工前，公寓几乎被本地家庭预订一空，只余2套。"1931年11月12日的英文《大陆报》报道。

同济大学华霞虹教授、《上海邬达克建筑地图》作者研究发现，当时因为租界人口和房产价格的一路飙升，各种住宅大楼在建成前通常已被大量预定。

在爱文义公寓兴建的20世纪30年代，上海的房地产公司纷纷致力于满足人们对现代公寓的巨大需求。

1931年《大陆报》的这篇报道就透露，"上海紧跟世界上其他大城市的发展，开始意识到公寓的好处。如今，住在公寓的人们无需操心拥有物业后的繁多琐事。相反，他们住在公寓里，从容地支付较高的租金。所以，在上海这样的城市里，建造两个大型公寓楼并在竣工前将其租掉是一件很平常的事，很少引起注意。"

报道还指出公寓受欢迎程度的两个其他原因，其中之一就是上海的租客们"有能力阅读并理解建筑图纸和图表，能够在大楼建成前想象公寓的模样"。

对此，华教授解释道："来预定的租客有不少是熟悉该工程的设计者，包括参与建设和审批的技术专家和公务员。这个项目的吸引力主要是其精致的功能布局、便利的交通和邻近的公共活动场地，并且只要支付少量租金就可以使用车库和电冰箱。"

而另一个原因是设计公寓的建筑师的知名度给租户带来信心，因为邬达克的公司曾负责设计建造上海很多最好的办公楼和公寓楼。

邬达克毕业于布达佩斯的匈牙利皇家约瑟夫技术大学建

筑系，1914年应征入伍参加一战，1916年不幸被俘。一战后奥匈帝国解体，在遣返途中的他隐藏了战俘身份，几经辗转，于1918年逃至上海，成为一位"国籍不明"的流亡者。

20世纪二三十年代的上海是远东最大的贸易、金融和工业中心，与纽约、伦敦、巴黎并称世界四大都市，房地产和建筑业蓬勃发展，邬达克身无分文且有腿伤，但这个受过专业建筑教育的年轻人正是当时上海需要的人才。他先在美国建筑师罗兰·克利（Rowland Curry）的克利洋行找到绘图员的工作，后自立门户，至1947年离开上海时，他设计建成了包括远东第一高楼——国际饭店、远东第一影院——大光明大戏院、远东第一豪宅——吴同文住宅、远东最豪华医院——宏恩医院、中国知名学府上海交通大学的扩建规划及其工程馆、中国最大的啤酒厂——联合啤酒厂等54个项目，近百个单体建筑。

2008年匈牙利驻沪总领馆和上海市政府举办"邬达克年"活

动，此后一系列邬达克活动和话题持续激发着公众对邬达克及其建筑的兴趣。上海市旅游局曾发布的"上海99个经典符号"名单里，邬达克作为唯一的外国人，与他的两件名作——国际饭店和武康大楼同时入选，被近百万参评者列为"喜欢上海的理由"。

根据《大陆报》报道，爱文义公寓的房型从一室到五室都有。大楼的外观宜人，内部宽敞，厨房和浴室铺设了瓷砖和水磨石。大楼设计有草坪、人行道和道路，提供私家车需要的设施。公寓位于城中富有吸引力的地段，靠近儿童游乐场。

值得一提的是，爱文义公寓的工程建造商是邬达克长期合作的洽兴营造厂（Yah Sing Co.）。洽兴营造厂由王才宏（1898—1987）创建于1925年，后办公室设在圆明园路209号806室，就在邬达克工作室的旁边。王才宏是与邬达克合作的最亲密的营造商，曾参与邬氏设计的闸北水电厂、真光、广学大楼、达华公寓、吴同文住宅、国际饭店等多个重要项目。

1935年9月14日《密勒氏评论》曾刊登一张摄于20世纪20年代的建筑照片，称这座由Dollar Company在霞飞路（今淮海路）和亚尔培路（陕西南路）转角处建造的大楼是上海第一座公寓大楼。

"在1920年之前的半个世纪中，住宅的标准形式是蓝色和灰色的砖结构建筑。当时，一扇门通往很多家庭的住宅是很罕见的。到了20世纪20年代，蒸汽供暖、现代化的抽水马桶和公寓房大约在同一时间出现……大多数公寓楼都是在上海建造的，这座城市的天际线已经完全改变。

全世界任何地方都找不到比上海这里更舒适和时髦的公寓了。"《密勒氏评论》报道写到。

根据1940年《大观园》杂志一篇题为《告上海寓公》的文章，上海公寓之所以受欢迎，是因为它们比旅馆生活起来更方便，房价因"包月"的关系收费也更便宜。

如今，红砖公寓是由三幢建筑组合而成，每座楼五至六层高。一位杨姓的物业经理透露，大多数公寓仍保留着昔日的格局，住户多为老年人。

华教授特别指出，今天的联华公寓包括三幢五至六层的板式住宅楼，这与邬达克最初的规划不尽相同。1931年规划的爱文义公寓只有两幢四层住宅楼，包含56套公寓。北面沿街设计有13个两层楼高的中国商店，其中一层用作店铺，二层为店主居室。住宅和商店之间是19个车库和一个锅炉房。今天沿北京西路建造的令人瞩目的六层弧形公寓和原来两幢楼的加层是何时何人所为，还有待进一步查证。

在这个现代公寓项目里，卧

室带有全套卫生设备，室内由新加坡红木铺地，设计有嵌入式壁橱。此外，公寓设有南北两套通行路线，业主和仆佣分别从南北入口进入。

爱文义公寓的建筑呈现现代风格，立面简洁。邬达克在窗间使用了清水红砖墙，在楼层间则使用米白色水刷石，两种颜色产生强烈的视觉效果。北面楼梯作竖向构图，南侧公寓沿哈同路形成流畅的弧面。阳台栏板中间和楼梯栏杆的铸铁花饰为艺术装饰风格。

当爱文义公寓在1931年被抢租时，邬达克正在迎来职业生涯的巅峰时期。他的三大代表作：国际饭店、大光明电影院和绿房

子，将在10年内沿着南京路陆续建成。

红砖的爱文义公寓虽然并非邬达克最知名的作品，但这个项目的热门为建筑师即将到来的成功打下伏笔。

昨天：爱文义公寓　**今日：**联华公寓　**地址：**北京西路 1348-1383 号
建造年代：1931-1932　**建筑师：**邬达克（L. E. Hudec）　**建筑风格：**现代风格
参观指南：可以在北京西路、铜仁路和南阳路欣赏这些建筑物。内部不对公众开放。

Opposite Laszlo Hudec's renowned "Green House" at the crossroads of Tongren Road (former Hardoon Road) and Beijing Road W. (former Avenue Road) are the architect's less well-known Avenue Apartments.

Situated at the edge of the International Settlement, the Avenue Apartments, widely known as Lianhua Apartments today, were financed by Union Real Estate Co., designed in 1931 and completed the following year. The 56 flats were much in demand.

"Before construction even started all the flats but two were snapped up by local families," *the China Press* reported on November 12.

Tongji University professor Hua Xiahong, author of the book *Shanghai Hudec Architecture*, added: "The buildings were constructed at a time when the population and real estate prices in the settlement were skyrocketing."

In the early 1930s, realty firms in Shanghai were accustomed to the enormous demand for apartments in new buildings.

"Shanghai had become apartment-conscious, following the trend of other big cities, and today persons who live here see no reason for worrying about the thousand and one details of home-owing," the 1931 *China Press* report stated.

"Instead, they live in apartments and calmly pay the higher rentals. The building of two large apartment blocks and the renting of them before completion, therefore, is a common and seldom a noteworthy event in a city like Shanghai."

The report also attributed the popularity to two other reasons.

One was that Shanghai flat-seekers were able to read and understand blueprints and diagrams.

"Many tenants were participating technicians or civil servants, who were familiar with the project," professor Hua said. "They were attracted by the functional layout, the convenient transportation and adequate facilities for public activity in the neighborhood. Permission to use the garage and refrigerators for only a small amount of money was an added bonus."

The other reason was the reputation of Hudec, whose firm had been responsible for a number of the best office and apartment buildings in the city.

Born in Beszterce Banya (now Banska Bistrica in Slovakia) in the Austro-Hungarian Empire in 1893, Hudec was involved in

54 architectural projects, including the Park Hotel and the Grand Theatre in the center of Nanjing Road, during his 29 years in Shanghai.

After he left for Switzerland in 1947 and later the United States, his name was nearly forgotten until the 2008 "Year of Hudec", organized by the Shanghai government and the Hungarian Consulate.

The event fired public interest in the legendary architect and Shanghai's architectural heritage which has proved long lasting.

In 2014 he was voted as a "Shanghai Symbol" by millions of Chinese in an online poll, the only foreigner in a galaxy of Chinese celebrities.

His two masterpieces, the Park Hotel and the Normandie Apartments on Wukang Road, were also listed in the "99 Shanghai Symbols" in a campaign launched by the city's tourism bureau to find "reasons for loving Shanghai".

There are two Hudec memorial rooms in Shanghai now. One opened in 2013, in Hudec's former English villa home on Panyu Road. The other opened last year in the architect's last Shanghai residence, the former Hubertus Court, now the Jinjiang Metro-Polo Hotel Classiq in Jing'an District.

Back in Hudec's hometown, part of a building designed by Hudec's father, Juraj Hudec, has been turned into the "Centre of architecture L. E. Hudec" showcasing the work of both father and son.

According to *the China Press*, the Avenue Apartments featured flats of one-room to five-room suites.

With a delightful exterior appearance, the Avenue Apartments were roomy inside. Tiling and terrazzo were liberally used in kitchens and bathrooms.

There were lawns, walkways and roads. Facilities for private motor cars were offered. Situated in an inviting section of the city, the apartments were close to the children's playgrounds.

The Yah Sing Construction Company, Hudec's long-time collaborating firm, was the contractor for the Avenue Apartments.

According to an article in a 1940 Chinese magazine *The Grand View*, the popularity of apartments in Shanghai was because they were more convenient and cheaper than hotels.

Today, the apartments are a cluster of three residential buildings, each with five to six floors. A housing manager surnamed Yang said most flats retain the original layout and many residents are elderly.

"The 1931 plan shows only two four-story apartments in 56 suites," professor Hua said.

"Fronting the street, there are a number of two story Chinese shops. The boiler room and 19 garages were installed between the residence and the shops."

In the initial design, each floor of the four-story apartments was divided into four sections. Every section contained suites ranging from one to five bedrooms, which were equipped with a bathroom, gas cooker and hot water sup-ply. A ventilating shaft was used to provide fresh air for the bathrooms lacking natural ventilation and lighting.

The rooms were paved with Singapore mahogany flooring and had in-wall closets.

The architect designed two entry and exit routes. Owners could walk in from the southern entrance which had a grand staircase, while the servants entered through the northern gate with a narrow staircase.

The buildings are essentially modern in style with a simple-cut facade.

Hudec used red-brick walls between the windows and a rustic finish between the floors. A strong visual effect is thus created by the contrasting creamy and red colors.

The northern staircase is in a vertical design while the southern facade constructs a fluent arc with Tongren Road. The balustrades over the balconies and staircases are graced by Art-Deco cast iron patterns.

When the Avenue Apartments were snapped up in 1931, Hudec was at the peak of his career. His three signature works, the Park Hotel, the Grand Theatre and the Green House, which were

admired as the No. 1 hotel, No. 1 cinema and No. 1 luxury residence in the Far East, were about to be built one after another in the following years along Nanjing Road.

The Avenue Apartments are certainly a lesser-known Hudec work, but their popularity led to the architect's future success that became part of Shanghai architectural history.

Yesterday: Avenue Apartments   **Today:** Lianhua Apartments
Address: 1348-1383 Beijing Rd W.   **Date of construction:** 1931-1932
Architect: L. E. Hudec   **Architectural style:** Modern Art Deco
Tips: The buildings can be appreciated on Beijing Rd W. Tongren Road and Nanyang Road. The interior is not open to the public.

　　上面这张照片摄于1920年代初。这是上海第一座公寓大楼,由Dollar Company在霞飞路(今淮海路)和亚尔培路(陕西南路)转角处建造。

　　与上海相比,世界上只有两个城市的建筑发生了相同的变化,分别是洛杉矶和底特律。然而,在这两个城市中,都没有像黄浦江畔那样逆转了本地建筑风格。在1920年之前的半个世纪中,住宅的标准形式是蓝色和灰色的砖结构建筑。当时,一扇门通往很多家庭的住宅是很罕见的。到20世纪20年代,蒸汽供暖、现代化的抽水马桶和公寓房大约在同一时间出现。奇怪的是,英国人在自己的国家里完全依赖老式壁炉,在那里身体的前面烤得很热,后背仍然冰凉。而在上海,他们却是所有国家里最坚决要求供暖的。英国人还与美国人竞争,宁愿选择公寓式的居住方式,也不愿使用层高很高、房间多的房屋。大多数公寓楼都是在上海建造的,这座城市的天际线已经完全改变。全世界任何地方都找不到比上海这里更舒适和时髦的公寓了。

The above photo, taken in the early 1920s, shows the first apartment building in Shanghai, built by officials of the Dollar Company at the corner of Avenue Joffre and Roi de Albert.

There are only two cities in the world where there has been an equal change in the building situated compared to Shanghai—namely Los Angeles and Detroit. In neither of those cities, however, has there been such a reversal of local architectural styles as there has been here on the banks of the Whangpoo. For half a century previous to 1920 the standardized form of dwelling house was a blue and grey brick structure. A door through which more than one family would enter their homes was indeed a rarity. Steam heat, modern flush toilets and apartment houses all came in about the same time, and curiously enough the British population, which in its own country is so thoroughly wedded to the old-fashioned fireplace, where you toast the front half of your body and freeze the rear part, has been the most insistent of all nationalities in Shanghai in demanding steam heat. The British have also vied with Americans in preferring the apartment style of living to the old-fashioned high-ceilinged house with many rooms, but mostly was built in Shanghai, the skyline has been entirely changed. Nowhere in the world are more comfortable and up-to-date apartment houses to be found than here in Shanghai.

摘自 1935 年 9 月 14 日《密勒氏评论》

Excerpt from *The China Weekly Review,* on September 14, 1935

神秘的共济会堂

Building Preserves Secrets of the Freemasons

美国作家丹·布朗（Dan Brown）的畅销书《达芬奇密码》（The Da Vinci Code）点燃了公众对神秘组织共济会的兴趣。在上海市中心的南京西路附近，一座新古典主义风格的共济会堂至今犹存。1931年，共济会堂从外滩迁到北京西路1623号现址，老会堂在被卖掉后遭拆除。

著名学者何新撰文提到，共济会在明清之际就进入中国，北京西路大楼是共济会在上海的一处遗迹。大楼正面的六芒大卫之星纹饰是共济会的重要标志之一，但关于这幢楼房的来历和资料，在目前已出版的介绍上海老建筑的书刊上都没有提到过，"好像这幢大楼从来不存在似的"。

圣约翰大学原校长卜舫济（F. L. Hawks Pott）在1928年出版的《上海简史》（A Short History of Shanghai）中提到，共济会在上海生活中扮演过重要角色。

"我们发现第一家分会——北华分会（Northern Lodge of China）——成立于1849年，紧随其后的是1863年的皇家苏塞克斯分会（Royal Sussex

Lodge），最早设在花园弄（Park Lane，今南京路）。而外滩共济会堂（the Masonic Hall）的奠基石是1865年7月安放的，那是在外滩滨水区最早出现的吸引人的建筑之一。"卜舫济写道。

上海历史学家吴志伟研究发现，共济会起源于欧洲中世纪的石匠组织。

"1843年上海开埠后，共济会在这里成立了十几个分支机构，其中的北华分会、皇家苏赛克斯分会和塔司干分会（Tuscan Lodge）共同建造了外滩共济会

堂。几个世纪以来，共济会的组织以神秘而闻名。作为世界上最大的秘密组织之一，其大部分的成员都是白人男性、自由思想者和社会精英。"吴志伟说。

外滩共济会堂的位置就在外滩29号东方汇理银行大楼和33号英国领事馆之间，原址如今是半岛酒店。共济会堂中文被译为"规矩会堂"，这是因为共济会的标志是圆规和矩尺——中世纪建造教堂的石匠们常用的两件工具。何新认为，会堂当年能在外滩这样的黄金地段占上一席之地，这从另一个方面也反映了共济会的实力。

规矩会堂每两年举行一次慈善募款舞会，此时会堂就会对公众开放。舞会是上海最大型的宴会活动之一，非常受欢迎，共济会的神秘特色也为活动增色不少。参加舞会的人数从1886年不到400人攀升到1910年的1200多人。原先宽敞的大厅变得拥挤，所以此时规矩会堂迎来一次改造。不幸的是，1918年一场大火部分损毁了这座美丽的大楼，后来共济会又把会堂卖给日本邮船株式会社（Japan Mail Shipping Line）。后者拆除了大楼，但却没有建造新楼。

1930年4月15日，英文《北华捷报》刊登了一张新规矩会堂的设计图，与今日北京西路1623号的建筑十分相似。

"可能大家会记得外滩旧规矩会堂在3年前卖给了日本邮船株式会社。今年初，共济会用这笔钱在爱文义路（今北京西路）和胶州路的东南角买到一块合适的基地。为了新会堂设计方案，共济会举行了一个小型设计竞赛，有6位建筑师参加。获胜的设计师J. E. March先生是英国皇家建筑师学会注册建筑师，来自英商马海洋行

THE NEW MASONIC HALL AS IT IS TO BE

（Messrs Spence, Robinson & Partners）。值得一提的是，这位建筑师还设计了1924年落成的外滩和平女神像纪念碑，1941年纪念碑不幸被日军拆毁。

报道提到，这张图显示设计方案面向爱文义路，建筑内部根据共济兄弟会的需求而规划，外观庄严美观。大楼将由英国、苏格兰和爱尔兰的共济会员使用，而美国分会（the American lodges）两年前已在贝当路（Avenue Petain，今衡山路）建造了一座会堂。

根据静安区房地局资料，这座共济会堂是一座砖混结构建筑，呈现新古典主义风格，顶部有三角形大山花，立面装饰有两根巨大的爱奥尼石柱。

20世纪50年代，这里由包括上海医学会在内的6家学会共同使用。1985年，三层高的会堂加建了一层，2003年和2015年历经两次大修。

如今，这里由多家医学会和机构使用。大楼仍保留着原始的柚木地板、楼梯和礼堂。浅绿色调的礼堂设计简洁，但仍装饰着神秘的图案与符号。礼堂的一扇门通往幽深的藏书室。藏书楼里有高达两层的巨大书架，有些神似电影《哈利

波特》中魔法学校的图书馆。

上海医学会图书馆副馆长张燮林介绍，这里藏有2000多本医学文献典籍，其中大多数都是中医书籍。上海医学会曾接待过前来参观的海外共济会员，他们辨认出了礼堂里的符号。这座大楼的红色木门仍装饰着共济会的标志——圆规和矩尺图案。

学者何新提到1949年以前，上海、威海、天津和厦门都有共济会的建筑遗迹。北京西路这座新共济会堂有一块石碑，上面刻有上海几位共济会成员的名字和大楼建造日期——1931年1月。

有趣的是，1931年在这块石碑上被写为"AL 5931"。"AL"是Anno Lucis的缩写，意思是"光年"。根据共济会的日历系统，公元1931是光历5931年，因此写成"AL 5931"。

"在维修大楼时，我们在这块石碑后面的墙壁里还发现了一个铁盒，里面装着《圣经》和两支古

董钢笔，还在发现一楼护墙板后的墙上刻有该建筑捐建者们的名字。"张馆长说。

2017年，这座鲜为人知的共济会堂被列入第五批上海市优秀历史建筑名录。

"我们计划将这座礼堂改造成一个面向医学专业人士和学者的'医学人文之家'，以促进更好的研究与交流。"张馆长说。

昨天： 共济会堂　**今天：** 上海市医学会　**建造年代：** 1931 年

建筑师： 马海洋行（Spence, Robinson & Partners）的 A.R.I.B.A. J. E. March

建筑风格： 新古典主义

参观指南： 该建筑物不对公众开放，但可以欣赏立面左下角奠基石上的原始铭文。

Dan Brown's best-selling novels *The Da Vinci Code* and *The Lost Symbol* aroused international interest in Freemasonry.

And while people may read the books and view the resulting movies to satisfy their curiosity, it is rarely known that a former three-story Masonic Hall in neoclassical style still stands in down-town Shanghai.

The society moved to the Beijing Road W. building near the former Bubbling Well Road after its structure on the Bund was sold and demolished in the 1930s.

"The building at 1623 Beijing Road W., now the office of the Shanghai Medical Association, is an important relic of Freemason-

ry in Shanghai," Chinese historian/economist He Xin wrote in his book *Who Rules the World*.

"However, the building is often missed out by publications on Shanghai historical architecture," He said, who has studied and written about the secret society.

"Shanghai, Weihai, Tianjin and Xiamen all have relics of Freemasonry before 1949," he noted.

According to F. L. Hawks Pott's 1928 book *A Short History of Shanghai*, Masonry played an important part in Shanghai life.

"We find that the first Lodge — the Northern Lodge — was established in 1849," Pott wrote.

"This was followed by the Sussex Lodge in 1863. Its first home was in Park Lane (now Nanjing Road). The foundation stone of the new Hall on The Bund was laid in July 1865, and was one of the first buildings of pleasing character to appear on the water front."

Shanghai historian Wu Zhiwei said the Freemasons have their origins in organizations for Medieval masons.

"Freemasonry founded over a dozen branches in Shanghai after the city opened as a port in 1843, among them were Northern Lodge of China, Royal Sussex Lodge and Tuscan Lodge that co-funded the construction of the Bund," Wu said.

They also had a reputation for

RT WOR BRO HENRY ....
D.G.M NORTHERN CHINA ENGLISH CONSTITUTION
RT WOR BRO F.G PENFOLD HON J.G.W.
D.G.M OF SCOTTISH FREEMASONRY IN NORTH CHINA &
WOR BRO STEWART C. YOUNG
PAST MASTER LODGE ERIN NO. 46.... 1913 CONSTITUTION
REPRESENTING THE ENGLISH IRISH AND SCOTTISH
CONSTITUTIONS IN THE PRESENCE OF MANY BRETHREN
ON ..... DAY OF JANUARY A.D. 1931 A.L. 5931

secrecy for centuries.

"As one of the world's largest secret societies nowadays, most of their members are white male Protestants, free thinkers and social elites," Wu added.

The site of the former Masonic Hall on the Bund is now occupied by the Peninsula Hotel.

The Chinese name "Kwei-Ken-Tang" meant "Compass and Square Hall" according to Masonic symbols "compass and square", two crafting tools used by masons who built stone churches.

The society's most revered room would be open to the public when hosting the famous biannual Masonic Ball for charity fund raising.

Symbolic mysteries added glamor to the ball, which was regarded as the city's largest feast and enjoyed great popularity.

The fewer than 400 participants in 1886 soared to 1,200 to 1,300 in 1910. The once spacious hall became crowded, which lead to a renovation in the 1910s. But unfortunately the building was partially damaged by a fire in 1918 and later sold to the Japan Mail Shipping Line (NYK), which demolished it and left the lot vacant.

On April 15, 1930, *the North-China Herald* published a drafting of the new Masonic Hall, which looks very like the one on today's Beijing Road W. .

"As may be remembered the old Masonic Hall on the Bund was sold to the NYK nearly three years ago," the article states.

"With the proceeds a desirable site at the southeast corner of the Avenue Road and Kiaochow Road crossing was bought at the beginning of this year. For the design for the new building a limited competition was held, six architects taking part. The author of the winning design is Mr J.E. March, A.R.I.B.A., of Messrs Spence, Robinson & Partners. The picture shows Mr March's design as it will front on Avenue Road (today's Beijing Road W.). The interior of the building is as well planned for the needs of the Masonic fraternity as the exterior is handsome and imposing."

The report noted that the building would house English, Scottish and Irish Masons. The American lodges had built a hall adjoining Avenue Petain (today's Hengshan Road) two years ago.

According to archives from Jing'an District House and Land Management Bureau, the building is a brick-and-concrete structure in neoclassical style with a triangle gable over the top. The facade is adorned with two gigantic Ionic Orders.

In the 1950s it was assigned to six academic societies, including the Shanghai Medical Association.

In 1985, a fourth floor was added to the building. The building was renovated in 2003 and 2015.

Currently housing a myriad of medical societies and organizations, the building is well preserved with the original teak wood flooring, staircase and most amazingly, a green-toned grand hall adorned with patterns and symbols.

A door in the hall leads to a dim-lighted old bibliotheca with a high ceiling and double-level book shelves, reminiscence of another era and a library in a *Harry Potter* movie.

Zhang Xielin, deputy director of the Shanghai Medical Association's bibliotheca, said it has more than 2,000 antique medical books, most of which are on traditional Chinese medicine.

Officer Hua Fei from the Shanghai Medical Society recalled receiving Freemason guests from overseas, who recognized symbols in the hall. Some red wooden doors of the building are still graced with the society's signature — "Compass and Square".

In his book, scholar He Xin

specifically mentioned a stone tablet in the new Masonic Hall, which is inscribed with the names of several Freemasons in Shanghai as well as the construction date — January 1931.

The year "1931" was also written as "AL 5931" on the stone according to a calendar system within the Freemason fraternity. "AL" is an abbreviation for Anno Lucis, which means "Year of Light".

"We found an iron case hidden in the walls behind this stone tablet which contained a bible and two antique pens," Zhang with the medical association added.

"Another wall behind the dado is inscribed with names of expatriates who gave donations for the construction."

To ensure protection for the building, which was not listed in 2012, He lobbied the municipal government.

In 2017, the building was listed in the fifth batch of Shanghai Historical Buildings.

"And we have a plan to renovate this bibliotheca hall into a 'family' for medical professionals and scholars for better research and communication," Zhang said.

Yesterday: Masonic Hall   **Today:** The Shanghai Medical Association
Date of construction: 1931
Architect: J. E. March, A.R.I.B.A., of Messrs Spence, Robinson & Partners.
Architectural Style: Neoclassic
Tips: The building is not open to the public but you can admire the original inscription at the left bottom base stone.

毗邻共济会堂的第一基督科学会堂
The First Christian Science Church in China

1934年11月4日（星期日），上海第一基督教科学教会在这幢新的教堂大楼内举行了仪式。新教堂位于爱文义路和胶州路转角处。

这是在中国建造的第一座基督教科学教堂，开幕式将是奉献典礼之一，教堂完工准备投入使用，没有任何债务。

1934年3月22日奠基的教堂结构已接近完成。这座建筑是一些人寄予目标和希望的物质体现。在过去的20年里。他们因为基督科学教而相识。

教堂根据哈沙德洋行（the firm of Elliott Hazzard，Architects）的设计建造，弧形立面所遵循的风格源自经典罗马风。

教堂用用灰泥覆盖的砖建造，其外观与浅黄色石灰石相似。入口门的上方用铜字写着"First Church of Christs' Scientist"（基督的第一教会的科学家），两侧是艺术设计的铸铁灯笼。

根据该建筑基地的形状，半圆形或扇形平面似乎是唯一可能的解决方案。

　　但这被证明是一个理想的机会，因为随之而来的安排特别适合于基督教科学教的仪式，从而允许面向读经师的桌子进行方便的座位安排。（注：基督教科学派或称科学教派The Church of Christ, Scientist是基督教新教的一个边缘教派，由Mary Baker Eddy于1879年创立，礼仪简朴严格，由读经师主持）

　　整个建筑的内部装饰在各方面都保持现代和艺术性，同时又简约而节制，其设计想法是保持一种安静庄严的氛围。必须承认，整个建筑无论内部外部，都是装饰性的经典设计方面一项令人称赞的成就，再加上最富有吸引力又很柔和的家具，为快速增长的上海精美建筑又添加了显著的一笔。

　　1914年，第一个基督教科学教派的阅览室开幕，自那时以来，阅览室一直运营，现在的阅览室位于南京路49号中央拱廊8b室。1915年，基督教科学派举行了第一次免费公共讲座。

　　1928年，该组织获得了足够的会员资格，成为上海基督科学派第一教会，就是今天的名字。.

　　教会仪式一直在外滩共济会堂举行。该建筑被拆除后，又在皇家亚洲学会位于博物馆路（今虎丘路）的建筑中进行。当美国共济会堂在杜福路（今乌鲁木齐南路）上建成时，他们就在那里举行活动，直到现在。

1934年12月2日晚9点15分，一个星期天的晚上，来自马萨诸塞州波士顿市的曾长期居住在科学教派创始人玛丽·贝克·埃迪（Mary Baker Eddy）家中的第一科学教派会员，将在这座新教堂发表演讲。

On Sunday, November 4, 1934, the First Church of Christ, Scientist, Shanghai held services in this new church building, located at the corner of Avenue and Kiaochow roads.

This is the first Christian Science church to be erected in China, and the opening service will be one of dedication, the edifice being finished and ready for occupancy, free from all debt.

The cornerstone for this building was laid on March 22, 1934, and this structure, now almost completed, is the material embodiment of the aims and hopes of a small group of people who, for the past twenty years, have met for the holding of Christian Science services.

It is built according to the designs of the firm of Elliott Hazzard, Architects, and the style adhered to in the curved facade is derived from the classic Roman.

Brick, covered with plaster, was used in its construction, and the exterior is similar in appearance to buff limestone. Above the entrance doorway, in bronze letters, are the words "First Church of Christs' Scientist", and wrought-iron lanterns of artistic design flank the central doorway.

In conforming to the shape of this building site, the semi-circular or fan-shaped plan seemed the only possible solution.

This necessity, however, proved a desirable opportunity, as the arrangement ensuing is especially well adapted to Christian Science services, permitting a convenient seating arrangement with respect to the Readers' desk.

The interior finish throughout of this building, while modern and artistic in every respect, has been kept simple and restrained, with the idea of preserving an atmosphere of quiet repose and dignity. It must be conceded that the entire edifice, within and without, is an admirable achievement in decorative and classic design, combined with most attractive though subdued furnishings, a notable and outstanding addition to the fast-growing collection of Shanghai's fine buildings.

In 1914, the first public Christian Science Reading Room was opened and since that time a Reading Room has been constantly maintained, the present one being located at Room 8b, Central Arcade, 49 Nanking Road. The first free public lecture on Christian Science was given in 1915.

In the year 1928 this Society had attained a membership sufficient to become organized as First Church of Christ, Scientist, Shanghai, and thus it is known today.

Services were held in the Masonic Hall on the Bund until that building was demolished, when they were held at the Royal Asiatic Society's building on Museum Road (today's Huqiu Road). When the American Masonic Temple was built on Route Dufour (today's Urumqi Road S.), they arranged to hold their services there, and have been in that location ever since.

The First Church of Christ, Scientist of Boston, Mass, and for many years resident in the home of Mary Baker Eddy, the founder of Christian Science, will lecture in Shanghai, in this new church edifice, on Sunday evening, December 2, 1934, at 9:15pm.

摘自 1934 年 11 月 7 日《北华捷报》
Excerpt from *The North-China Herald, on* November 7, 1934

购物中心里的石库门
Shikumen House in a Shopping Mall

南京西路静安嘉里中心的建筑风貌十分独特：几座白色通透的现代建筑环绕着一行深褐色石库门里弄房。其中门牌号码为"安义路63号"的一间是1920年毛泽东旧居，这一行石库门因此得以保留，成为上海现存不多的早期石库门住宅之一。

藏在购物中心广场里的石库门虽然面积不大，映射的历史却很丰富。这里原为安义路民厚南里，与安义路北侧的民厚北里同为犹太富商哈同的房产。

1910到1912年，哈同以旧式里弄建筑风格，投资建造了民厚南里和民厚北里这两个"现代

社区"，租售房屋获利。民厚南里有七条弄堂，兴建有砖木结构二层石库门房屋203幢，建筑面积21733平方米。而民厚北里有五条弄堂，建有同样的石库门房屋135幢，建筑面积15884平方米。为方便居民生活，哈同还在这里兴建了一座现代菜场，招徕菜贩和商户入驻经营，提供"配套服务"。后来因为哈同的房产都改成以"慈"字当头，这两个社区也分别改名为"慈厚南里"和"慈厚北里"。

时筠仓所著的《静安石库门》一书记载，慈厚南里曾有两套门牌号，一套是哈同为收房

租而使用的，另一套是管理公共
租界的工部局收房捐时用的。
1934年后工部局的门牌号重新编
过，后来上海革命历史纪念馆调
查小组在安义路63号找到了遗留
下来的哈同使用过的门牌号码：
"民厚南里29号"。1920 年 5
月 5 日至 7 月 7 日，年仅27岁
的毛泽东曾寓居在"民厚南里 29
号"。

　　《静安历史文化图录》记载
了毛泽东早年到访静安寺路的经
历。1919年3月他到上海参加寰球
中国学生会（World's Chinese

Students' Federation）召开的
第一二批赴法留学生欢送会。学生
会早期会址在静安寺路（今南京西
路）51号，后迁卡德路（石门二
路）191号。1920年5月，毛泽东
又作为湖南驱逐督军张敬尧运动的
赴京请愿团代表来上海，居住在
民厚南里29号，直至7月7日离开
上海去长沙。1924年2月中旬毛泽
东再到上海，6月夫人杨开慧携儿
子毛岸英、毛岸青前来团聚，全家
寓居慕尔鸣路（今茂名南路）甲秀
里，直到12月去湖南。

　　1949年后，根据毛泽东致同

乡、北京大学中文系主任兼文学院院长黎锦熙(邵西)信函,确定毛泽东1920年在上海的寓所为哈同路(铜仁路)民厚南里29号,并于1959年5月26日公布为上海市文物保护单位。

据李思安回忆,民厚南里29号是她作为"驱张代表团"成员在上海出面租借的,用作湖南改造促进会会员到上海活动的住处。1920年5月5日毛泽东抵沪,开展了驱逐湖南军阀张敬尧的斗争活动,探讨了湖南改造问题,并参加"半淞园会议",讨论了新民学会会务问题,其间的两个月都是居住在哈同路民厚南里29号。

毛泽东在民厚南里的日子艰苦而充实。他睡在二楼靠北的落地窗下的板床上,每月仅有3元零用钱,大家轮流做饭,常吃廉价的蚕豆煮米饭、青菜豆腐汤,还要为人洗衣服。但他每天阅读上海出版的报纸、杂志和介绍西方学术思想的译著。在此期间,他还多次拜访陈独秀,与之讨论马克思主义,酝酿创建中国共产党,并在报刊上发表宣扬革命的"激扬文字",积极投身革命活动。毛泽东曾说过,

这个时期在他一生中可能是关键性的时期。

在20世纪20年代的上海,这片石库门里弄还入住了一批近代名人,如郭沫若、田汉、张闻天、施蛰存、徐悲鸿、严复、廖仲恺、何香凝、左舜生、戴望舒等,成为中国现代文学史、思想史上重要的文人聚集区。他们和毛泽东一样,当时大都在意气风发、充满理想的年纪,从世界和全国各地汇聚在这片静安寺路石库门里弄,在各自的领域里探索、学习、交流。

日本作家村松梢风在1924年出版的小说《魔都》中,对民厚南里和民厚北里的中国文人有着生动细致的回忆。

他先拿着佐藤春夫的介绍函,去了静安寺路上的中华书局编辑部拜访当时还是文学青年的田汉。他描述静安寺路是"一条电车不通的住宅街,道路很宽,两边尽是很大的宅邸,纯然西式景象"。

"田君的家就在附近的民厚北里。折入一条弄堂一直往里走,在尽头处有一扇大门,一丈左右高的木门半掩着。约有门两倍高的围

墙将邻家隔了开来，其处有一棵似是朴树的古木枝叶繁茂。房子看上去很大，楼下一侧的房间可看见上了年纪的老妇人等的身影。田汉噔噔地快步走上了狭窄的楼梯，将我带到了二楼他自己的书房。房间里放着一张简朴的床，有个二十岁左右的年轻人睡在那里，我们进房间时，那人醒了，走了出去。瞧了一下书架，见上面放满了英文的小说和日文的文学书，书桌上放着一部文稿的校样。" 村松梢风在《魔都》（徐静波 译）中写道。

他提到，二十六岁的田汉读托尔斯泰、陀思妥耶夫斯基的作品，将来想当一名剧作家。

在小说中的另一篇文章里，他写到在田汉家与郭沫若、林伯渠、黄日葵等人餐叙后，应郭沫若邀请去他民厚南里的家做客。

"走出了混凝土地面的犹如隧道般的民厚北里，有个小小的市场。穿过这条街，就到了民厚南里的入口。这是一条相当整齐的弄堂，中间是一条笔直的道路，左右两边则是对称的横向小弄堂。在东头第五个横向弄堂拐进去，就是郭君的家了。最前面的一个像是玄关一样的房间里，放着桌子、椅子和塞满了洋书的书橱。" 村松梢风写道，他发现郭沫若的太太是日本人。我来到了自己所尊敬的外国人的家里，结果他的太太是自己的同胞，这事情总觉得像是奇迹一般。总而言之，我沉浸在一种感慨而激动的心绪中。觉得很兴奋。"他写道。

根据《静安石库门》一书，民厚北里大部分为坐北朝南、砖木结构的穿斗式木构架二层石库门住宅，仅沿安南路（现安义路）一排为坐南朝北的店房建筑，毛泽东居住过的29号（现安义路63号）为其中一间。开间宽度3.6米，主体为木结构承重，横墙为五柱落地立帖式构架，圆柱杉木。木楼板由杉木长板条组成，楼梯均为木楼梯，外墙面及室内隔墙采用黏土青砖。

1960年，上海文物局收回安义路61-67号四幢房屋，迁出原居民，并计划复原63号，将61号改作办公室，65号和67号用作接待。上海民用设计院进行复原设计

后，1963年旧居修缮完成，但并未对外开放，仅竖有旧居碑石。1995年因建造延安中路，民厚南里和民厚北里均被拆除，只留下安义路61-67号这一排房子。

安义路毛泽东旧居也是上海保存较好的早期石库门住宅，现在作为"1920年毛泽东旧居"向公众开放。旧居建筑面积83平方米，一楼原为客堂间，楼上是卧室，据说当年毛泽东睡在靠北的落地长窗旁的板床上。旧居的展陈空间非常迷你，却可以了解早期石库门住宅的内部结构，回味百年前在这片土地上激荡的青春岁月。

2020年12月26日毛泽东诞辰127周年之际，上海市委党史办与静安区委在安义路63号举行"初心足迹：毛泽东在上海"红色研学线路首发仪式。这条路线串起了毛泽东在不同时代到上海的足迹，其中一站就是静安嘉里中心里的这间石库门。

昨天： 民厚南里 29 号　**今天：** 1920 年毛泽东旧居　**地址：** 安义路 63 号
参观指南： 安义路旧居对公众开放，建议参观毛泽东位于静安区的另外两处旧居纪念馆：茂名北路 120 弄旧居和三曾里（现浙江北路 118 号中共三大后中央局机关历史纪念馆）。

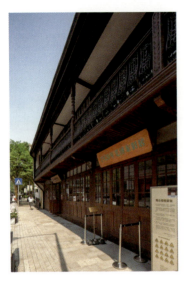

The Jing'an Kerry Center on Nanjing Road W. features a unique architectural scene: a line of dark brown Shikumen (stone-framed gate) lane houses are encircled by white, transparent modern buildings. One of the lane houses, No. 63 Anyi Road is Chairman Mao Zedong's former residence in 1920. Thanks to this, the line of lane houses has been preserved in the center of a shopping mall.

The lane houses are small in size, but rich in history. No. 63, Anyi Road was formerly No. 29, South Minhou Lane on Hardoon Road (today's Tongren Road) which was later changed to No. 29, South Cihou Lane. South and North Minhou lanes were both Shikumen residential compounds developed by Jewish tycoon Silas Hardoon between 1910 and 1912. Hardoon built the two "modern communities" and profit from collecting rents.

Covering an area of 16,735 square meters with a floor area of 21,733 square meters, South Minhou Lane features 203 Shikumen houses in seven lanes which are two-story brick-and-wood structures. North Minhou Lane is a bit smaller in scale, containing 135 Shikumen houses in five lanes. Hardoon even constructed a modern wet market for the convenience of residents.

The house at 63 Anyi Road was the residence where Mao Zedong, at the age of 27, lived from May 5 to July 7 in 1920.

According to the book *Jing'an History and Culture Catalogue*, Mao Zedong's early footprints in Shanghai were along the former Bubbling Well Road (today's Nanjing Road W.).

In March 1919, he came to participate in the farewell party for Chinese students setting off to France. It was organized by the World's Chinese Students' Federation. The meeting site was at 51 Bubbling Well Road, which was moved to 191 Carter Road (today's Shimen Road 2).

In May 1920, Mao came to Shanghai again as a representative of the movement in Hunan Province to expel warlord Zhang Jingyao. During the two months living here, Mao attended meetings, visited revolutionist Chen Duxiu many times to discuss Maxism with him and published articles themed in Chinese revolution. He called the time in Shanghai a crucial period of his life.

In February 1924, Mao visited Shanghai again and was joined by his wife Yang Kaihui and their two little sons Anying and Anqing in June. The Maos lived in Jiaxiu Lane on Moulmein Road (today's Maoming Road S.) before they left for Hunan in December.

After 1949, according to an old letter from Mao Zedong to Li Jinxi, dean of the Chinese Department of Peking University, it was decided that Mao's residence in Shanghai in 1920 was No. 19, South Minhou Lane. It was announced as a Shanghai Municipal Cultural Relics on May 26, 1959.

In the 1920s, this community was also home to a galaxy of modern China's cultural elites, such as literati Guo Moruo, playwright Tian Han, artist Xu Bei-

hong, translator Yan Fu etc.. Like Mao Zedong of the times, they were also young people with passions and spiritual pursuits. They came from all over the world and all around China to gather in this Shikumen community, to explore new ideas and creations.

In his 1924 novel *Mato (The Magic City)*, Japanese writer Shofu Muramatsu recalls visits to homes of Chinese literati in North and South Minhou lanes.

He described the Bubbling Well Road as a wide residential street flanked by very large mansions, featuring "a purely Western-style scene".

According to his writing, Tian Han's home in the North Minhou Lane was behind a tall wooden gate and fronted by an old tree. A narrow staircase led to Tian's study on the second floor. There were English novels and Japanese literary books on the bookshelf and a manuscript on the desk. The Japanese writer mentioned that the 26-year-old Tian Han read the works of Tolstein and Dostoevsky and wanted to be a playwright in the future.

In another article in the novel, Muramatsu noted that he was invited by Guo Moruo to his home in South Minhou Lane after a din-

ner.

"This was a fairly neat alley with a straight road in the middle. There were symmetrical horizontal smaller lanes on the left and right sides. Turn in from the fifth horizontal lane at the east end was Guo's home. The front room was like a hallway, with a table, chairs and a bookcase stuffed with foreign books," Muramatsu wrote, who was excited to find that Guo's wife was Japanese.

According to the book *Shikumen Houses in Jing'an District*, most Shikumen residences here are two-story brick-and-wood structures with wooden frames. The line of surviving houses on Anyi Road used to have shops on the ground floor sitting south to north along the street.

Mao's former residence has a floor area of 83 square meters. The width of the bay is 3.6 meters. The horizontal wall features a five-column vertical frame with cylindrical fir. The stairs are made of wood. The exterior walls and interior partition walls are built with clay bricks.

In 1960, the Shanghai Municipal Bureau of Cultural Relics took back the houses at 61-67 Anyi Road for renovation. The old residence was renovated in 1963 but it was not open to the public. Only a stone monument was erected here. In 1995, both North and South Minhou Lanes were demolished due to the construction of Yan'an Road M.. Only the line of houses at 61-67 Anyi Road remained.

Today, the residence is open to the public as "the Former Residence of Mao Zedong in 1920".

It's also a precious example of early Shikumen residence in Shanghai.

The ground floor which originally had a sitting room is now an exhibition hall. Upstairs is the bedroom where Mao had slept on the slatted bed next to the French window on the north. The exhibition space of the old residence is very small, but it showcases the layout of early Shikumen residences and the youthful years of Mao and others on this land century ago.

On December 26, 2020, on the occasion of the 127th anniversary of Mao Zedong's birth, the Shanghai Municipal Office of the History of the Communist Party and the Jing'an District Government launched a visiting route named "Initial Footprint: Mao Zedong in Shanghai" in front of the 1920 residence. This route features Shanghai buildings where Mao had lived or worked in different eras. One of the stops is certainly the dark brown Shikumen house in the center of a shopping mall.

Yesterday: 29 South Minhou Lane
Today: The Former Residence of Mao Zedong in 1920   **Address:** 63 Anyi Road
Tips: The residence is open to the public. It is recommended to visit Mao's other two residences at 120 Maoming Road N. and 118 Zhejiang Road N.

茂名北路甲秀里毛泽东旧居
Mao Zedong's Former Residence on Maoming Road

　　1924年2月至12月，毛泽东曾在上海慕尔鸣路（现茂名北路）甲秀里寓居，这是毛泽东一生中在上海居住时间最长的地方。

　　毛泽东旧居位于茂名北路120弄，初名甲秀里，建于1915年，是1924年毛泽东到国民党中央上海执行部工作时的寓所。

　　同济大学钱宗灏教授认为，甲秀里旧居是典型的里弄石库门住宅，二层砖木结构，毗连式布局，一客堂一厢房形制。弄内共有两排五幢房屋，坐南朝北，北面一排为两幢一客堂两厢房形制，而南面一排为三幢一客堂一厢房形制。由于甲秀里北通威海卫路（威海路），西通慕尔鸣路，1934年公共租界市政部门重编门牌时改为威海卫路583弄。

　　1960年党史部门对毛泽东寓所旧址进行调查时访问了当年到过该处的张琼、杨之华等人，但对威海路583弄内5、7、9号三幢中的哪一幢无法确定，就将此三幢均列为上海市文物保护单位。1977年旧居列为上海市文物保护单位，1999年中共静安区委、区人民政府对旧居进行了修缮，同年12月作为毛泽东旧居陈列馆对外开放。

1924年寓居上海工作的10个月中，毛泽东全方位地提升了领导水平和工作能力。离开上海后，他继续摸索救国之路，认识到农民和武装斗争是中国革命的两大基本问题，大力开展农民运动，开创了农村包围城市、武装夺取政权的革命道路。

这里也是见证毛泽东一家难得温馨相聚的地方。1924年6月毛泽东夫人杨开慧携儿子毛岸英、毛岸青前来团聚，全家一起在此居住了6个月。

杨开慧在这里照顾幼子、料理家务，协助毛泽东整理文章，晚上还去工人夜校教课，过着充实忙碌又幸福的生活。故居里还陈列着老式藤编摇篮和木制童车。据说杨开慧忙得手脚不停，用脚摇摇篮，同时帮毛泽东修改文章。

在这里，杨开慧母子三人拍摄了在沪期间唯一的合影，未出镜的拍摄者很可能是毛泽东。在这张珍贵的照片上，乌黑短发的杨开慧穿一身白衣，腿上抱着还是婴孩的毛岸青，身边倚靠着年幼的毛岸英。

也许为了弥补毛泽东一家人没有合影的遗憾，2003年毛泽东诞辰110周年时，旧居纪念馆委托北京中央美术学院雕塑家制作"毛泽东一家"的雕塑，陈列在甲秀里旧居的院落中。

The former residence of Mao Zedong in 1924 is located at 120 Maoming Road N., which was originally named Jiaxiu Lane. Mao resided here when he came to work in the Kuomintang Central Shanghai Executive Office from February to December 1924. This is the place where he lived in Shanghai for the longest time in his life.

The residence is a two-story, brick-and-wood structure built in 1915 in typical Shikumen style of the 1920s and 1930s. With a contiguous layout, the house features a guest hall and a wing room. There are two rows of five houses in the alley that sit south to north. The north row features two houses, each with one guest hall and two wing rooms. The south row has three houses, each with one guest hall and one wing

room.

Owing to the fact that Jiaxiu Lane connects to Weihaiwei Road (today's Weihai Road) in the north and Moulmein Road (today's Maoming Road N.) in the west, Shanghai Municipal Council changed the residence's address to Lane 583 Weihaiwei Road during the reorganization work of house numbers in 1934.

During an investigation in 1960, Zhang Qiong and Yang Zhihua among others who had visited Mao's residence were all interviewed. However, it was impossible to determine which of the three buildings at No. 5, No. 7 and No. 9 in Lane 583 Weihai Road was Mao's residence in 1924. Therefore, the three buildings are all listed as Shanghai Municipal Cultural Relics for Preservation. In December 1999, the residence opened to the public as an exhibition hall after a revamp project conducted by the Jing'an District government.

During the 10 months that he lived and worked here in 1924, Mao Zedong improved his capabilities and leadership in all aspects.

This is also a place to witness the rare reunions of Mao's family. In June 1924, Mao Zedong's wife Yang Kaihui and his sons Mao Anying and Mao Anqing came to live with him in the Shikumen house for six months.

His wife Yang Kaihui lived a full, happy life here caring her little children, doing housework, assisting Mao to revise articles and teaching at an evening school for Chinese workers. An old-fashioned rattan cradle and a wooden stroller are exhibited here to revive life of this young family.

Also exhibited here is a precious photo of Yang and her two sons, which was most likely taken by Mao Zedong in Shanghai in 1924. Yang is dressed in white, holding her younger son Mao Anqing on her lap while the eldest son Mao Anying leans beside.

Perhaps in order to make up for the regret that Mao is absent in this photo, the residence museum made a sculpture of the Mao Zedong Family in the courtyard in 2003, on the 110th anniversary of Mao's birth.

常德公寓是一座装饰艺术风格的大楼，东立面两侧的长阳台与中部竖线条形成对比，十分别致。1939年后，女作家张爱玲（1920-1995）曾在这里居住和写作，迎来职业生涯的巅峰。

静安区房管局档案显示，常德公寓原为爱林登公寓（Eddington House），是一座高达8层的钢筋混凝土建筑，米黄色拉毛外墙，建筑面积约2789平方米。1936年竣工的大楼平面呈凹形，两翼向后，入口处雨棚及两侧墙面均采用水平横向线条作为装饰，顶部两层退台收进。投资兴建大楼的是意大利律师兼地产商拉乌尔·斐斯。

张爱玲曾在这座公寓生活过六年多时间。1939年她与姑姑张茂渊第一次入住51室，后去香港读书，1942年回上海后与姑姑第二次搬入60室，直到1947年9月。

她们俩各有独立卧室和盥洗室，中间有厨房相连，需要见面开门即可，也能从消防门进出保留各自的私人空间。

在爱林登公寓，这位年轻的女作家开始尝试职业写作，展露才

华。她陆续写出并发表《倾城之恋》《金锁记》《封锁》《心经》《花凋》等重要作品，在沦陷的上海迅速走红，掀起一股"张爱玲热"。至1947年，她又随姑姑搬入位于南京西路另一端的卡尔登公寓（今黄河路65号长江公寓），直至1952年夏赴海外。20世纪80年代后她在美国洛杉矶创作的最后一部作品《小团圆》中，仍回忆了居住在此的故事。

常德公寓所在的常德路，原来叫赫德路。这座公寓大楼建于1933年，当时正是上海近代公寓建筑的黄金年代。同济大学钱宗灏教授研究发现，上海租界早期的住宅多为石库门——一种为小刀会起义后涌入租界的移民建造的联排建筑。根据中国人的习惯，石库门设有天井和厢房。20世纪20年代上海出现成套的里弄公寓，高约三层，钢窗蜡地板与煤卫齐全，现代舒适。

近代公寓的建筑形态、建造技术与建筑设备都与传统低层居住建筑有很大不同，但这种新的居住模式更适宜上海这样人口高密度的都市，也对日后的住宅建筑产生了深远的影响。

"上海的地价不断上涨后，开发商又开始兴建6—9层的高层公寓。虽然高层公寓中每套平均房的面积更小，但因为更现代的设计和设施，居住品质反而提升了。"钱教授说。

同济大学左琰教授研究上海近代公寓的室内设计后发现，公寓大楼的邻里关系没有里弄住宅那样通透外向，显得更为独立和私密，这与公寓环境的安静、隐蔽和内向感有关。高级公寓的居住者多为中等资本家、高级职员、律师或大学教授、医师、艺术家等，大都受过西式教育，在洋行里做事或有留学经历，有些是外侨来沪短暂工作，住上两三年或数月不等。

"张爱玲笔下的公寓是最合理想的逃世的地方。她居住的常德公寓地处今常德路与南京西路的交叉口，靠近哈同花园，是当年的高档住宅。有着"十里洋场"之称的南京路是上海的中心繁华地带，南京路车水马龙，但过了西藏路（今名），南京西路（今名）的环境就幽静许多。公寓门前原来有两座街心花园，种植百来株银杏，树影婆娑，可谓闹中取静，很适合文人居住。"左教授在题为《上海近代公寓居住文化和历史风貌变迁研究》的论文中写到。

上海的公寓大楼多分布在旧公共租界或法租界的商业区，位于今天的黄浦、静安、徐汇、长宁和虹口区。早期公寓建筑设计为古典风格和文艺复兴风格，20世纪20年代晚期后公寓建筑转向装饰艺术风格或现代风格。到了20世纪30年代，高层公寓已变得十分流行。张爱玲在南京路先后住过的两座公寓大楼——爱林登公寓和卡尔登公寓——都是装饰艺术风格的高层公寓楼。

1931年英文《大陆报》专门报道，"上海终于快速地成为一座公寓楼之城"。当时上海公寓建筑流行的原因之一是比酒店居住起来更方便，而价格却更便宜。

根据静安区房地局档案，常德公寓的2至5层每层有三户、6、7层每层两户，第8层为电梯机房和水箱等用房。最底层原来是汽车间，后来改成复式住宅。每层房型都不同，有两室、三室和无客厅的公寓，每层楼设有后阳台和保姆专用的卫生间。房间铺设木地板，装有壁炉和热水汀，卧室配备小衣帽间和独立卫生间。厨房沿西外廊布置，双阳台连通客厅和卧室。

"常德公寓因上部缩退和下部平面不一致，公寓顶层有两个2室2卫单元（带浴缸的大卫生间）。进单元门，走廊一边是两间厨房，外间有4个灶眼带烤箱的管道煤气灶，里间是配餐；另一侧安排了两间卧室，前方的主卧室有一个朝东的阳台。"左教授提到。

她认为，这些高层公寓将国外摩登的生活方式带到了上海，水门汀、热水汀、木地板及奥的斯电梯，一下子让生活在公寓里的人多了几分光彩和神气。与上海老洋房相比，高层公寓不仅代表了新的生活方式，更代表了新潮的思想观念。因此，有能力购买或租住这些公寓的，一般都是社会的上层人士，足以让人刮目相看。

钱教授提到，上海公寓建筑的建造活动从20世纪20年代一直持续到20世纪40年代。1949年后，上海政府兴建了许多工人新村，如曹杨二村。这些工人新村在老上海公寓的基础上加入苏联特点，配套建有学校、菜场和邮局。在工人新村开始兴建的20世纪50年代，张爱玲从南京路另一头的爱林登公寓（今常德公寓）搬到卡尔登公寓，当时的她已与胡兰成离婚。

如今，常德公寓保持昔日风貌。在车水马龙的静安寺，装饰艺术风格的外立面上有一块标有"张爱玲故居"的铭牌，吸引张粉无数。

昨天： 爱林登公寓　**今天：** 常德公寓　**地址：** 常德路 195 号　**建造年代：** 1936 年

设计师： Cumine & Co. Ltd.　**建筑风格：** 装饰艺术风格

参观指南： 大楼底部有一间张爱玲文学主题的咖啡馆，陈列着不少这位知名女作家的作品。

Changde Apartments, a striking Art Deco building, will always be associated with celebrated author Eileen Chang (1920-1995).

Archives from Jing'an District Housing Management Bureau reveal the building was called the Eddington House when Chang lived there. And the days spent at Eddington House saw Chang at the zenith of her writing power.

Decades later, even on the other side of the globe, she kept writing about this part of her life.

"Eileen Chang first lived in this apartment building with her mother and aunt in 1939 but later went to study in Hong Kong. When she returned to Shanghai in 1942, she moved into Room 60

with her aunt, and became a freelance writer until September 1947. Here, Chang completed the most important several novels of her life," the archive record shows.

The eight-story Eddington House building was erected in 1936 during the golden era (1920s-1940s) of modern Shanghai apartment buildings. Listed among the second batch of historical buildings, the construction features vertical lines as the centerpiece, which is flanked by long, horizontal balconies as a contrast. In addition, the canopy to the entrance and the walls on two sides are also adorned by horizontal lines. The top two floors are set back and showcase a strong Art

Deco feature.

The research of Tongji University professor Qian Zonghao revealed the city's early residential buildings were mostly shikumen (stone-gate) houses, which were built after refugees from neighboring provinces flooded into the foreign settlements of Shanghai following the upheavals of the Taiping Rebellion in the 1850s.

The new-style three-story "lane apartments" emerged in the 1920s. Every flat in a lane apartment had an en suite, and was equipped with a kitchen, steel-framed windows and a wax wooden floor.

"As Shanghai's land price continued to soar in the 1920s, tall-er apartment buildings were built with up to six and nine floors. Though every flat in the taller buildings was smaller than before, the living quality of flat dwellers improved due to modern design and facilities. Tall apartment buildings were in either Art Deco or modern style," Qian says.

After researching dozens of the city's modern apartment buildings, another Tongji University professor, Zuo Yan, discovered apartment dwellers appeared to be more independent and behaved in a more "privacy-sensitive way" compared with those living in local lane houses.

Most of the apartments' residents were medium-level capital-

ists, senior executives, lawyers, professors, doctors or artists, who either worked for foreign companies or had the experience of studying overseas. Some residents were expatriates who came to Shanghai for work for a period of two to three months.

Apartments under Chang's pens were ideal places to be secluded from the world. Perched at the crossroad of Changde Road and Nanjing Road W., Changde Apartments, where she lived for six years, was an upper-class residence close to the garden of tycoon Silas Hardoon. Nanjing Road, nicknamed "Shi Li Yang Chang", or "10-mile-long foreign metropolis", was a prosperous, bustling area in downtown Shanghai. But passing Xizang Road, the western stretch of Nanjing Road appears to have a more elegant and quieter environment.

"The apartment buildings were formerly fronted with gardens planted with gingko trees. It was a tranquil place at a prominent location pairing sophistication and eccentricity, great for a writer to live in," professor Zuo wrote in her thesis "A study on the changes of apartment-living culture and historical features in modern Shanghai".

According to the book *Old Shanghai Classic Apartments*, Shanghai's apartment buildings were mostly located in commercial areas in the former International Settlement or the French Concession areas, covering today's Huangpu, Jing'an, Xuhui, Changning and Hongkou districts.

Early apartment buildings were in classic or Renaissance style, whose facades were embellished with architraves and carved brick decorations. Most apartment buildings changed toward a more modern style and simple-cut form since the late 1920s. In the 1930s taller apartment buildings, such as the Eddington House at 195 Changde Road and the Carlton Apartments at 65 Huanghe Road were prevailing in Shanghai.

A *China Press* report in 1931 noted "Shanghai has finally rapidly become a city of apartment buildings". Another article in a 1940 Chinese magazine *The Grand View*, noted the popularity of apartments in Shanghai was because "they were more convenient and cheaper than hotels".

The Jing'an District Housing Management Bureau archives say an Italian developer invested heavily in the Eddington House.

The building features three

apartments on each level from the second to fifth floor. The upper two floors contain two apartments each. The eighth floor is used for facilities and equipment. The apartments differ in sizes from two to three bedrooms, with or without a sitting room. Each floor is designed with a back balcony and servants' bathroom. The rooms are all paved with wooden floors and equipped with fireplaces and a heating system. The bedroom has a cloakroom and bathroom inside while the kitchen is arranged along the western veranda. Double balconies connect the sitting room and bedroom.

"Owing to the set-back struc-ture, the upper and lower parts of the building have different layouts. The top floors are two-bedroom, two-bathroom flats. Inside the gate, the corridor features two kitchen rooms, both on one side. The outer kitchen room has a four-burner gas stove while the inner kitchen room is a pantry. On the other side, there are two bedrooms. The master's bedroom has a balcony facing the east," professor Zuo recalled on her visit to Changde Apartments.

She said that compared to the garden houses, these tall apartment buildings not only embraced new life style, but also showed a more avant-garde concept.

Professor Qian added that the construction of the apartment buildings in Shanghai started from the 1920s and continued until the 1940s.

"After 1949 the government built many residential compounds for local workers, the style of which were based on Shanghai apartment buildings, yet featuring characteristics of those residential compounds in the former Soviet Union," Qian said.

Today, Changde Apartments is well preserved inside and out. The Art Deco facade is still eye-catching and a nameplate saying it's Eileen Chang's former residence on average attracts dozens of visitors a day. However, it is not open to people without an invitation. There's a bed and breakfast in the building themed on the famous writer, while many of Chang's books are on display in the cafe on the ground floor.

Yesterday: Eddington House   **Today:** Changde Apartments
Address: 195 Changde Road   **Built in** 1936   **Architects:** Cumine & Co. Ltd.
Architectural style: Art Deco
Tips: The building is not open to the public without an invitation. There's a bed and breakfast in the building themed on the famous writer, while many of Chang's books are on display in the cafe on the ground floor.

卡尔登公寓
The Carlton Apartments

长江公寓原名卡尔登公寓，是一座摩登的高层公寓，也是张爱玲在上海的最后一个家。大楼建于1935年，浅褐色砖铺就的立面设计简洁，仅装饰有几个弧形的长阳台。卡尔登公寓和许多市中心的老上海公寓楼一样，底层为商铺，楼上是公寓。

根据1929年《大陆报》报道，卡尔登公寓属于名为"卡尔登地产"的综合开发项目。该项目位于今南京西路黄河路路口，除了卡尔登公寓，还包括卡尔登剧院、舞宫（Palais de Danse）、美艺公司的产业和商铺等。卡尔登公寓原计划建10-12层，最终建了8层。

卡尔登公寓体量大，有四架电梯，楼梯铺有厚地毯，后面还有一个嵌入式的花园。公寓的地段无敌，附近有国际饭店、卡尔登剧院和大光明电影院，上海跑马厅和南京路商业街步行5分钟可达。

她和姑姑住在公寓301室期间，创作了电影剧本《不了情》《太太万岁》，小说《十八春》《小艾》。由《十八春》改写的《半生缘》被拍成多部深受欢迎的影视剧。

1952年这位女作家离开了卡尔登公寓，先赴香港后到美国定居。她再也没有回来，但上海成为她作品中反复出现的城市。

Changjiang Apartments, formerly called Carlton Apartments, was one of the many tall apartments which upgraded the city's residential life.

Built in 1935, the Carlton Apartments was designed in such a simple-cut way that there are only several long, curved balconies gracing the facade. The ground floor features shops and the floors above are residential. The flank is painted in a warm chocolate tone, chic and modern.

According to a 1929 report in *The China Press*, the project for constructing Carlton Apartments was part of a large property transaction. Known as the "Carlton Property" situated at the corner of Bubbling Well Road (today's Nanjing Road W.) and Park Road (today's Huanghe Road) facing the former race course, the site included buildings such as the old Grand Theater, the Carlton Theater, the late Palais de Danse, premises occupied by Arts and Crafts, shops and houses. The initial plan for the now eight-floor Carlton Apartments was taller, up to 10 to 12 floors.

After divorcing her husband Hu Lancheng, Eileen Chang moved into the Carlton Apartments from Eddington House. In Flat 301 of Carlton Apartments, which Chang shared with her aunt, Chang completed several novels and movie scripts including "Eighteen Springs", which she revised to a well-known novel *Affair of Half a Lifetime* in the US in the late 1970s and early 1980s. The novel was later adapted to a popular movie and TV series.

Eileen Chang left the Carlton Apartments in 1952 for Hong Kong and later the U.S. . She never returned to the city but Shanghai was forever a theme in her writings.

百乐门的光芒
Gateway to 100 Pleasures

百乐门舞厅是一座装饰艺术风格的剧院，引人注目的塔楼熠熠生辉。百乐门的光芒下，一幕幕历史故事华丽上演。

1933年12月5日百乐门舞厅开业，英文《大陆报》称这个项目投资百万，可能是中国或远东地区最奢华的舞厅。作为老上海四大舞厅之一，百乐门是一座西式建筑，却是华人建造的项目，由浙江商人顾联章等人投资，开业时还包含一座设计精美的酒店，套房都带有阳台。

"舞厅摩登现代，用美好的色彩设计而成，乐队、服务和娱乐都妙极了。百乐门称自己的大舞厅是太平洋此岸最美丽的夜总会，确实名副其实。"《大陆报》报道写道。

报道还透露，百乐门装饰奢华，经营团队努力为客人们提供最好的娱乐享受，在采购装饰织物和设备时主要考虑的是效果，而不是价格。

上海档案馆研究员张姚俊发现，百乐门的舞厅分为两层，可容纳数百人。其中第一层铺设跳舞专用的弹簧地板，而楼上则是一种玻璃制成、灯泡点亮的"水晶地板"。1936年，刚演完《摩登时代》的英国著名演员查理·卓别林（Charlie Chaplin）与宝莲高黛

（Paulette Goddard）曾在这摩登舞厅共舞。

《大陆报》报道提到，这种弹簧地板很出色，对于表现舞步和剧场效果效果非常好。而被点亮的"水晶地板"是为楼上的客人而准备，他们使用包房，不想下楼去大舞厅。百乐门有两个宽敞的大包房，可以举行大型派对。

1934年1月，《中国建筑》杂志刊登题为《百乐门之崛兴》的文章，透露了百乐门舞厅设计两层舞厅的原因。文章提到，如果舞厅过分庞大，假日或宴会时佳宾满座，平日间少数宾客置于硕大无垠之广厅中，"即有寥落岑寂之感"。大华饭店（Majestic Hotel，已拆除）就是一个例子，在平日晚间赴宴人数少的时候，"如入古宫旧刹，减却欢乐不少"。据统计，当年每周六晚舞厅的宴客者常常较平日晚增加五倍以上。

百乐门的解决方案很巧妙：将舞厅划分为几个空间，添建楼座，并增设两间包房。宾客先就大舞厅楼下而坐，楼下坐满后客人会自然地上楼到楼座。楼座满员再开包房。这样楼下可坐400人，楼座容纳250人，包房各75人，从百余人到800人"皆可应付裕如，不觉拥挤，而不觉寥落矣"。

张姚俊说，百乐门的中英文名字是投资人顾联章想出的。百乐门的英文名为"Paramount Ballroom"，其中"Paramount"是"至高无上"的意思，显示了业主打造远东第一舞厅的雄心。而中文名"百乐门"寓意通往欢乐世界，朗朗上口。百乐门舞厅的中英文名都十分贴切好记，盛大开幕后也好评如潮。

"舞厅灯光柔和，墙壁美丽，有适宜舞步滑行的绝佳地板。乐队令人着迷，提供娱乐表演的明星艺人充满魅力，这里确实如其中文名表达的，是'通往百种欢乐之门'。所有吸引品位高尚的现代男女的豪华舒适的方式，都在舞厅里愉快而和谐地组合在一起。我敢肯定，在座的以及未来经常光临的其他许多朋友会发现，这里是度过休闲时光并获得最大享受的最佳场所。" 1933年《大陆报》刊登的开幕预告引用了一位宾客的评价。

百乐门不但由华人投资，也是华人建筑师杨锡镠的作品。在一次介绍中国近代建筑师上海作品的

讲座中，同济大学郑时龄院士特别提到南洋公学（上海交通大学前身）土木工程科毕业的杨锡镠，称他是本土培养的建筑师中的佼佼者。

"杨锡镠曾担任中国建筑学会书记，同时又负责出版委员会。我们现在要了解上海的近代建筑往往去查一本《中国建筑》杂志，就是他主编的。同时他还兼任沪江大学商学院的建筑科教师。" 郑时龄介绍。

郑院士认为杨锡镠具有当时中国建筑师的特点，既做设计，又在大学教书兼课，所以既有理论研究，又有设计实践。杨锡镠的代表作有鸿德堂、南京饭店、上海第一特区法院、国立商学院和百乐门舞厅等，其中最出名的就是百乐门舞厅。

"他用'声、光、电'来设计，非常华丽，又用弹簧地板让跳

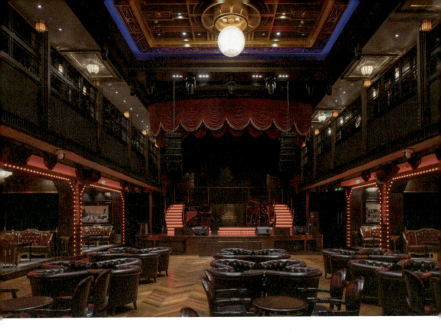

舞有不同的感觉，这是中国建筑师较早设计的娱乐建筑。不过，百乐门舞厅经过了历史的很多变迁，重新整修过风格已经不是原来的那种。"他说。

杨锡镠的职业生涯延续很长，1949年后还曾参与新中国十大建筑的设计工作。让他名垂建筑史的百乐门舞厅在开业后，成为一座高端的舞厅。

"百乐门是个'销金窟'。一杯茶要5毛钱，在当时可以买9斤面粉。一块牛排1元，一瓶香槟16元，工薪阶层是消费不起的。百乐门的客人非富即贵，飞虎队将

军陈纳德和陈香梅就在百乐门举行了订婚仪式。"张姚俊说。

他提到，百乐门最出名的就是舞女陈曼丽遇刺事件。陈曼丽曾是百乐门最红的舞女，曾与中国实业银行总经理刘晦之结婚，后来又回到百乐门的舞女生活。

根据1940年2月28日英文《北华捷报》报道，案件发生在2月26日深夜约12点45分左右。当时陈曼丽与两名男客人坐在靠百乐门门口的一张桌边，突然遭到一位刺客5发子弹袭击。陈曼丽和一位客人身亡，另一位受轻伤。当时乐队正在演奏最新的华尔兹舞曲，灯

光暗下来，舞伴们进入舞池。一位穿着西式服装的人偷偷摸摸地靠近了漂亮的陈曼丽，他拿出藏在衣服里的一把军用手枪向这个年轻的姑娘射击。舞厅里惊叫声四起，酒瓶和杯子砸到地面，舞厅的一侧人们纷纷逃散，而另一侧的舞客们还在跳着华尔兹，对刚刚发生的悲剧毫无知觉。突然间，音乐戛然而止。凶手后来逃离了案发现场。来自静安寺路警局的警察来到案发现场。

陈曼丽遇刺的原因至今仍是谜团，有不同的说法。而此后的岁月里，百乐门的生意也渐渐地不景气。

上海社会科学院历史研究所专家马军在论文"光芒与阴影：上海百乐门的创办和经营"中写道，"虽然百乐门成功地赢得了'舞厅之王'这一文化品牌，但就企业经营本身而言，由于受制于

内外各种因素，它长期处于亏损状态。想象的百乐门和真实的百乐门之间，存在着相当大的落差"。

2017年春，百乐门历经三年修缮装修，成为一家风格奢华繁复的舞厅，对外营业。据说，很多重新走进百乐门的客人都与上海有着很深的缘分。

昨天：百乐门　**今天**：百乐门　**地址**：豫园路 218 号　**建筑师**：杨锡镠　**建筑风格**：装饰艺术
参观指南：舞厅对客人开放，提供下午茶、餐饮等服务。

The Paramount Ballroom, a glistening Art Deco theatre, was not only at the forefront of entertainment in the heart of Shanghai in the early 20th century, it was patronized by Hollywood superstars, such as Charlie Chaplin, became a den of iniquity for city gangsters and provided the scene for one of the metropolis' most mysterious murders.

"The Paramount Ballroom was one of four major theatres in old Shanghai. It was a Western-style architectural building but it was mainly invested in by a wealthy Chinese merchant named Gu Liancheng from Nanxun of Zhejiang Province," Zhang Yaojun, a researcher from Shanghai Archives Bureau, said.

When the ballroom threw its doors open in 1933 on December 15, *The China Press* reported that the new million-dollar establishment was perhaps the most luxurious structure of its kind ever attempted in China or the Far East.

"Modern in every respect, with a fine color scheme, excellent orchestra, service and entertainment, the ballroom lived up to its boast of being the most beautiful nightclub this side of the Pacific," the newspaper said.

The China Press revealed the theatre was decorated on a lavish scale and the owners of the establishment had tried to provide the best in entertainment.

"The illumination is a little short of spectacular while the draperies, fixtures, et cetera, have been purchased with an idea of effectiveness rather than any thought of saving money," the report said.

Zhang added that the ballroom featured two kinds of outstanding dance floors, large enough to accommodate hundreds of dancers.

"One was a spring floor and upstairs was a kind of crystal floor made of glass and illuminated by light bulbs," he said.

The spring floor was where silent film legend Chaplin danced with his movie co-star and companion Paulette Goddard on his one and only night in Shanghai in March 1936.

The China Press said the spring floor was outstanding for dancers and for the presentation of ballroom acts and theatricals.

The crystal floor, however, was effectively illuminated for the use of the Paramount's patrons, who were using private dining rooms upstairs and did not wish to walk down a flight of steps to the main dance floor. There were two private dining rooms in the place, both large enough to accommodate large parties.

Zhang added that it was an in-

vestor named Gu that gave the ballroom both English and Chinese names.

"With the intention of building it as the ultimate, No. 1 music hall in the Far East, he named it "Bai Le Men", literally meaning the gateway to 100 pleasures in Chinese, which was easy to remember and had a good meaning," Zhang said.

It seems the Paramount Ballroom had a fitting name and got rave reviews after its grand opening.

"The ballroom with its soft lights, beautiful walls has an excellent floor for gliding feet. The enchanting dance orchestra and charming star entertainers is truly a gateway of a hundred pleasures, as its Chinese name well suggests. All means of luxury and comfort that appeal to modern men and women of good taste are happily and harmoniously assembled in this ball. I am sure that friends present here and many others that will frequent the ballroom in the future find it the best place in which to spend their leisure hours with the maximum amount of enjoyment," a guest was quoted in the preview of the new ballroom in 1933.

At the opening, the Paramount

Ballroom had a hotel section which was fitted with a large number of suites, all decorated and fitted out on a lavish scale. These suites were each fitted with a sun porch and verandah, giving occupants an accommodation few establishments could boast of at that time. And in the tower of the building there is a bridge room with three or four tables.

The paramount establishment was not only a Chinese investment, but the building was designed by a Chinese architect named Yang Xiliu.

In a lecture on the Shanghai practices of modern Chinese architects last year, Tongji University professor Zheng Shiling introduced Yang who graduated from Nanyang College, predecessor of today's Shanghai Jiao Tong University.

"He was an excellent architect, an architectural teacher and editor-in-chief of an architectural journal named *The China Builder* which was an important reference book for studying modern Shanghai architecture," Zheng said.

"Like other Chinese architects of his time, Yang not only conducted design work as a profession but also taught lessons in university. So he was good at both

theoretical research and design practices. His signature works include a Christian church named Hong De Tang, the Nanking Hotel, the Paramount Ballroom, the Stadium of Nanyang College, to name just a few."

Zheng added that among them, the Paramount Ballroom was Yang's most famous work, which had encountered many historical changes and was renovated from top to bottom in recent years to be far different from the original style.

"Yang used a lavish style of sound, light and electricity and a spring floor to design this building. It was an early practice of entertainment architecture designed by a Chinese architect, his exploration of modern Chinese style," Zheng said.

He notes that many of Shanghai's historical buildings are the work of China's remarkable first generation of architects. Other examples include the Majestic Theatre by Fan Wenzhao and the Shanghai Concert Hall by Fan Wenzhao and Zhao Shen along Nanjing Road.

He explains that traditionally the profession of an "architect" did not exist in China — only builders and craftsman. But things changed after the first series of Chinese, who studied architecture overseas, returned to the country in the 1910s and took advantage of a building boom that was just under way.

The city was undergoing massive architectural changes as more people poured into the "Paris of the East" and places for living, working and entertainment were built with amazing speed.

When Chinese students returned from overseas with architectural degrees, they joined foreign architectural enterprises, or later opened their own companies like the Allied Architects.

There were also Chinese architects who received training at home and designed excellent buildings like the Great World Amusement Center in the vicinity of the People's Square.

"The work of Chinese architects has been undervalued and lesser known to the public compared to foreign architects like Park Hotel designer Laszlo Hudec," the professor said.

Yang's career was long and he participated in the 10 signature buildings of new China designed after 1949.

The well-designed Paramount Ballroom used to be an expensive nightclub for the upper class.

"Paramount Ballroom was a 'money-squandering den' where the working class could not afford the entertainment. A cup of green tea was priced at a half yuan which could buy 4.5 kilograms of flour at that time. A steak cost 1 yuan and a bottle of champagne 16 yuan. So guests were mostly the wealthy or notables. It was where General Chennault,

commander of the Flying Tigers during World War II, and Anna Chan engaged," Zhang said.

He mentioned the most famous incident in the ballroom was the murder of its most renowned dancer Chen Manli:

"As the most popular dancer in the Paramount, Chen was taken as a concubine by one of her guests, bibliophile/banker Liu Huizhi, the Shanghai branch manager of the National Industrial Bank of China," Zhang said.

The North - China Herald reported Chen later returned to her profession of "taxi dancing" after her husband Chu Shui-fu, manager of the Kiu Fu Company, died.

A gunman fired five shots at her as she sat at a table with two Chinese men friends. One friend was fatally wounded, while the other escaped with a slight injury. Chen died a day after the attack on February 26, 1940, from wounds to the abdomen, back, neck and shoulder.

It is still a mystery why she was killed. The Paramount Ballroom did not churn out a profitable business for long and it encountered twists and turns in the following years.

"Although it successfully gained the cultural brand of 'King of the Dance Halls', in terms of business operation, Shanghai Paramount lost money for a long time due to internal and external factors. Between the imaginary Paramount and real Paramount, there exists a considerable gap," scholar Ma Jun from Shanghai Academy of Social Sciences wrote in his essay named "Light and Shadow: Founding and Operation of Shanghai Paramount".

In the spring of 2017, after a three-year lavish renovation, the ballroom threw open its doors to the public again for ultimate enjoyment of music and dance.

Many guests of the ballroom have some roots or a nostalgia link with old Shanghai.

Yesterday: Paramount Hall   **Today:** Paramount Ballroom   **Address:** 218 Yuyuan Road
Architect: Yang Xiliu
Architectural style: Art Deco
Tips: The ballroom opens to the public for afternoon tea, dining and night club.

斯蒂尔·威尔逊将领衔百乐门常驻乐团
Styrl Wilson to Head Paramount Resident Orchestra

今天，斯蒂尔·威尔逊（Styrl Wilson）和他的新百乐门舞厅交响乐团将乘日本女王号从底特律抵达上海。此前他们在底特律利兰德饭店（Leeland Hotel）长期驻演，乐团曾被美国国家广播公司（NBC）报道。

在过去的一年里，威尔逊和他的乐团为维克多公司（Victor Company）录制了许多唱片。这些唱片中最富有本地特色的一张是《我的黑鸟现在是蓝鸟》（*My Blackbirds are Blue Birds Now*）。

本来这支乐团已经被芝加哥最新的一家夜总会预定开演冬季音乐季，但此时百乐门公司的管理层提供了一份合同，邀请他们来上海的豪华新舞厅。由于决定权是在芝加哥和上海之间摇摆，前者没有机会。这些男孩们带来了那种平滑的、可跳舞的节奏，这将使百乐门成为真正热爱跳舞的人们的圣地。

今天抵达的百乐门艺术家中，有一位布罗姆利·豪斯先生（Mr. Bromleigh House）。这位男中音歌唱家的声音据说异常柔和而丰富。他刚刚结束与底特律密歇根剧院的合作。另一位是比利·海兹

（Billy Heads）先生，他的幽默妙趣横生，舞技绝妙，有望在这座上海娱乐中心占有一席之地。

海兹先生与"公爵"（Duke Ellington 1899–1974，美国作曲家、钢琴家，爵士乐史最有影响力的人物之一）和保罗·阿什（Paul Ash）都曾一起演出。了解娱乐圈的人们应该会重视这不同寻常、富有前途的履历。百乐门舞厅将于12月初开放。

Arriving here today on the Empress of Japan will be Styrl Wilson and his new Paramount Ballroom Orchestra, direct from a long engagement at the Leeland Hotel, Detroit. The orchestra has been featured over the National Broadcasting Company.

Styrl Wilson and his music have made numerous recordings for the Victor Company during the past year. One of the most locally of these recordings was *My Blackbirds are Blue Birds Now*.

The orchestra was booked to open the winter season at one of Chicago's newest night clubs when the management of the Paramount offered them a contract to come here to open Shanghai's luxurious new ballroom. With the decision resting between Chicago and Shanghai, the former didn't have a chance, and here the boys are bringing with them the sort of smooth, danceable rhythms that will make the Paramount a mecca for those who really love to dance.

Among the Paramount artists arriving today is Mr Bromleigh House, possessor of a baritone voice that is said to be exceptionally smooth and rich. He has just completed an engagement at the Michigan Theater, Detroit. Another is Mr Billy Heads, whose sparkling humor and sensational dancing is expected to secure him a place in the hearts of pleasure-loving Shanghai.

Mr. Heads has been featured by both Duke Ellington and Paul Ash. Persons who know good entertainers should appreciate this record as promising entertainment out of the ordinary. The Paramount will open early in December.

摘自 1933 年 11 月 21 日《大陆报》
Excerpt from *The China Press*, on November 21, 1933

华丽忧伤的大理石大厦
Tears and Joy of the Marble Hall

1924年，嘉道理爵士的新家大理石大厦被称为"上海最美丽的豪宅"。

犹太富商嘉道里家族在上海拥有大量房产，其中最著名的就是位于静安寺的大理石大厦，又名嘉道里大厦。这座宫殿般的豪宅用料考究，工程总造价高达100万两白银，占地1.5万平方米，室内面积3300平方米，包含大小客厅和20多个房间。

嘉道理家族是1880年从巴格达来到远东地区定居的塞法迪犹太人（Sephardi Jews）。嘉道理家族的财富由埃利·嘉道理（Sir Elly Kadoorie）和埃利斯·嘉道理（Sir Ellis Kadoorie）创造。他们都是商业领域的巨擘，先后创办香港上海大酒店有限公司（Hongkong & Shanghai Hotel Co.）和中华电力有限公司（China Light and Power Co. Ltd.）等产业。

"大理石大厦"的主人埃利·嘉道理爵士（Sir. Elly Kadoorie）1867年出生于巴格达，曾经为沙逊洋行工作，后离职创业。他后来成为一名相当成功的

房地产商人、酒店业主、商业银行家和橡胶种植园主。

上海社科院王健教授研究发现，1840年到1949年间共有三批犹太人移民到上海，分别是19世纪中期到20世纪初期来自中东的塞法迪犹太人、20世纪初来自俄国的犹太人和20世纪30年代末从德国、奥地利和其他中欧国家逃至上海的犹太难民。

嘉道理家族是上海塞法迪犹太人中最著名的家族之一，以贸易和房地产业起家，获得巨额财富。1924年大理石大厦建造时，英文《北华捷报》刊登了整版配图报道，详细介绍了这座不一般

的豪宅。

"我们许多商业巨子都因建造美丽住宅而赢得了持久的声誉，这些房屋被优雅布局的庄园所环绕。已故爱德华·埃兹拉先生（Mr. Edward Ezra）、穆勒先生(Mr. Moller)、帕克太太(Mrs. Parker)、马立斯先生（Mr. H. E. Morris）等人的宅邸在英国的一些乡间别墅中也名列前茅。而位于静安寺路延伸段的大理石大厦也加入到上海豪宅的名录中。大理石大厦是嘉道理先生的家，堪称上海最美丽的房子，具体的理由后面会讲到。上海将为此而感到特别

骄傲。"1924年3月22日《北华捷报》报道。

这篇报道透露，原来的想法是建造一个犹太乡村俱乐部。随着工程推进，"很显然一切对于犹太社区那方面的需求来说都规划得尺度太大了，因此嘉道理先生就把这里用作自己的宅邸了。"

建筑原来由赉丰洋行设计（Messrs. Lafuente & Wootten），但不幸毁于火灾。嘉道理邀请英商文格罗白郎事务所（Messrs. Graham-Brown & Wingrove）的嘉咸宾（Graham-Brown）重新设计这件"建筑的瑰宝"。

这个设计项目后来与思九生（Robert Ernest Stewardson）合作完成。

王健教授提到，大理石大厦高达1百万两白银的造价在当年是一笔天价，富丽堂皇的主厅是上海上层社会的社交中心之一。

如今，大理石大厦位于延安西路54号，建筑的宏伟华丽依然让每个到访者感到震撼，形容这是一个国王居住的宫殿也不为过。

建筑师使用了大量的白色意大利大理石——墙面、柱式、壁炉、楼梯和露台，到处都是，"大理石大厦"的美名因此而来。室内装饰的色调也很别致，以醋绿色（vinegar green）和奶油色为主。主厅20米高，25米乘50米见方，有装饰精美的白色天花板、巨幅镜面和水晶吊灯，美得让人目眩神迷。大理石大厦的二楼是主人和客人的卧室。

《北华捷报》报道提到，嘉道理先生许诺，这套宅邸和场地可供任何慈善组织使用，不限国籍和种族，而他会支付所有的费用。

"这里非常适合此类慈善活动，有宽敞漂亮的沙龙，长达225英尺（68米）的美丽外廊，大宴会厅仅比卡尔登咖啡馆略小几平方英尺，厨房可满足招待大量客人的需求。室外空间除了可以用于多种活动的铺石板的场地外，还有6个网球场和其他草地运动场地。"报道写到。

大理石大厦建成后，嘉道理一家在此举办了犹太社区和其他组织的很多活动，包括社区聚会和犹太节日的大型派对、宴会和舞会。

虽然拥有如此华丽的大理石大厦，嘉道理家族却经历了不少磨难与起伏。

1919年，嘉道理的爱妻劳拉（Laura）在家里发生的火灾中去世，震惊了外侨社区。二战期间，日军把嘉道理一家关入闸北集中营。由于嘉道理年事已高，经过特许返回大理石大厦与两个儿子——劳伦斯（Lawrence）和霍瑞斯（Horace）被软禁在原先的佣人房。嘉道理先生于1944年8月8日去世。

1945年劳伦斯与霍瑞斯离开上海去香港发展。嘉道理家族的产业在战争中损失不小，不过，这对兄弟在香港努力发展，再创辉煌。目前家族企业由劳伦斯的儿子米高·嘉道理（Michael Kadoorie）掌舵，他拥有中电集团、香港上海大酒店有限公司等产业，名列2020胡润全球富豪榜之一。20世纪80年代，嘉道理家族还参与投资兴建了深圳大亚湾核电站。半岛酒店也是嘉道理家族的产业。

而老嘉道理和妻子劳拉则长眠在上海虹桥路的原万国公墓。他们的墓碑上写着"逝者真正的墓地在活者的心中"。

如今，万国公墓已成为宋庆龄陵园。1953年就在中国福利会的创始人宋庆龄的倡议下，嘉道理故居成为中国福利会少年宫，成为儿童学习文化艺术的课外活动乐园。

每年六一儿童节，中国福利会少年宫都会举办大型游园活动。大理石大厦变为五颜六色的游戏海

洋，飘荡着孩子们的欢声笑语。

米高·嘉道理曾多次访问中福会少年宫，表示他和父亲都很高兴看到昔日家园成为有天赋的孩子们的乐园。半个多世纪来，数不清的孩子们在这座童话般华丽的大房子里度过愉快时光，也为这座最美的豪宅画上完美句号。

昨天：嘉道理故居　**今天：**中国福利会少年宫　**地址：**延安西路 54 号
建筑师：嘉咸宾（Graham-Brown）、思九生（Robert Ernest Stewardson）
参观指南：建筑内部只对参加活动的儿童开放，可以看看大草坪，或从南京西路欣赏外立面。

The "Marble Hall", Sir Elly Kadoorie's former residence was called "the most beautiful of all stately homes in Shanghai" in 1924.

"The Kadoorie family owned many properties in Shanghai, the most renowned of all being the Marble Hall near the Jing'an Temple. The palatial building is made of refined marbles imported from Italy," said Professor Wang Jian from the Shanghai Academy of Social Sciences.

The Kadoorie Family, Sephardi Jews, emigrated from Baghdad in 1880 to settle in the Far East.

The family fortunes were founded by Sir Elly Kadoorie and Sir Ellis Kadoorie, who were pivotal players in the development of business giants, such as the Hongkong & Shanghai Hotel Co. and China Light and Power.

Born in Baghdad in 1867, Sir Elly Kadoorie, owner of the Marble Hall, had worked for David Sassoon & Sons' Company but left to start his own business. He became a successful real estate and hotel owner, merchant banker and rubber plantation owner.

According to Professor Wang, there were three groups of Jews emigrating to Shanghai between 1840 to 1949—Sephardi Jews from the Middle East since the mid-19th century to early 20th century, Russian Jews from the early 20th century to late 1930s and Jewish refugees from Germany, Austria and other central European countries between the 1930s-1940s.

The Kardoori family was one of the most famous Sephardi Jewish families that made a fortune from the trade and real estate business in old Shanghai.

When the Marble Hall was built in 1924, *the North-China Herald* dedicated a full page feature with pictures to the news.

"Many of our commercial princes have done lasting credit to themselves by the beautiful homes they have built, surrounded by tastefully laid-out estates. The houses of the late Mr. Edward Ezra, Mr. Moller, Mrs Parker, Mr. H.E. Morris and others, would rank high even amongst some of England's old country houses. To the list of Shanghai's 'stately homes' Marble Hall must be added, in Bubbling Well Road extension, the residence of Mr. E.S. Kadoorie, which must be regarded as the most beautiful of all, and for reasons which will be given later Shanghai will feel particularly proud of it," *the North-China Herald* reported on March 22, 1924.

The report revealed that the original idea was to construct a Jewish Country Club. But as the

work progressed "it was obvious that everything had been planned on too large a scale for the needs of that section of the community and so Mr Kadoorie has taken the place for his own residence".

The original building designed by Messrs. Lafuente & Wootten was gutted by fire and then Kadoorie commissioned Messrs. Graham-Brown & Wingrove to redesign the "architectural gem".

Professor Wang added that the most stately home was built with a steep price of around 1 million taels of silver (Most taels were equivalent to 1.3 ounces of silver).

"The major hall at a height of 65 feet (20 meters) is extremely magnificent which has been a social center of the city's upper-class

gatherings," he said.

The Marble Hall is now numbered at 54 Yan'an Road W. Every visitor was shocked at its incredible grandeur and luxury. Covering an area of 1,500 square meters, the two-story mansion with more than 20 rooms was fit for a king.

White Italian marble is everywhere — on the walls, columns, fireplaces, staircases and platforms. The inside is unique in color with vinegar green and cream hues.

The stunning ballroom is 20 meters high, 25 meters long and 50 meters wide with an exquisite white ceiling, giant mirrors and crystal chandeliers.

A room on the first floor, originally used for playing poker, has an exotic ceiling in a curved shape with golden patterns. The second floor features mostly bedrooms for the hosts and guests.

According to *the North-China Herald*, Kadoorie promised to place the whole of the house and grounds at the disposal of any charitable society, of any nationality or creed, for any worthy money-making purposes and "he will pay all expenses so far as the house goes".

"The place is admirably suited for such purposes, with large and handsome salons, a wonderful verandah 225 feet long (68 meters), a ballroom only a few square feet less than the Carlton Café, a kitchen capable of attending to the wants of a very large gathering, and outside, ground for six tennis courts, and other lawn games, besides a great flagged court which could be utilized for many purposes," the report stated.

In the following years, Kadoories hosted many activities for the Jewish Community and other organizations in the house. Large-scale parties, banquets and dancing balls were held here for community meetings and Jewish holidays.

Despite the magnificence of Marble Hall, the wealthy Kadoorie family suffered many ups and downs.

In 1919, Kadoorie's beloved wife Laura died in a fire in their home, which sent shock waves throughout the expatriate community of old Shanghai.

During World War II, the Japanese put some Kadoories family members into a detention camp in Zhabei District in 1943, where Sir Elly Kadoorie died on August 8, 1944.

Elly's sons, Lawrence and Horace, were placed under house

arrest in Marble Hall before they left Shanghai for Hong Kong in 1945.

The two brothers continued the family businesses, which had encountered loss during the wars, and became wealthier following their move back to Hong Kong.

The family is today headed by Lawrence's son, Sir Michael Kadoorie.

Sir Elly Kadoorie, who built the Marble Hall, and his wife Laura Kadoorie were both buried in Shanghai, in the former Jewish Cemetery on Hongqiao Road. The inscription on the Kadoories grave reads: "The true grave of the dead is in the heart of the living."

Today the cemetery is a quiet graveyard known as the Mausoleum of Soong Ching Ling, widow of Dr Sun Yat-sen and the late Honorary Vice Chairwoman of China.

The Kadoories' former home became the China Welfare Institute Children's Palace in 1953 under the advice of Madame Soong, who was also founder of the China Welfare Institute. From then on, the palatial Marble Hall became a place for Chinese children to enjoy recreation and cultivate hobbies.

The institute often hosts festive celebrations on June 1, International Children's Day. During that time, the Marble Hall turns into a sea of games and laughter inside out.

Michael Kadoorie has visited the house several times, and said both he and his father Lawrence were happy to see their home become a paradise for gifted children.

The children love the fairy tale house and it provides a happy ending to Shanghai's most beautiful home.

Yesterday: Former Residence of Kadoorie's
Today: Children Welfare Institute Children's Palace   **Address:** 54 Yan'an Rd W.
Architects: Messrs. Graham-Brown & Wingrove
Tips: The building is not open to the public but it can be admired from Nanjing Road W. and on the lawn fronting it.

　　"要描述建筑物本身，只能说它是富丽堂皇的。它的尺度庞大，但并不夸张。到处都使用了大理石，总共有150吨，但却并不庸俗，有着出色的品位，在很容易被用力过猛的地方取得了最令人愉悦的视觉效果。建筑用地几乎占据了由静安寺路（Bubbling Well Road现南京西路）延伸段、地丰路（Tifeng Road现乌鲁木齐路）和大西路（Great Western Road现延安西路）围合的整个街区。入口处是漂亮的铁门，上面有厚重的黄铜栏杆，门柱横梁也有丰富的黄铜装饰。穿过主要的东入口进入草坪，可以看到长达300英尺的建筑立面。这座建筑从草坪以上数英尺的高度升起，是自由复兴风格的鲜明代表，体现了意大利文化的影响。它有一个被漂亮的青铜灯装点美化的宽阔石阶，雕塑装置正准备在那里安放，然后是长达225英尺、宽约30或40英尺的精美玻璃封闭阳台。

To describe the building itself, one can only say that it is palatial. It has been built on a lavish scale, yet at the same time it is not ostentatious. There is marble everywhere—150 tons of it altogether –but without a suggestion of vulgarity, the work having been executed with wonderful good taste, giving a most pleasing effect where it would have been so easy to overdo it. The grounds occupy nearly the entire block bounded by the Bubbling Well Road extension, Tifeng Road and Great Western Road. At the entrance are handsome iron gates with heavy brass balusters and brass enrichments in the architraves. Passing by the main east entrance to the lawns one has a magnificent view of the 300 feet frontage. Raised several feet above the lawns, the building is a striking example of the free Renaissance style, with a suggestion of the Italian influence. It has a wide stone terrace further beautified by handsome bronze lamps, whilst sculptured sets are on their way for erection there, and then the fine glass enclosed verandah, 225 feet long and some 30 or 40 feet in width.

摘自 1924 年 3 月 22 日《北华捷报》

Excerpts from *the North-China Herald,*on March 22, 1924

身世传奇的静安公园
The Legendary History of Jing'an Park

在繁华的静安寺商圈，静安公园是一块珍贵的绿地。

这里曾是静安寺公墓（Bubbling Well Cemetery），由上海的外侨经营使用长达70多年，被本地居民称为"外国坟山"。静安寺公墓因为环境优雅宜人，也像今天一样吸引游人。

1843年上海开埠后，旅居这座城市的外侨人数不断增长。根据陈蕴茜和吴敏合著的论文《殖民主义影响下的上海公墓变迁》，上海公共租界1843年仅26人，但到1865年已增至2297人，1910年达13536人，法租界也多达1476人。1869年苏伊士运河开通前上海到欧洲的航程至少为期4个月，运送客死上海的侨民回国归葬是一项巨大的工程。为此，不少人选择安葬上海。

1846年，英国人在外滩附近建成上海第一座公墓——山东路公墓，到1868年入葬者已达540人，当时整个墓区已无拓展空间，不得不于1871年关闭。1929年12月7日英文《北华捷报》的一篇报道透露，有一份档案手卷显示山东路公墓早期安葬的大多是20多岁

的青年外侨男女。

此后，随着租界不断扩大，旅沪外侨人数增加，西式公墓的数量也随之而持续增加。

"西式公墓均有专门机构管理，体制完善，既节省土地资源，又保护环境卫生，体现出优雅、恬静的园林化风格，有的公墓成为旅游胜地。外侨扫墓风也极为特别，成为上海一道独特的风景。如每年的4月26日和5月30日，租界里美国侨民及驻军有祭扫墓地的习俗。"陈蕴茜和吴敏在论文中写道。

当公共租界从外滩沿着静

安寺路（今南京西路）向西扩张后，管理租界市政的上海工部局于1896年在静安寺南侧购买了一块郊野空地，建造新的静安寺公墓，以满足对西式公墓不断增长的需求。

法国里昂第二大学东亚学院历史系教授安克强（Christian Henriot）发现一个有趣的现象：上海的公墓多位于租界以外的乡村，但随着城市发展，公墓所在地很快成为市中心。静安寺公墓就是一个例子。在城市扩张的过程中，公墓随移民迁移到西部廉价的土地上，城市空间点缀着这些永久公墓，后来基本都位于市区内。山东路公墓旧址如今是黄浦体育馆，八仙桥外国坟山改建为淮海公园，而静安寺公墓成为今天的静安公园。

1896年，工部局为修建静安寺公墓共投资白银56200两，购置了64亩土地。新公墓当时的选址偏西，远离租界中心，但是城市最终还是扩张到了此处。静安寺公墓占地面积39300平方米，内有苗圃和一座小教堂，园内设化骨炉及骨灰陈列室。葬礼大多在教堂里举行。

根据上海市静安区志，工部局建造的新公墓有6214个墓穴，到1949年时已使用5353个，大都为外侨使用，很多墓穴的水泥盖竖立着大理石安琪儿。由于公墓靠近静安寺，称静安寺公墓，老百姓习惯称其为"静安寺外国坟山"。华人通过预约也可以使用公墓。

由于地段方便，静安寺公墓被上海外侨社团认为是"最好的公墓"，葬礼费用也比其他公墓，如1926年开放的虹桥公墓更高。

这里是许多上海近代史上著名的外侨的安息地，如本书写到的德国医生宝隆（Erich Paulun）和英国地产大王雷士德(Henry Lester)。1899年，宝隆医生在南京西路东端长征医院现址开办了收治中国穷人的同济医院，后来又创办同济德文医学院，是今天上海和武汉两地的同济医院及同济大学的前身。而拥有南京路大量地皮的雷士德1926年去世后，留下遗嘱在上海捐建三个医疗教育机构，包括南京西路附近的雷士德医学研究院。宝隆是两岁就失去父母的孤儿，雷士德终生未婚孑然一身，这

两位在南京西路沿线工作、生活的外侨却为上海这座城市留下丰厚的爱的遗产。他们都被安葬在这座宁静宜人的公墓。

上海社科院历史所研究员张生还找到近百年前一段关于这座著名公墓的珍贵记忆。"这墓地的历史，我也不大明白，但以从门口起就一直排着，直到中心的礼拜堂屋后为止的，那两排齐出的洋梧桐树看来，少算大约也总已有六十几岁的年纪……从亭子间的南窗望出去，正好是静安寺公墓的所在，

那墓地里每一座坟的水泥盖上，竖立着的大理石安琪儿，也都历历可数。"王映霞在《我与郁达夫·半生杂忆》中写道。

1928年二月初，她与著名文人郁达夫在上海结婚，三月迁入上海赫德路（今常德路）嘉禾里1476号居住。王映霞形容，"新搬的这一间小屋，真也有点田园野趣。"这就是近百年前静安寺一带的城市风貌特征。

王映霞的回忆与1947年2月23日《新民报》刊登的一篇题为

《静安寺公墓巡礼》的文章不谋而合："这是闹市中惟一的一片干净土，战争、夺取、欺诈，都不在这里进行。"

这篇文章发表的六年后，上海市人民政府将静安寺外国坟山改造为静安公园，于1955年10月3日对公众开放。

如今，公园是高楼环绕的一片绿洲。中外游客与市民在这里漫步、锻炼、看书、遛娃，享受静谧的自然气息。

静安公园历经数次修缮改造，增加了450平方米的池塘，塘泥堆成小山，修整了道路，加建了茶室。1998年，还建造了一个2300平方米的"园中园"，在园中重现了"静安八景"，包括原在静安寺山门前的著名"涌泉"，那是南京西路英文名"Bubbling Well Road"的由来。

负责静安公园改建的静安区园林管理所所长黄彩娣撰文透露，改建工程慎重保护原有的历史遗产，如一座纯白色大理石亭，还有32棵见证许多人间悲欢的"洋梧桐树"。

昨天： 静安寺公墓　**今天：** 静安公园

参观指南： 公园免费对公众开放，适宜漫步发呆。静安八景园小巧雅致，门票3元，供应中国茶。

Jing'an Park is a precious, pleasant oasis in the busy Jing'an Temple area. In the 19th century it was known as Bubbling Well Cemetery for foreigners in Shanghai, renowned for its tranquil environment, which attracted visitors just like it does today.

"Adjacent to the Bubbling Well Temple (today's Jing'an Temple), the Bubbling Well Cemetery was managed and used mainly by expatriates for more than 70 years. The Chinese called it 'Wai Guo Fen Shan' (Hill of Foreign Tombs)", said scholar Zhang Sheng from Shanghai Academy of Social Sciences, who did a research of urban and architectural history around Jing'an Temple.

After Shanghai opened its port in 1843, the city saw a growing number of expatriates.

According to a study by scholars Chen Yunqian and Wu Min from Nanjing University and Suzhou Middle School respectively, the foreign population in Shanghai International Settlement rose from only 26 in 1843 to 2,297 in 1865. As the journey by sea from Europe to Shanghai took over four months, before the Suez Canal opening in 1869, many deceased expatriates were buried in Shanghai instead of being transported home.

The first foreign cemetery on Shandong Road near the Bund was built by the British in 1846 and had up to 469 tombs when it was closed in 1871. According to a report in *the North-China Herald* on December 7, 1929, a hand-bound volume revealed early burials at the cemetery mostly consisted of young men and women in their 20s.

More Western cemeteries were constructed following the first cemetery as foreign settlements expanded and the population of expatriates continued to grow.

"Managed by special institutions, these well-designed Western cemeteries made economic use of land, maintained a hygienic environment and presented an elegant, quiet garden ambience, many of which even became scenic spots. Some ceremonies, such as the annual U.S. Memorial Day for honoring those fallen while in the service of their country often attracted local visitors," Chen and Wu wrote in their co-authored pa per titled "The Change of Shanghai Cemeteries under the Influence of Colonialism".

As the city expanded from the Bund to the west along Bubbling Well Road (today's Nanjing Road W.), Shanghai Municipal Council purchased some empty land fronting the southern facade of the Bubbling Well Temple in 1896.

On the then suburban area, the council built a new cemetery and crematorium to meet the growing demand for Western burials and funeral services.

French historian Christian Henriot, who currently teaches at the Department of Asia Studies, Aix-Marseille University, pointed out an interesting phenomenon, that all the early foreign cemeteries were located in today's downtown Shanghai as "the city has been developing and expanding so fast in the past decades".

He said the Bubbling Well Cemetery was a typical example. During urban expansion, cemeteries which were built on cheaper land on the western outskirts of Shanghai were later included in the city area.

As a result, Shanghai today is dotted with "cemetery" relics of yesterday through continuous urban renewal projects. The Shandong Road cemetery became Huangpu Stadium, the Baxian Bridge Cemetery was trans-

formed into Huaihai Park and the Bubbling Well Cemetery is now Jing'an Park.

"The Shanghai Municipal Council invested 56,200 taels of silver to build the cemetery which experienced several renovations but its scale remained basically unchanged," Henriot wrote in his paper titled "The Study of Public Cemeteries in Shanghai's International Settlement".

Covering an area of 39,300 square meters, the new cemetery contained a nursery garden, a small chapel, a crematory and a room for bone ashes. The burial ceremonies were mostly hosted in the chapel.

According to Jing'an District annals, the cemetery had 6,214 tombs, with 5,363 of them occupied by 1949. The Chinese could also use the cemetery through bookings.

Owing to the convenient location, the Bubbling Well Cemetery was widely regarded as "the best cemetery" by the Shanghai foreigner community and therefore higher prices were charged for funeral services than the other cemeteries, such as the Hongqiao Cemetery which opened in 1926.

It was also the burial place for many prominent expatriates in Shanghai, including the German doctor Erich Paulun, who established the German Medical School for Chinese in Shanghai, and Henry Lester, a British architect, merchant and philanthropist in Shanghai.

The Tung Chee Hospital for Chinese, which Paulun founded in 1899 together with the German doctor Oscar von Schab, treated poor Chinese patients for free, which later evolved into today's Chang Zheng Hospital and the Medical School of Tongji University.

British tycoon Henry Lester

made a fortune from Shanghai's old real estate but donated almost all of his assets to the education of Chinese people. It included a medical institution that still stands a few minutes' walk from Nanjing Road W. and a foundation that still sponsors Chinese scholars studying in the UK today.

The two men, who had lived and worked along the Bubbling Well Road and whose legacies had a lingering influence in Shanghai, were both buried in the Bubbling Well Cemetery.

Scholar Zhang Sheng from Shanghai Academy of Social Sciences also scooped a vivid Chinese memory of this famous cemetery in the late 1920s.

"I was not clear about the cemetery's history. But I remembered there were two lines of plane trees, which were around 60 years of age, stretching from the gateway through the back of the chapel in the center. From the south window of my small room over the kitchen, I could see the Bubbling Well Cemetery. On each tomb, there stood marble angles," Wang Yingxia wrote in her diary soon after she married Yu Dafu, a popular short-story writer and poet in the 1920's China, and moved into an alleyway house on Hart Road (today's Changde Road).

Her account was echoed in an article titled "A Visit to the Bubbling Well Cemetery" published on February 23, 1947, in a Chinese newspaper, which was a predecessor of today's *Xinmin Evening News*.

"It was the only clean land in the bustling downtown, where wars, tricks and cheats were not conducted," says the writer in the 1947 article.

Six years later, the clean land was turned into a public space. According to the book *Jing'an History and Culture Catalogue*, Shanghai government moved the tombs to another "Hill of Foreign Tombs" in Pudong and transformed the downtown cemetery to Jing'an Park which opened to the public on October 3, 1955.

Since then the park has been an oasis in the bustling commercial center of skyscrapers and busy traffic. People come to the park to walk, practice tai chi, read newspapers, play chess or meditate. During weekends, the big green lawn is an outdoor activity paradise for kids.

The park was renovated several times and a pond, a rockery and a two-story teahouse were later added. In 1998, the park was upgrad-

ed again. The project's highlight saw a 2,300-square-meter garden created to revive eight famous scenes in Jing'an Temple history, starting from East Jing Dynasty (AD 317-420), including the famous Bubbling Well, which Nanjing Road W. was named after in English.

Huang Caidi, the then director of Jing'an District Landscaping Bureau, who headed the project, notes that some historical relics were well-preserved, including the white marble pavilion and 32 100-year-old plane trees lining the avenue, which witnessed the life and death of Shanghai expatriates from a bygone era.

Yesterday: The Bubbling Well Cemetery   **Today:** Jing'an Park
Tips: It's free and nice to wander in this incredibly beautiful park in downtown Shanghai. The mini garden that revived eight scenes in the history of Jing'an Temple is small and elegant which serves Chinese tea. The Jing'an Park is free for entrance and the mini garden charges 3 yuan (US$0.43) per person.

美侨社区举办阵亡将士纪念日活动
The Memorial Day

5月31日是美国阵亡将士纪念日，是美国纪念为国捐躯的将士们的全国性的纪念日。在这一天，上海美侨社区以令人印象深刻的方式举行了纪念日活动。

当天凌晨，美国妇女俱乐部的成员们用自己和上海美侨社区其他人捐赠的花朵装饰了虹桥、八仙桥和静安寺公墓的墓地。这种墓地装饰习俗在美国各地很普遍，当地富有公共精神的女性为此所做的工作值得尊敬。对于阵亡将士纪念日而言，这是完美的一天，装饰精美的墓地也是对爱国将士们致以的敬意。

当天的主要活动在静安寺公墓举行，由美国总领事坎宁安（E. S. Cunningham）先生主持，所有美国组织在上海的代表都参加了活动。

上午8时30分，游行队伍在跑马场集合。在这里，康奈特上尉率领第四司令部的第2、19、25和26支美国海军陆战队组成了支队。海军乐队演奏音乐。

其他出席的还有西班牙战争退伍军人、索尔上尉（W. E. Sauer）的万国商团美国队、哈尔科姆上尉（C. P. Holcomb）的万国商团美国队，以及两排来自匹兹堡海军的"蓝夹克"。在四名锡克族骑兵的带领下，游行队伍于上午8点30分快速出发，沿着静安寺路前往墓地。

位于教堂台阶上的正式代表除了坎宁安先生、领事雅各布先生（J. Jacobs）和美国地区检察官萨莱特（G. Sellett）博士以外，还有其他人。台阶的左侧集结着女童军（The Girl Guides），右侧是西班牙战争退伍军人，海军陆战队沿着通向入口的大道排列。其他出席的人们尽可能靠近发言者。

美国社区教会的牧师陆考科（E. W. Luccock）牧师进行了祈祷，随后是萨莱特（Sellett）博士，他在纪念日上对阵亡将士纪念日的重要性及其在美国国定假日中的地位进行了演讲。

Memorial Day, the United States national occasion for honoring those fallen in the service of the Republic, was celebrated on May 31, in an impressive manner by practically the entire American community in Shanghai.

Early in the morning members of the American Women's Club decorated the graves in the Hongqiao, Baxianqiao and Bubbling Well Cemeteries with flowers gratefully donated by themselves and others in the American community. This custom of grave decoration is universal throughout the United States, and the local public-spirited women did an estimable work. It was a perfect day for Memorial Day, and the beautifully adorned graves were a fitting tribute to the patriotism of those being honored.

The main event of the day was the celebration at the Bubbling Well Cemetery presided over by Mr E. S. Cunningham, American Consul-General, and participated in by representatives of all American organizations in Shanghai.

A parade was formed at 8:30am at the Race Course where detachments were drawn up of the 2nd, 19th, 25th and 26th US Marines' companies under Capt. Cornell with the 4th Regt. Marine Band furnishing the music.

Other units present were the Spanish War Veterans, American Co S. V. C. under Capt W. E. Sauer, American Troop, S. V. C. under Capt C. P. Holcomb, and two platoons of bluejackets from the USS Pittsburgh. With four Sikh troopers leading, the parade left promptly at 8:30am along Bubbling Well Road for the cemetery.

The official group on the chapel steps included in addition to Mr. Cunningham, Mr. J. Jacobs, Consul and Dr. G. Sellett, U.S. District Attorney. The Girl Guides were grouped on the left of the steps and the Spanish War Veterans on the right with the Marines ranged along the path leading to the gate. The other units took up positions as close as possible to the speakers.

The Rev E. W. Luccock, pastor of the Community Church, offered prayer and was followed by Dr Sellett, who addressed the gathering on the significance of Memorial Day and its place on the list of American national holidays.

摘自 1929 年 6 月 1 日《北华捷报》

Excerpt from *the North-China Herald*, on June 1, 1929

红尘中的静谧
Temple of Repose, Purity and Peace

上海静安寺的旧英文名叫"Bubbling Well Temple"（涌泉寺），因为寺前曾有一座古井，井内泉水如沸腾般日夜涌动。20世纪60年代，涌泉被填埋，但静安寺却保存至今，还大幅扩大了规模。

上海社科院历史所研究员张生发现，关于静安寺最早的文字记载出现在南宋绍熙年间（1190—1194年）刊印的《云间志》。

"静安寺原是濒临古吴淞江(今苏州河)的一座寺庙，因寺址逼近江岸，不断遭受江涛袭击，寺屋时有倾圮之虞。南宋嘉定九年(1216年)发生一场洪水，静安寺果然被江涛冲垮，其后，寺僧仲依将寺庙迁至芦浦沸井浜畔，也就是现在的上海市静安区南京西路1686号这个地方。"张生在《上海静安嘉里中心历史文化底蕴研究》一文中写到。

他认为按照《云间志》记载，静安寺已有1680多年历史，不但是上海一座最古老的佛寺，而且也是江南地区最古老的佛寺之一。不过《云间志》只是孤证，史学界无法获得相应的史料佐证，为稳妥起见，后人一般把静安寺的始建年代称作"相传建于赤乌年间"。

根据上海市静安区规划与土地管理局编制的《静安地名追踪》一书，静安寺初名沪渎重元（玄）寺，寺址位于吴淞江（今苏州河）北岸，唐代该寺更名为永泰禅院，北宋大中祥符元年（1008年）始名静安寺。

古老的静安寺迁至涌泉浜后，在元代发展为一座大型寺庙。静安寺不仅规模大，风景也很美，有著名的"静安八景"，其中之一就是被誉为"天下第六泉"的涌泉。

随着时光变迁，"静安八景"都消失了，不过静安公园1998年建造了一个2300平方米的"园中园"，在园中重现了"静安八景"，包括"涌泉"，那也是南京西路英文名"Bubbling

Well Road"的由来。

　　"古代中国寺庙经常成为文人墨客吟咏游玩的场所。最迟自元代起，静安寺已成沪地一座著名的游览景观。静安有八景：赤乌碑、陈朝桧、虾子潭、讲经台、沪渎垒、涌泉、芦子渡、绿云洞。明、清两代，慕名前往游览者络绎不绝，留下不少题咏，散见于旧志及各家诗集中。"张生说。

　　1923年12月29日，英文《北华捷报》刊登了一位名叫希克莫特（A. G. Hickmott）的外侨撰写的静安寺游记。他首先描绘了静安寺涌泉里的"浑水、碳酸和沼气"。

　　"这座寺庙是一个干净整洁的地方，但由于缺乏资金而有不少缺陷。穿过几个小厅堂和院落，来到主殿，据称它有千年历史。这是真正的'静''安'（静默、纯净与安宁）寺。首先看到的神佛是三兄弟：分别为天神、地神和水神——他们的名字代表着所掌管的事物，以及那些生日分别在阴历一月、七月和十月十五的人。所有佛像都穿着鲜红色的长袍。"他写道。

　　进入寺庙时，希克莫特看到了一尊金佛，高约20英尺的佛像坐在荷叶上，还供奉着其他佛像。

"所有东西，包括门、桌子和神殿，以及神灵本身，都经过精心雕刻，引人注目。锦缎、窗帘和挂毯很漂亮。"他描绘道。

当他参观时，僧侣们正要做晚课。住持敲击三下铃铛后开始了仪式，他快快慢慢地敲铃，发出叮叮当当的声音，而另一位和尚则击打了木鱼，产生了一种中空的声音。方丈长而轻柔地吟诵了几句话，然后在几分钟内，其他僧侣相继加入，诵经、呢喃、哼唱，直到聚会终于散去。

张生研究发现，静安寺一带曾经是一个城市信仰生活的共同体。一年一度的静安寺庙会为幽静的古寺增添了一份热闹。庙会是设在寺庙内或附近的中国传统市集，一般在佛教节日举行，如农历二月十九、六月十九和九月十九观音菩萨诞生、成道及涅槃日，三月初三弥勒佛涅槃日和四月初八释迦牟尼佛诞辰日等。上海寺庙有习俗在四月初八举行浴佛会，用梁香、安息香、附子香、丘隆香和郁金香浸制的五色香水浇灌佛像，僧人诵佛祛灾祈福，乡民信徒前来礼佛设摊。

20世纪二三十年代是静安寺庙会的鼎盛时期，寺庙周边的人行道（如今是华山路、南京西路、万航渡路和愚园路）都挤满了摊贩。1937年后庙会的人气逐渐衰落，1963年举办最后一次庙会后宣告结束。静安寺庙会方便了城乡民众购销物品，交流物资，对上海商品经济的发展做出了贡献。

《静安地名追踪》一书提到，2000年时古老的静安寺开始新一轮寺庙整体改建工程，于2011年结束。改建后的静安寺占地总面积9705平方米，比原静安寺占地面积5500平方米扩大76.5%。这座长方形的寺庙建筑群落有钟楼、鼓楼、山门、大雄宝殿等10座建筑单体。

其中，大雄宝殿高26米，庑殿重檐，以铜瓦为顶，殿内竖立着46根巨大的柚木柱子。殿内供奉一尊15吨纯银铸造的释迦牟尼佛

像，大殿底层是千人讲经堂，地下为1000平方米的藏书阁。

负责静安寺行政事务的亚蕴法师介绍，静安寺如今由20多名年龄在30到50岁的僧人负责日常事务，此外还有很多志愿者帮忙。因为地段方便，每天静安寺要接待近1000名来宾，其中有很多境外游客和旅居上海的外籍人士。这里也是国际佛教交流的窗口，接待过来自美国、欧洲、日本、韩国和东南亚的佛教代表团。

他还提到，静安寺曾有佛学院，培养了很多佛教高僧。如今，静安寺也吸引很多对佛教文化感兴趣的白领。

"佛教的智慧和慈悲促进身心健康、家庭和睦和社会稳定，对于现代社会压力大的人特别有益。

静安寺也做了大量救助老弱病残的慈善工作。"他介绍。

静安寺钟楼的底楼有一个复建的涌泉。这座寺庙曾以昔日的"天下第六泉"而得名，并因此而闻名。站在南京西路看静安寺，这座位于繁华商圈的古老寺庙显得金光灿烂。但是，走进山门就仿佛来到另一个世界——香烟缥缈的内院给人宁静的感受，"静""安"寺名副其实。

昨天： 静安寺　**今天：** 静安寺　**地址：** 南京西路 1686 号
建造年代： 建于 1216 年，于 2000 年改造
参观指南： 上午 7 点半到下午 5 点对公众开放，门票 50 元。

The old English name of Jing'an Temple was Bubbling Well Temple as there was an ancient well bubbling all day and night in front of it. The well was filled up in the 1960s but the temple still survives today and has grown much grander in scale in the heart of Jing'an District.

"The temple formerly perched on the bank of old Wusong River (today's Suzhou River), which was constantly attacked by river waves, finally crashed in a flood in 1216. After that the temple was moved to the bank of Bubbling Well Creek, which is the present site of 1686 Nanjing Road W. today," said scholar Zhang Sheng

from Shanghai Academy of Social Sciences who has researched the urban and architectural history around Jing'an Temple.

After researching a Songjiang record named *Yun Jian Zhi or Record among the Clouds*, published in the 1190s, Zhang traced the temple's history to more than 1600 years, which made Jing'an Temple the oldest Buddhist temple in the southern region of Yangtze River. He and other historians are still searching for more sources to prove this fact.

According to the 2013 book, *Traces of Place Names in Jing'an District*, edited by the district's urban planning and land management bureau, the temple was first named Hudu Chongyuan Temple, renamed Yongtaichan Temple during the Tang Dynastry (618-907) and got the present name Jing'an Temple in 1008 during the Song Dynasty (960-1279).

After moving to Bubbling Well Creek, the ancient temple gradually expanded and grew to be a gigantic temple in the Yuan Dynasty (1271-1368). The temple was not only big, but also beautiful. It boasted eight famous scenes, one of which was certainly the "Bubbling Well" fronting its main gate acclaimed as "the Sixth Spring of the Earth".

As times went by, all the eight scenic spots disappeared, but were revived in a Chinese garden inside Jing'an Park. Small rivers, a stone tablet, bubbling well, rockery, flowers and woods were arranged in an elegant way so the "Garden of Jing'an Eight Scenes" covers an area of 2,300 square meters.

"Ancient Chinese temples had often been a place for writers to wander and jot down their thoughts and feelings. Poems of the Jing'an Eight Scenes had been edited into collections. The temple attracted a continuous stream of visitors and people wrote about their tours in old records or poem

collections," said Zhang.

In his *Guide to Shanghai*, an expatriate named A. G. Hickmott wrote about his tour to the temple in great details, which was recorded in *the North-China Herald* on December 29, 1923.

The writer first described the well-known "Bubbling Well" with "its muddy water, carbonic acid and marsh gas".

"The temple is a clean and well-kept place, but is greatly handicapped through lack of funds. Passing through several small halls and a couple of courtyards one comes to the main building, which, it is claimed, dates back some 1,000 years. This is the real Ching-an-tz, 'Temple of Repose (Silence), Purity and Peace'. The first gods that greet one are three brothers — the Gods of Heaven, Earth and Water — whose names signify what they rule and those birthdays fall on the 15th day of the 1st, 7th and 10th moons. All are gorgeously dressed in scarlet robes," he wrote.

Going into the main temple, Hickmott was welcomed by a golden Buddha, which was around 20 feet high, sitting on lotus leaves and occupied the chief shrine. In the hall were the nine companions of his life and a similar number of other gods.

"Everything, including the doors, tables and shrines, and the gods themselves, is exceedingly well carved and attracts not a little attention. The brocades, curtains and tapestries are beautiful," he said.

The monks were just about to meet for evening prayer when the writer entered. Having struck his bell three times, the abbot began the service by beating fast and slow, and produced a tinkling sound, while another monk struck a wooden shell drum, which produced a hollow sound. A few words were chanted by the abbot in long, drawling tones and in a few minutes this was followed by the other monks present joining in, chanting, murmuring and singing in succession for some time before the meeting finally dispersed.

Scholar Zhang Sheng added that the history-rich temple had become a common place for urban religious life, which is reflected in the annual temple fair.

He explains that the Chinese Buddhist temple regularly hosts Buddhist ceremonies such as the "Buddhist Bathing Festival". At this festival, monks bathe Buddhist statues with fragrant water made from five aromatic herbs and chant scripts to ask for blessings.

"Jing'an Temple was located in the western suburbs of Shanghai and its Buddhist festival drew many local villages to visit for burning joss sticks and praying for good life. The villagers often brought with them agricultural products and handicrafts for sale and exchange for farm implements and households they needed. So more and more peddlers set up their stalls around the temple, which gradually became an annual temple fair for pilgrims, tourists and shoppers," Zhang said.

During the fair's peak time in the 1920s and 1930s, the promenades of the neighboring streets, which are today's Huashan Road, Nanjing Road W., Yan'an Road W., Wanhangdu Road and Yuyuan Road, were all crowded with peddlers' stalls. After 1937, the fair started to decline and finally terminated after 1963.

"The temple fair has contributed to the economy in the Jing'an Temple region and even the city's commerce, which made it easier for urban and country people to exchange products. It also mirrored the time, background and social condition of Jing'an Temple area," Zhang said.

According to the book named

Traces of Place Names in Jing'an District, the temple started a big-scale renovation in 2000, which was completed in 2011. The temple now covers an area of 9,705 square meters and is an architectural complex of 10 buildings including a bell tower, drum tower, main gate and main hall.

The grand main hall as high as 26 meters was built with 46 teak wood columns in enormous sizes and topped by copper tiles. The centerpiece of the main hall is a Buddhist statue made of 15 tons of silver. The ground floor of the hall has a capacity for housing up to 1,000 people for a ceremony while a 1000-square-meter bibliotheca is located underground.

"The temple is operated by 20 to 30 monks, mostly aged between 30 to 50, and many volunteers. Owing to the temple's convenient location, we receive around 1,000 visitors every day including many foreign tourists or expatriate residents. It's also a window of in-

ternational Buddhism cultural exchange and we had visiting delegations from the US, Europe, Japan, Korea and Southeast Asia," said Ya Yun, who has worked in the temple for more than 20 years and acts as Jing'an Temple's administrative office director.

He adds that Jing'an Temple once had a Buddhist school and nurtured several famous Buddhist monks. Today it attracts "white-collar" professionals who want to learn about Buddhism.

"The wisdom and mercy of Buddhism improves physical and mental health, family harmony and social stability, which benefit stressful people of modern society. Our temple also did extensive charity work to help the elderly, the poor and the young children lack of education," Ya Yun said.

On the ground floor of the bell tower is a new revived bubbling well, a replica of yesterday's "Sixth Spring of the Earth", which the temple was named after and is famous for. From the outside, Jing'an Temple looks golden and extravagant in the middle of the city's shopping malls and office skyscrapers. But the inner yard of the temple gives a serene, peaceful atmosphere and lives up to the name of a temple—repose, purity and peace—after one step into the main gate formerly fronted with a famous bubbling well.

Yesterday: Bubbling Well Temple   Today: Jing'an Temple
Address: 1686 Nanjing Road W.   Built in 1216, renovated in 2000
Tips: The temple is open to the public from 7:30am to 5:00pm at an admission of 50 yuan.

繁华的静谧

2019年7月18日，我应上海市静安区历保委邀请，在南京西路街道福民会馆做了一场讲座。当时，我的南京路专栏正好写到南京西路，于是就第一次尝试着向公众讲述整条南京路的故事，包括南京东路、人民广场和南京西路。

大学毕业后，我一直在威海路上海报业大楼里的上海日报工作，从我们40楼办公区的落地窗就能欣赏蜿蜒伸展的南京西路，虽然离得那么近，但是却一直没有好好地去认识它，直到我开启了南京路专栏。

据说上海早期的外国侨民认为外滩是一把弓，而南京路是一支箭，一路向西，射向近代上海城市发展的方向。不知不觉，我沿着上海之箭的方向，从外滩到静安寺，一座楼一座楼，写完了整条"十里洋场"。

在调研南京路的过程中，我发现曾经作为上海城市象征的这条著名商业街，无论是南京东路还是南京西路，似乎没有一本记录它最新面貌又适宜公众的书籍。

福民会馆的讲座后，我就想与更多的读者朋友分享整条南京路的故事，重温这次难忘的探索之旅：从外滩出发，逛逛新的南京路步行街，环绕人民广场兜一圈，再漫步南京西路，体会南京东路与西路两种截然不同的风情，感受历史街区深厚的底蕴和能量。

2020年1月我开设了建筑可阅读主题的微信公众号"月读上海"，希望架设一座建筑保护业界与大众之间的桥梁。上海三联书店编辑杜鹃女士看到"月读上海"后来电约稿新书，我想正好尝试一下，就利用2020年疫情期间的一段宁静时光完成第一本书稿。8月，讲述南京东路和人民广场33个建筑故事的《阅读南京路》在疫情防控严密的上海书展首发。9月，我带着这本"小橙书"见证了南京路步行街东拓开街仪式。11月，"小橙书"被上海市政府新闻办选入第三届进博会新闻中心城市形象传播平台，成为热门书籍之一。

《阅读南京路》完稿不久，我便开始了《阅读南京西路》的策划写作。仿佛时光轮回，在2021年初疫情反复期间完成了新的书稿。

在采访过程中，我得到了静安区府办、静安区房管局和沿线南京东路街道、南京西路街道、石门二路街道、江宁路街道和静安寺街道等单位的热心帮助。他们不仅提供历史建筑资料，还陪同实地考察。我发现南京西路沿线的文保单位运用新理念和新技术建立历史建筑档案、监测保护历史建筑、制作二维码文物牌。

　　写作期间，我还有幸在南京西路参加了两场"建筑可阅读"活动。2020年9月13日，我应静安区文旅局邀请在安义路毛泽东故居举办"月读静安·南京路"腾讯直播讲座，吸引近30万观众收看。2020年12月26日，我应邀担任上海市委党史办与静安区委主办的"毛泽东在上海的足迹红色研学路线"直播访谈专家。活动前我特意重走了20世纪20年代青年毛泽东在上海的"足迹"，包括书中写到的安义路故居和茂名南路故居。

　　我在"月读上海"发刊词里写到："上海是一座伟大的城市，愿'月读上海'为这座城，洒落一点温润的月光。"如今，"月读南京路"的心愿终于完成了。希望这本《阅读南京西路》继续陪伴你，探索这条马路上繁华的静谧。

乔争月

2021 年月 3 月

上海武康路月亮书房

Exploring Bubbling Well Road

On July 18, 2019, at the invitation of the Historical Preservation Committee of Shanghai Jing'an District, I gave a lecture on Nanjing Road at a local community center of Nanjing Road West Sub-district named "Fumin Hall" or "Hall of Lucky Civilians".

At that time, my Shanghai Daily column series—"On Nanjing Road Trails" was near the end, so it became my first trial to tell the public stories of the entire Nanjing Road, including Nanjing Road East, the People's Square and Nanjing Road West.

Through the windows of my office on the 40th floor of the Shanghai United Media Group building on Weihai Road, the winding Nanjing Road West looks just like a stone's throw away. After writing about Nanjing Road East and the People's Square, I continued along and finally started to explore Nanjing Road West, a rather familiar street to me.

In preparation for the column, I found that this famous commercial street, though a symbol of Shanghai, does not seem to have a book that records its latest developments.

After the lecture at the "Fumin Hall" in 2019, I wished to share with more readers the stories of the whole Nanjing Road and my unforgettable journey along the road: starting from the Bund, walking on the new Nanjing Road Pedestrian Street, circling around the People's Square and finally strolling along Nanjing Road West.

In January 2020, I opened a WeChat public account "Yue Du Shanghai" or "Moon's Reading of Shanghai" to share my amazing findings about Shanghai architectural history and build a bridge between the circle of architectural conservation and the public. After reading my articles, Ms. Du Juan, the editor of Shanghai Joint Publishing Company called for co-operation of publishing my new books. I agreed to give it a go. In the spring of 2020, as we all had to slow our normal work and life pace due to the outbreak of the epidemic, I took on the fight to complete the first manuscript in that unusual peaceful period.

In August 2020, *Shanghai Nanjing Road*, which tells the 33 architectural stories of Nanjing Road East and the People's Square, debuted at the Shanghai Book Fair. Soon after, the opening ceremony of the new Nanjing Road Pedestrian Street was held in September. In November, the book was recommended by the Shanghai Municipal Information Office to the 2020 CIIE News Center and became one of the most popular books among international and domestic journalists.

After that, I started the planning and writing of this *The Bubbling Well Road* of Nanjing Road West. As if time was recurring, I completed the second manuscript during the recurrence of the epidemic in early 2021.

During the exploration, I received warm helps from Jing'an District Government and five sub-district governments—Nanjing Road E., Nanjing Road W., No. 2 Shimen Road, Jiangning Road and Jing'an Temple sub-districts along the former Bubbling Well Road. Their staffs not only provided information of historical buildings, but also accompanied me on field trips. And through them I was glad to know new concepts and technologies were adopted to establish architectural archives, monitor and protect historical buildings and increase the public awareness through heritage plates with digital information of building stories.

While writing this book on Nanjing Road West, I happened to have two relevant events on this road. On September 13, 2020, I was invited by the Bureau of Culture and Tourism of Jing'an District to give a live lecture of Nanjing Road on Tencent at Mao Zedong's 1920 residence on Anyi Road, which attracted nearly 300,000 online viewers. On December 26, 2020, I served as an expert for a live talk on "Mao Zedong's Early Footprints in Shanghai". Both have contributed to the new book.

It is my sincere hope that my two books can help you to get a new picture of Nanjing Road through a new perspective, to understand the connections and dif-

ferences of Nanjing Road East and Nanjing Road West, to feel the historical meaning and vital energy of this historical street.

In the launching article for my WeChat account "Yue Du Shanghai", I wrote that "Shanghai is a great city and I hope 'Moon's Reading of Shanghai' will sprinkle some gentle moonlight onto this city". Now with two years' efforts, my wish to share stories of the whole Nanjing Road finally becomes true today, and I do hope *The Bubbling Well Road* can be your guide in exploring this prosperous and peaceful street.

Michelle Qiao

March 2021

Moon Atelier, Wukang Road, Shanghai

参考书目

南京西路一百四十年（1862-2002） 静安年鉴编辑部 上海社会科学院出版社 2003

上海史 The History of Shanghai（英） 兰宁 库寿龄 著 朱华译 上海书店出版社 2020

上海百年建筑史 1840-1949（第二版） 伍江著， 同济大学出版社，2008

上海近代建筑风格（新版） 郑时龄著 同济大学出版社，2020

上海建筑指南 罗小未主编，上海人民美术出版社，1996

上海近代建筑史稿 陈从周、章明著，上海三联书店，1988

老上海南京路 沈寂 主编 上海人民美术出版社 2003

走在历史的记忆里——南京路 1840s-1950s 上海历史博物馆编 上海科学技术出版社 2000 年

上海城市之心 马学强 主编 上海社会科学院出版社 2017

绿房子 上海市城市规划设计研究员 上海现代建筑设计集团 同济大学建筑与城市规划学院 编著 同济大学出版社 2014

鸿达 上海的匈牙利超现代主义建筑师 Eszter Baldavari （代表匈牙利建筑师协会）著 2019

上海邬达克建筑地图 华霞虹、乔争月等著 同济大学出版社 2013

邬达克 ［意］卢卡．彭切里尼 ［匈］尤利娅．切伊迪 著 华霞虹 乔争月译 同济大学出版社 2013

静安地名追踪 上海市静安区规划和土地管理局 组编 复旦大学出版社 2013

静安历史文化图录 龚德庆 张仁良 主编 同济大学出版社 2011

海上第一名园——张园史料图文汇编 上海市静安区文物史料馆编 上海社会科学院出版社 2012

风华张园 张爱华主编，王曼隽，张伟执笔 同济大学出版社 2013 年

静安石库门 时筠仑 上海交通大学出版社 2020 年

我在上海修历中建筑 1997-2017 上海章明建筑设计事务所 上海远东出版社 2017

魔都 ［日］村松梢风 徐静波 译 上海人民出版社

范文照 黄元炤 编著 中国建筑工业出版社 2015

开埠后的上海住宅 曹炜 著 中国建筑工业出版社 2004

犹太人在上海 潘光主编 上海画报出版社 2005 年

同济老照片 陆敏恂主编，同济大学宣传部编 同济大学出版社 2007 年

德国对华政策中的同济大学 1907-1941 李乐曾著 同济大学出版社 2007 年

老上海百业指南，道路机构厂商住宅分布图 吴健熙选编 上海社会科学院出版社 2008 年

Shanghai, a handbook for travellers and residents to the chief objects of interest in and around the foreign settlements and native city C. E. Darwent. Hazell, Watson and Viney, LD

A Short History of Shanghai by F. L. Hawks Pott, D.D China Intercontinental Press， 2008

近现代英文报刊

《字林西报》及其周末版《北华捷报》*North China Daily News & North China Herald*

《大陆报》*The China Press*

《密勒氏评论》*Milliard's Review*

《社交上海》*Social Shanghai*

《上海泰晤士报》及其周日版 *Shanghai Times & Shanghai Sunday Times*

《大美晚报》*Shanghai Evening Post*

《以色列信使报》*Israel's Messengers*

《文汇报》

《解放日报》

《新民晚报》

《中国建筑》

《大众画报》

The China Builder

部分图片来源
Part of the Picture Sources

上海市体育总会：
P019，P025

国际饭店：
P39，P40，P43，P44

廖方：
P50

上海大光明电影院：
P52，P54

上海历史博物馆：
P62,P63

王浩娱：
P125

匈牙利驻沪总领馆：
P193

永安百货：
P225，P235，P236，P237

上海市静安区文化和旅游局：
P334

静安寺：
P409

部分图片说明
Part of the Picture Captions

P31:
斯裔匈籍建筑设计师邬达克
Architect Laszlo Hudec

P38:
摘自 1934 年《大陆报》
Excerpt from the China Press in 1934

P53:
斯裔匈籍建筑设计师邬达克
Architect Laszlo Hudec

P55:
1928 年电影院原有的外墙砖柱一直
保存至今
The original exterior brick columns of
the 1928 cinema have been preserved
until today (fronting No. 2 Cinema hall
on the second floor).

P72:
同济德文医学堂（现上海理工大学）
File photo of Tongji German Medical
School(Now Shanghai University of Science and Technology)

P74:
1908 年同济德文医学堂正门照片
File photo of Tongji German Medical
School, front gate, in 1908

P90:
乐福德设计的礼查饭店孔雀厅
The Peacock Hall of Astor House designed by Abelardo Lafuente

P125: 中国设计师陆谦受
Chinese architect Luke Him Sau

P185: 匈牙利建筑师鸿达
Hungarian Architect C.H.Gonda

P190:
鸿达手绘的犹太学校设计图
C.H.Gonda's drawing of Shanghai Jewish School

P199:
建筑师李锦沛
Architect Poy Gum Lee (Li Jinpei)

P240:
颜料大王贝润生
Pei Runsheng

P251:
报业大王史量才
Shi Liangcai

P261:
史量才在杭州为沈秋水修建的秋水山
庄
The Qiushui Villa built by Shi Liangcai
for Shen Qiushui in Hangzhou

P281: 建筑师雷士德
Architect Henry Lester

P303:
斯洛伐克发行的邬达克邮票
The Hudec's stamp of Slovakia

P304:
斯洛伐克邬达克建筑中心
Hudec Architecture Center in Slovakia

P371:
埃利 · 嘉道理爵士
Sir. Elly Kadoorie

P377:
嘉道理爵士和儿子们
Sir. Elly Kadoorie and his sons

图书在版编目（CIP）数据

阅读南京西路 / 乔争月著. -- 上海:上海三联书店,
2021.7

ISBN 978 - 7 - 5426 - 7448 - 7

Ⅰ.①阅… Ⅱ.①乔… Ⅲ.①城市史—
上海 Ⅳ.①K295.1

中国版本图书馆CIP数据核字(2021)第110784号

阅读南京西路

著　　者 / 乔争月

责任编辑 / 杜　鹃
封面设计 / 0214_Studio
版式设计 / 一本好书
监　　制 / 姚　军
责任校对 / 王凌霄

出版发行 / 上海三联书店
　　　　　（200030）中国上海市漕溪北路331号A座6楼
邮购电话 / 021-22895540
印　　刷 / 上海南朝印刷有限公司

版　　次 / 2021年7月第1版
印　　次 / 2021年7月第1次印刷
开　　本 / 787 X 1092　1/32
字　　数 / 360千字
印　　张 / 14.75
书　　号 / ISBN 978-7-5426-7448-7 / K·647
定　　价 / 72.00元

敬启读者，如发现本书有印装质量问题，请与印刷厂联系 021-62213990